694

A SHORT HISTORY
OF THE
CHINESE

THE FOUR HUNDRED MILLION

A SHORT HISTORY OF THE CHINESE

BY MARY A. NOURSE

Mount Vernon Seminary, Washington, D. C.
Formerly of Ginling College, Nanking, China

THIRD EDITION

THE NEW HOME LIBRARY
NEW YORK

THE NEW HOME LIBRARY EDITION PUBLISHED FEBRUARY, 1943
BY ARRANGEMENT WITH THE BOBBS-MERRILL COMPANY

COPYRIGHT, 1935, 1938, 1942, BY THE BOBBS-MERRILL COMPANY

A SHORT HISTORY OF THE CHINESE was formerly published as
THE FOUR HUNDRED MILLION

THIRD EDITION

THE NEW HOME LIBRARY, 14 West Forty-ninth Street
New York, N. Y.

CL

PRINTED IN THE UNITED STATES OF AMERICA

PREFACE

FORTY years ago and more, when our Secretary of State, John Hay, was laboring for the "open-door" policy, he voiced his ideas regarding the understanding that the West needed to have of China in the following words, "Whoever understands that mighty Empire socially, politically, economically, religiously, has a key to world politics for the next five centuries."

Until 1937, when Japan opened up war upon China, we as a nation have known little of China and have probably cared less. But when with almost nothing in the way of modernized equipment she was able to withstand Japan's onslaught, our admiration and sympathy were aroused. Now that over five years of war have passed and she is still resisting her enemy, our admiration grows, and also the feeling voiced by John Hay that we should know something about this country of China (empire in his day, republic in our own).

The American people have watched with great interest not only the military resistance that China has shown but also the political, social and economic progress she has made while undergoing the hardships of war. Pushed to the western part of her country, cut off from all sea communications, hemmed in by high mountains, she has given birth to a new China. Her capital, Chungking, has become a beehive of activity. Chinese refugees have migrated to this new China, students carrying books, industrialists burdened with ma-

PREFACE

chinery, and common people with their small belongings. There they have created new homes, set up colleges and schools and built manufacturing and mining establishments. Cut off from their old lines of communication, they have carved out new ones over and through the mountains, almost entirely by hand labor, to Burma, India, Iran and Siberia.

Moreover, her new strength has given China a place of growing weight in international relations. Her officials have entered into A B C D discussions and Lend-Lease agreements in Washington, and Americans, army officials, political leaders, economists and engineers, have visited Chungking. In the Far East, Indian and Chinese leaders have exchanged visits. All this indicates that China's importance in postwar arrangements will be very great. With her population of one-fifth of the people of the world, with her advancement of the last decade, she bids fair to be the leader of east Asian peoples.

Of such a virile people we wish to know more. What has been their history, their culture? What are their characteristics which have made this rebirth possible? Are they democratic? Do they possess qualities of leadership?

Hu Shih, eminent scholar and Chinese ambassador to the United States for four years (1938-1942), has toured our country from end to end, lecturing on the culture and characteristics of his people. He has greatly informed us and endeared his people to us. Other lecturers, Chinese and American, have been engaged in like activity as well as radio broadcasters and contributors to magazines.

Of books on China we have many. For the specialist on the subject of trade relations and diplomatic intercourse there are learned treatises, but so full of detailed and technical knowledge that they are of little use to the general reader. At the other extreme there are superficial accounts of the traveler who has tarried but a short time in coastal cities of

PREFACE

the Orient or at most penetrated only to the more accessible cities of the interior. Brief but authentic accounts of China's civilization and culture, her distinctive contributions to the story of world civilization, are sadly lacking.

Because of my conviction that there is a desire on the part of the general reader and young student in the United States for a history of China told in broad strokes with the principal persons and events sketched in high relief, I have attempted this short and informal history of the Chinese. I have placed emphasis, not on the political details, but on the economic and social phases of their progress; the beginnings of industrial arts, the growth of religion, literature and philosophy, the more intimate contact with her neighbors by the overland route across central Asia in Roman times and later by modern water routes.

My periods of residence in China created for me an atmosphere and background which have constantly been of value in interpreting China's past history and in understanding current events. The years of my stay covered a remarkably significant span of time; the last years of the famous Empress Dowager and the Revolution of 1911, then, the exciting beginnings of the Republic, later, the régime of various war lords and the coming of the Nationalists. On my last trip in 1937, just before the outbreak of the war with Japan, I found Nanking (then the capital) alive to the dangers that lay ahead and energetically preparing for the ordeal. The spirit of Nanking has become the spirit of Chungking, which pervades the present period in China's long and eventful history.

M. A. N.

Washington, D.C.

PREFACE

The Orient are at most penetrance only to the most accessible parts of the interior. Brief but authentic accounts of China's civilization and culture, her distinctive contributions to the heritage of world civilization, are sadly lacking.

Because of my conviction that there is a desire on the part of the learned reader and young student of the United States for a knowledge of China told in broad strokes with the principal events and epochs depicted in high relief, I have attempted this short and informal history of the Chinese. I have placed emphasis not on the political details, but on the economic and social phases of their progress, the beginnings of industrial arts, the growth of religion, literature and philosophy, the recent intimate contact with her neighbors by the overland route across central Asia in Roman times and later by modern water routes.

My periods of residence in China created for me an atmosphere and background which have constantly been of value in interpreting China's past history and in understanding current events. The visits of my stay covered a remarkably significant span during the last years of the famous Empress Dowager and the Revolution of 1911, then, the exciting beginnings of the Republic, later the régime of various war lords and the coming of the Nationalists. On my last trip in 1937, just before the outbreak of the war with Japan, I found Nanking (then the capital) alive to the dangers that lay ahead and energetically preparing for the ordeal. The spirit of Nanking has become the spirit of Chungking, which pervades the present period in China's long and eventful history.

M.A.N.

Washington, D.C.

CONTENTS

CHAPTER   PAGE

PART ONE: THE FIXING OF CUSTOM

I	A Panoramic Glimpse of China	17
II	Mythical Beginnings	23
III	Legendary Heroes	27
IV	Archaeology Finds the Shangs	36
V	The Chou Dynasty. The Fixing of Custom	45
VI	The Eastern Chou Dynasty. An Age of Creative Thought and Literature	59

PART TWO: EXPANSION AND INTERCOURSE

VII	The Ch'in Dynasty. A Unified Empire	75
VIII	The Hans	83
IX	The Dark Ages in China	100
X	The Golden Age of the T'ang Dynasty	110
XI	The "Five Little Ages" and the Sung Dynasty	130
XII	The Mongol Rule	141

PART THREE: THE SHUT-IN PERIOD

CHAPTER		PAGE
XIII	The Ming or Bright Dynasty	161
XIV	The Chinese Again a Conquered People	182
XV	Foreign Trade Advances	201
XVI	The Tai Ping Rebellion	214
XVII	The Empress Dowager	227
XVIII	China's Vast Empire Is Shrinking	239

PART FOUR: REFORM AND REVOLUTION

XIX	Reform and Reaction	251
XX	The Empress Dowager Again and the Last Manchu Emperor	267
XXI	Reform Changes into Revolution	277
XXII	Students and War Lords	298
XXIII	The Nationalists Come into Power	308
XXIV	The Nationalist Regime	318
XXV	Nationalism Prepares for a Test	335
XXVI	The "Popular Front" Faces Japan	349
XXVII	China at War	358
	Citations	373
	Additional Bibliography	385
	Index	393

PART ONE

THE FIXING OF CUSTOM

THE FOUR HUNDRED MILLION

CHAPTER I

A Panoramic Glimpse of China

BEFORE we step back some thousands of years into the past to trace the early beginnings of what is now China let us pause to take one brief panoramic glimpse of China today. It will probably be easier to follow the historic narrative if we review a few basic points about the physical scene in which the story unfolds.

In size and position China more nearly matches the United States than any other country in the world. It stretches across the great central part of Asia as the United States does across North America. Siberia lies to the north of it as Canada lies north of our country and the long peninsula of India borders it on the south much as Mexico borders the States. There is, however, one great difference between the two countries—both on the east and west of America are great oceans, whereas China is bordered by water on her eastern side only. In this she is not so fortunate as America, for it limits her opportunities for foreign commerce. China's western border is hemmed in by the all but impassable Himalayas on the south and deserts on the north. The Himalayas and deserts, however, help as well as hinder for they protect her from attack.

If you should fly over China in an airplane you would see a country divided quite distinctly into halves, one brown, one green. For mile after mile and province after province as you moved over southern China you would look down on a countryside more intensely green than America ever is, for there is no green so vivid as rice, the universal crop of southern China. You would see a vast checker-board spread out, each square carpeted with green rice blades, each square bordered by dike paths covered with green grass. Along the streams and the canals in phalanx after phalanx these rice paddies lie; on the mountain sides they rise in terrace after terrace.

In narrow valleys between mountain ranges in odd corners grow the tea shrubs, their evergreen leaves a thick leathery green, punctuated in the spring by bright green leaf buds. The leaves of the mulberry on which the silkworms feed are a duller green and around the farmhouses you would see the feathery, ever-green bamboo; around the temples and tombs, the cypress. All these greens are the shining greens that come with much rain. Mist, rain and green fertility—that is southern China.

This great fertile tract, the largest of China's agricultural regions, extends along the great Yangtse Valley and along the eastern coast. To the southwest the land is more rugged and less fertile.

But when you have flown across the Yangtse and left its valley behind, quite suddenly the country changes. North of the Yangtse the sun shines almost as many days as rain falls south of it. Great stretches of plain, brown and fertile, and great stretches of desert, brown and sterile, stretch away into the distance. Wherever there is moisture enough for crops you see beans and wheat and the giant millet called *kaoliang*. Its corn-like leaves early turn yellow and it puts forth heavy heads of red brown grain. The soil, too, in the north is red-brown. Out of it the peasants make their mud houses. Except for the July rainy season it rarely rains in the north, and often whole sections are without rain for two or three years. Sunshine and red-brown earth, red-brown huts, red-brown crops—that is northern China. Here the fertile sections are scattered, many of them small, but we notice two sizable ones: the smaller a more southerly one lying in the delta of the Yellow River and the other to the northeast, the newly formed land of Manchukuo.

China, like America, has great variety in climate and thus of agricultural products. In the north by late November the thermometer often registers many degrees below zero; in the south in that same month the chrysanthemums are blooming. This divergence of climate makes it possible for China to grow most of the grains, fruits and vegetables that the world knows. Wheat, millet, corn and rice grow in plenty; apples and persimmons thrive in the north and oranges in the south and in between tea and the mulberry tree. Somewhere in the vast country of China are raised all the vegetables that we enjoy and many with which we are not so familiar, such as bamboo and water chestnut. Sir Robert Hart said: "China has the best food, rice; the best drink, tea; and the best clothing, silk."

China's mineral resources are in comparison with other countries limited. According to recent surveys it is well established that supplies of oil, iron, copper and probably sulphur are small. Copper has been mined since ancient times but never has been found in rich ores or large deposits, so mines have continually been opened in new localities only to be quickly exhausted. Iron is distinctly limited and of poor quality. Of gold and silver there is little and that toward the Siberian border in the new state of Manchukuo. However, the country is rich in two minerals—coal and antimony. The supply of coal is plentiful and of good quality. One half lies in the northern province of Shansi. Of antimony eighty per cent of the world supply is mined in China.

Lumber supplies are pathetically meager. In the northern loess lands there apparently never were any forests and those in other sections have been cut down long ago. In the northwest, wood is used only for roof beams, simple farm implements and coffins. Benches, beds and tables are made of mud. Even in the rich agricultural regions of central and southeastern China wood for house building is limited to the frames of houses, window-frames and doors, the walls being built of mud and the roofs of tiles. The people clip the hillsides closely for stubble to burn in their tiny clay stoves.

Three great river systems cross China from west to east. The Yellow River runs through the brown loess land. It is known as "China's Sorrow," rightly called, for every year it overflows its banks, destroying crops and scattering stones over the fields, making them untillable. For practically the whole of its journey from west to east across China it is turbulent and unnavigable, offering the Chinese little opportunity to use it as a highway of trade.

The Yangtse, rising in the remote peaks of the Himalayas, cuts its way through the very heart of Asia, four thousand miles to the Yellow Sea, dividing China in two, separating the green half from the brown. For six hundred miles it is navigable for ocean-going steamers and for smaller steamers for fifteen hundred. Then it, too, becomes turbulent and unnavigable. It, too, floods its banks, but although it often destroys the crops, its floods have also a beneficial aspect. Fertile plains along its shores are its gift. The silt carried in suspension and finally deposited along the coast adds a mile of rich alluvial land to its delta each sixty years.

The West River, the third of China's great waterways, flows through the green expanse of southern China. For many miles it offers a highway to the Chinese. Junks and

A PANORAMIC GLIMPSE OF CHINA

steamers move back and forth carrying the products of the fertile south down to the coast, and bringing back things made in Japan, America and England.

Water power is plentiful in the south where already many power sites have been developed. To the west great development is possible in the Yangtse gorges but in the north the rivers are too variable for hydroelectric power.

In all this modern China there are but a few hundred miles of railroads, all of them near the coast. China, today, as she has for centuries, depends in the south on her three great river systems and her network of canals built long ago, and in the north on her roads worn into deep ruts by the continual passage of the carts. Within the last few years in coastal provinces the construction of automobile roads has been making rapid headway. For carrying on foreign commerce she has a goodly number of seaports, eight or nine, scattered along her seacoast much as we have on our Atlantic coast. The most important of these are Canton, Amoy, Swatow, Shanghai, Tsingtao, Chefoo and Tientsin.

Today four hundred millions of people inhabit the plains and mountains of this vast country. The Chinese people, like the country, can be divided into two main divisions: northern and southern—two distinct types. The northerner is tall and broad-shouldered, slow of speech and slow to anger; the southerner, short, slender and agile, excitable and fiery of temper. In this difference of temperament lies much of China's history. Speech also shows something of a twofold division, but the dialects are numerous and widely varied. Those of the northern and western provinces maintain enough similarity so that they can be understood even though sometimes with difficulty by each other. But in the southeast we find dialects varying so sharply that the men of one province cannot be understood by those of another province of the same section much less by the Chinese of the west and north.

Within the Great Wall is China proper, which is divided into eighteen provinces. Bordering the eighteen provinces on the north and west are districts which at times have come under China's sovereignty, and at other times have been independent. Today they are in various conditions of independence or semi-independence. On the northeast lies the newly formed independent country of Manchukuo and west of it Inner and Outer Mongolia, the latter with large Russian and the former with Japanese influence. On the northwest corner is Chinese Turkestan, largely Mohammedan, while south of it lies Tibet where British interests loom large.

The Chinese people are estimated to comprise one-fifth of the population of the world. This great mass has grown in numbers and developed in civilization since the days of primitive China when they were but groups of peasants scattered here and there in the Yellow River Valley with barbarian neighbors, wild horsemen of the deserts, on their northern and western frontiers. The amalgamation of these groups of peasants into a nation and their constant struggles with the "Barbarians" is China's historical story.

CHAPTER II

Mythical Beginnings

LIKE all primitive people the early Chinese sought to explain their own origin and that of the world in a series of myths. China's story of creation differs from either the Greek story or our own as told in the Bible in the greater recognition it gives to the slow evolution of earth and man. The Chinese did not conceive of a god dwelling above in the heavens and creating a world. God and the heavens were made later. First chaos alone existed, a waste of water that bubbled and surged, finally producing two powers or forces, *yin* and *yang*, which after long ages brought forth a man named P'an Ku. Shortly P'an Ku began to shape this chaos of which he was the center, and which had now inexplicably turned from water into stone.

With a mallet and chisel he worked for eighteen thousand years, splitting and carving, and shaping the great blocks of granite which floated in space. Out of them he made the earth, the sun, the moon and the stars. From some mysterious source came the divine dragon, phoenix and tortoise to aid him in his work. P'an Ku grew into a gigantic man, each day adding six feet to his stature as gradually he was absorbed into the world he was creating. His head made the mountains, his breath the vaporous mist and clouds. This mighty man, now hundreds of thousands of feet tall, spoke and his voice boomed across the earth in thunder. His veins became the great rivers of the earth; his skin and hair the trees. His teeth and bones became the metals hidden deep in the earth. The dropping sweat of this hard-working giant turned into rain. And last of all, the insects which crawled across his body took the form of human beings who peopled the earth. Then he died. But he lived again in his own handiwork—the earth, the heavens and mankind. Thus in naïve fashion and with many inconsistencies do the Chinese tell the story of creation. This P'an Ku myth did not originate apparently until the third or fourth century A. D. At least it was not written until then.

Other myths carry the story farther down in the progress of the world. Some time before P'an Ku had finished chiseling out his heavens and earth, in some mysterious way five ancients took shape. The first was called the Yellow Ancient and he became the ruler of the earth. The second, the Red Lord, ruled over fire, and the Dark Lord over water. The Wood Prince had charge of the wood, and the Mother of Metals presided over the metals of the earth. Of course, according to the story of P'an Ku, earth, fire, water, wood and metal had not yet been created. But that did not matter to the makers of the myths. In these far-off beginnings of the world all sorts of miraculous things could happen.

And then came one known as the True Prince, and the five Ancients begged him to rule as the Supreme God, so he ascended above the thirty-three heavens that some time during the eighteen thousand years P'an Ku must have made. He was called the White Jade Ruler and dwelt in the Jasper Castle of White Jade looking down on the thirty-three heavens and the world spread out at his feet.

All the five Ancients helped him to rule over the thousand tribes of men. The Dark God dwelt in the north and the Red God in the south. The Wood Prince found his home in the east and the Mother of Metals in the west. That left but one Ancient homeless—him they called the Yellow

Ancient. To this one was given the task of teaching mankind the arts. We infer that he dwelt in the midst of mankind. Many, many centuries afterward the Yellow Ancient was supposed to be born again, not as a baby but as an old man with white beard and hair. He was called Lao-tzŭ, Old Ancestor. Later—some time during the sixth century B. C.—the Yellow Ancient appeared again on the earth in human form. This time he was known as the Old Man of the River. Even today he is a great favorite among the Chinese. He appears over and over again in their pictures, and figures of him are often found in the shops carved out of wood or jade. Usually he carries a staff and he has a very large head with a bulging forehead, indicating great knowledge.

One of the most interesting figures in all Chinese mythology is the dragon. A strange and gorgeous animal, he has the head of a camel, horns of a stag, eyes of a demon, neck of a snake, claws of an eagle. The soles of his feet are those of a tiger, and he is covered with glowing scales of gold. He has a beard under his long snout, a hairy tail and shaggy legs. In his mouth the dragon holds pearls worth a hundred pieces of gold. When he spits them forth they fall to the earth for man's use. The dragon loves all precious stones and dislikes iron. The dragon both destroys and protects. One hundred and seventeen of his scales are imbued with powers of good and thirty-six with powers of evil.

There are many dragons but all of them are intimately connected with water. They dwell in pools, in the rivers, in the ocean. When they ascend to the clouds they bring rain; when they rise to the surface of rivers there are floods; when they rise to the surface of the ocean the tide comes in; when they sink from sight the tide goes out. The season of drought is winter when the dragons sleep in their pools.

In the spring they stir from their sleep and leap into the sky to fight one another. Then comes the thunder, and the rain pours down in torrents. When the battle lasts too long there is a flood on the earth. When a province suffers drought and the sky is a cloudless blue, the governor orders the people to go out and beat upon iron, making a great noise to rouse the dragons sleeping within the pools. They throw iron into the pools and the dragons rise to the surface to protect their eyes. Then comes rain. If the rain continues for too long a period the dragon must be driven back into his home beneath the water.

The dragon has played his part throughout all Chinese history. The emperor was closely connected with the dragon god. His throne was called "The Dragon Throne." When wars and revolutions came, it was because the priests and the emperor failed to control the dragons. Then the indignant and ruined peasantry had a right to overthrow the dynasty and start a new line strong enough to control the dragons. Until the days of the revolution in 1911 the Chinese flag was a great dragon upon a yellow background. That flag has gone now and so too has the Dragon Throne, but the people still believe in the dragon.

CHAPTER III

LEGENDARY HEROES

SOME tens of thousands or perhaps hundreds of thousands of years after P'an Ku's creation of the earth and of mankind, we come to a group of kings and emperors whose names are well known and revered among the Chinese for their divine character and beneficent works. They have undoubtedly been evolved from a combination of fact and fancy. Though these personages are largely and some of them no doubt wholly fictitious, still they have become heroes to the Chinese and are as much a part of the life of the Chinese people as Homer's heroes are a part of the literature and life of the Greeks. These legendary emperors may be divided into two classes: first, a group of discoverers to whom are attributed the inventions which started the Chinese on their march toward civilization; and, second, a group revered as exemplars of conduct.

The earliest of these legendary personages are called "Divine Emperors," some of them half man, half dragon. The first one according to the confused legendary chronology[1] is Sui Jen, the Producer of Fire. The Chinese characters that form his name mean that he brought fire down from heaven and used it in cooking food. Whether or not there ever was such a man, the legend is an attempt to tell the story of what was probably the first discovery that the Chinese, like other people, stumbled upon which began to lift them out of the savage state. To this great discovery of Sui Jen another divine ruler, Fu Hsi, added several others. He taught his subjects how to catch animals and to fish with nets, hence his name Fu Hsi, Conqueror of Animals. He also taught them how to rear domestic animals and use them for food, thereby acquiring the name Po Hsi, Butcher of Animals. The legends also add that Fu Hsi invented musical instruments, among them the thirty-five-string lute. To him is ascribed also a form of picture writing which took the place of an earlier system of tying knots.

After Fu Hsi many thousand years pass, and then appears yet another divine ruler, Shen Nung. He taught the people the art of agriculture, thus acquiring the title "God of Agriculture." He also taught the use of herbs for medicine and even today in medicine shops there stands a figure of Shen Nung and before it a bowl of burning incense.

Again a lapse and then another inventive emperor steps forth whose fame has endured through the centuries. Huang Ti is his name and to him is attributed the making of the first boats, carts, bows, arrows, utensils of wood, and pottery. He gives the people a calendar and a system of reckoning time by dividing it into the year of the cat, the rat and so on to twelve different animals repeated five times in each period of sixty years. To this day the Chinese count the years thus in cycles of sixty years. Huang Ti was also a great soldier and the inventor of armor. He is supposed to have opened a copper mine and started the coinage of copper coins. He built a temple, a palace. He improved agriculture by determining the time for sowing cereals and planting trees. A remarkable record for one emperor even if his reign was a hundred years as legends say!

The Chinese legends add one more to the list of discoverers. To Sui Jen, the producer of fire; Fu Hsi, the conqueror of animals; Shen Nung, teacher of agriculture; and Huang Ti, maker of boats and carts, they add the Empress, Su Ling, wife of Huang Ti, who gave them the great gift of silk. Su Ling, so the old tales in the classic poetry go, taught her people how to cultivate the mulberry and to feed the silkworm upon the mulberry leaves. Just when they learned to unwind the silk from the cocoons, spin it into thread, and weave it into silk cloth we do not know.

But we do learn from the old records that from early times the care of silkworms was the work of women and also that the King and his wife dignified the industry by giving it their sanction. The lady, Su Ling, endeared herself to all posterity by caring for silkworms herself. All subsequent queens were regarded as patronesses of silk culture even as the kings were patrons of agriculture. In the spring, the Emperor went forth and plowed the first furrow and the Empress blessed the silkworms. The old records say that in the last month of the spring the Empress purified herself and offered a sacrifice to the goddess of silkworms. She went into the eastern fields and collected mulberry leaves. She forbade noble dames and ladies of statesmen adorning themselves and excused her attendants from their sewing and embroidery in order that they might give all their care to the rearing of silkworms. When the work of the season was ended the women carried their cocoons to the ruler whose wife in royal dress received them. She "caused a sheep and a pig to be killed and cooked to treat the ladies. This probably was the ancient custom at the presentation of the cocoons."[2]

The Chinese attribute the invention of spinning also to women and worshiped these first spinners as goddesses. An old myth tells us of a young girl who promised to marry a white horse. For this her father killed her. Some days later the neighbors found the girl wrapped in a horse's hide hanging from a tree, and as they watched she turned into a worm and wove a cocoon for herself. When the cocoon was taken down a girl stepped out and spun the silk of the cocoon into silk thread and took it to the market place and sold it. Later the girl rode away on the horse hide saying, "Heaven has assigned me to the task of watching over silkworms. Do not yearn for me." Thus did the goddess of the silkworms come into Chinese mythology. Modern scholars believe that the Chinese legends are right in placing this discovery very early in their history and that silk spinning was known before the Bronze Age.

What a fascinating sight it would be if we could look back into those far-away ages and see the prehistoric Chinese living along the banks of the Yellow River on the flat brown loess land, discovering the cocoon of the silkworm and then finding that that cocoon could be unwound. Ancient records tell us that to loosen the strands of the cocoon they moistened them in their mouths. How did they first learn this? Did some starving man start to eat one of the cocoons and put it in his mouth to suck and by accident find the moistened silk could be unwound? Who later thought to put the cocoon into boiling water, thus loosening the strands of many cocoons at one time? And how did they learn that when it was unwound they could twist several of these strands, delicate as spider webs, into a thread strong enough to be woven into cloth? None of these questions can be answered. The knowledge of these things was buried thousands of years ago with the inarticulate men of that age who did not know how to record their achievements.

The second group of legendary heroes are rulers who have been revered by the Chinese for their righteous conduct. To both emperors and people they have been held up as the perfect men whom all should copy; Yao and Shun, models of virtue and propriety; Yü, the Chinese Noah, and lastly T'ang, the virtuous, who was willing to sacrifice his own life to the people.

Yao and Shun have become objects of the greatest national veneration, the Chinese historian, Li Ung Bing, saying as late as 1914 that no greater honor can be paid to a Chinese emperor than to compare him favorably to Yao and Shun. As the Anglo-Saxon builds his ideal of chivalry around King Arthur and his Round Table so moral teachers of the Chinese have built the national ideal of simplicity around Yao and Shun. Legend pictures Yao a heroic figure in a yellow cap and dark tunic, riding in a chariot with white horses. Off duty he did not use jewels, and his clothes were simple and without variety. In summer he affected a simple garb of hemp, in winter deer skins. The eaves of his thatch were not trimmed, and the beams had no ornamental ends. He drank his lentil broth from a clay dish with a wooden spoon. Yet was he "reverential, intelligent, accomplished and thoughtful. He united the various parts of his domain in bonds of peace so that concord reigned among the black-haired people."[3]

In the tales handed down through the centuries Yao is credited with making the "black-haired" people so honest and virtuous that no one ever shut the doors of his house at night. So kind, simple and tolerant was the "model emperor" that anyone might appeal to him, writing his plea on a tablet which was placed outside the palace for the emperor to see. Anyone might voice his grievance or his desires. He had but to strike the drum which stood outside the emperor's house. The wants of this simple agricultural people were not many. Only when food was insufficient did they seek out the emperor. They labored in their fields intent on their crops and their families. A peasant song of the time goes:

> "We rise at sunrise
> We rest at sunset
> Dig wells and drink
> Till our fields and eat
> What is the strength of the Emperor to us?"[4]

In their folk tales, the Chinese tell of the calendar trees that grew at the court of Yao. On one hand stood a tree which put forth a leaf every day for fifteen days as the moon waxed, and then as the moon waned daily for fifteen days it shed a leaf. Thus they measured the months. On the other hand stood a tree which put forth a leaf once a month for six months, and then shed its leaves each month until the year was ended. Thus they measured the years.

As the end of Yao's days drew near he looked around for a successor who would be able to rule in a difficult situation for the people were suffering from a famine, the result of an overflow of the Yellow River. This model Emperor was so disinterested that he passed over his son whom he did not consider worthy and chose Shun. Shun was an unmarried man of the people, a man noted for his filial piety. His father was obstinately wicked, his mother insincere, his half-brother arrogant. Yet he was able by his filial piety to live in harmony with them and to lead them gradually to self-government so that they were no longer filled with great wickedness. Yao married him to his two daughters, made him co-ruler and successor to the throne.

In the ancient records Shun, like Yao, has been featured as a model character, wise, and vigilant for the welfare of the people. He improved the methods of astronomy, he created new forms of worship to *Shang Ti* (the Supreme God) and to the presiding spirits of the land. In the government too, he was busy; he divided the land into twelve states. He, like Yao, was noted for his wisdom and justice in the administration of the government. This is his charge to his Minister of Education: "The people are wanting in affection for one another, and do not docilely observe the five orders of relationship. It is yours as the Minister of Instruction, reverently to set forth the lessons of duty belonging to those five orders." Much effort he spent on the control of floods and preserving the land for agriculture. To the Minister of Agriculture he said: "The black-haired people are suffering from famine. Do you, O prince, sow (for them) the various kinds of grain."[5] The reigns of these two, Yao and Shun, are styled "The Golden Age." It is China's millennium.

Shun, at the end of his reign, followed the example of Yao and appointed his successor, Yü, his surveyor general. Yü was China's Noah. For China too has the story of the flood and Yü is the hero. In a literary work, the *Tso Chuan*, the people cry:

> "How grand was the achievement of Yü
> How far reaching his marvelous energy
> But for Yü we should all have been fishes."[6]

Legge has given us a translation of the story of the flood as Yü himself is supposed to have told it.

> ". . . the inundating waters seemed to assail the heavens and in their vast extent embraced the mountains and over-topped the hills so that people were bewildered and overwhelmed. I mounted my four conveyances, carts, boats, sledges, and spiked shoes, and all along the hills hewed down the woods at the same time along with Yi showing the multitudes how to get flesh to eat. I opened passages for the streams throughout the nine provinces and conducted them to the streams at the same time along with Chi sowing grain and showing the multitudes how to procure the food of toil along with flesh meat. I urged them further to exchange what they had for what they had not, and to dispose of their accumulated stores. In this way all the people got grain to eat and all the states began to come under good rule."[7]

So grand was the achievement of Yü that ancient literature of the seventh century B. C. makes him a god of hills and rivers and a later passage calls him God of Shê (God of the Soil). And yet another says, "Yü, whose labors extended over the whole earth, was after his death, Shê."[8]

It is now believed by modern Chinese historians that these model emperors were created by Confucius and other scholars writing from the sixth to the third centuries B. C. The period was one of chaos and warring among the various small states of China. The philosophers of the time, of whom Confucius was foremost, hoped to end the warfare and disaster then universal in all China by exhorting kings, military leaders and people to follow the example of the ancients. In the time of Yao and Shun and Yü, they pointed out, emperors were intent on the welfare of the people, the people were honest and faithful so that in all the land none need lock his door. This is now called the "Model Emperor Lore"[9] or known as the Confucian theory of history. It is believed that it was built up to teach the people lessons of sobriety and peace. These emperors may or may not have been real men but at least it became the custom to look back into bygone ages for examples of perfection.

And finally one more legendary hero appears, T'ang, but about him there is somewhat more evidence of authenticity. The legendary story is that T'ang, a virtuous prince of the little principality of Shang, part of modern Honan, distressed by the ruin of the country by the wicked emperors, became convinced that he was called by Heaven to save the empire. He conquered the imperial forces and ascended the throne with his capital at Po. It is recorded in the *Shu Ching* that he announced to the people that he had not desired to usurp the throne but had acted under the command from Heaven. A drought of seven years brought great distress to the people, so great that they thought a human victim should be sacrificed to appease the wrath of Heaven. In this crisis T'ang proved his nobility of character by offering to be that victim. Accordingly, he fasted for seven days and then proceeded in the white robes of mourning to a mulberry grove, the place chosen for the sacrifice. But High Heaven intervened and sent a heavy rain as he knelt praying. The legends make T'ang the founder of a new dynasty known as the Shang or Yin which lasted roughly from 1700—1100 B. C. But at this point the findings of archaeology begin to supplement the legendary history of the ancient writings.

CHAPTER IV

Archaeology Finds the Shangs

ARCHAEOLOGY in the modern sense is only beginning in China, but some approach to it was made in antiquarian studies of earlier centuries. During the first hundred years of the Sung Dynasty, in the tenth and eleventh centuries A. D., Chinese scholars were interested in collecting antiques, mainly bronzes, jades and coins. They gave much labor to the cataloguing of the pieces, reproducing pictures of the objects, and interpreting the inscriptions found on them. After a lapse of five hundred years the movement was revived. It followed much the same methods but included the writing of treatises on the objects. It also broadened the range of objects to include bricks, tiles and seals. Only in the last thirty to forty years has archaeological research of modern character, including excavations, been undertaken.

China has not been fortunate, compared with many ancient countries, in the manner in which her relics of antiquity have been handed down to modern times. In Egypt, for example, the Pyramids built nearly five thousand years ago have served as a storehouse for objects of antiquity—utensils, jewelry, and the very bodies of the people preserved as mummies. In the paintings and inscriptions on the walls of the tomb chapels and in the models of houses and boats there has been preserved a record of the customs of the people in their proper historical setting. These huge buildings were possible to Egypt because of the cliffs of stone and rock which formed the banks of the Nile River.

But Nature was not so kind, in this respect, to China. The valley of the Yellow River, the center of the earliest Chinese civilization, was shifting sand, and the early Chinese found no stone with which to build large tombs and temples. Over all northern China there are thick layers of loess consisting of great accumulations of wind-borne soil which were formed long before historic China, probably contemporaneously with the Riss-Würm glaciation of Europe. Mr. Cressey describes the loess as it looks today: "Sprinkled over the countryside as though by a giant flour-sifter a veneer of fine wind-blown silt blankets over a hundred thousand square miles of the northern provinces."[1] It is thought improbable that there have ever been forests in recent geological times as the loess is not suitable for dense forest growth. Ancient writers describe the plains as vast areas of grass and, where the rivers overflowed, as expanses of shallow lakes and marshes. Under these conditions there was no material for buildings of a permanent nature. The fact that this stretch of loess was the home of the ancient Chinese seems to be sufficient explanation why so few ancient relics have been preserved.

Furthermore, the articles so far excavated have not been found stratified according to the chronological era to which they belong. Objects from various periods are found together, which makes dating and chronological sequence difficult to discover. In spite of these handicaps and although, as we said, scientific excavation began only recently, Chinese and Western archaeologists who have been digging on various sites in northern China, have already progressed far enough to furnish much material on the Neolithic Age. They have been working in the modern provinces of Kansu, Shensi, Shansi and Honan. The Japanese excavating in Manchukuo, Mongolia, Korea and Siberia have found much material which supplements the work in China proper.

Just below the present layer of loess and even in it are found many traces of the Neolithic culture. One of the most interesting sites for this period, discovered by J. G. Andersson,[2] is that of Yang Shao Ts'un in the province of Honan. The finds consisted of broken bits of pottery, stone implements including adzes, rectangular knives, slate and bone arrowheads, spinning whorls (some of stone and some of clay), stone mattocks used in primitive agriculture, mussel shells, bone sewing needles and awls. As there was no metal with these remains nor any writing, Mr. Andersson concluded that this is the site of a prehistoric village of the late Neolithic Age. Some of the pieces of pottery are from vessels shaped like those of the early historic period indicating that the people of this Neolithic village were ancestors or relatives of the historic Chinese.

Summarizing the information gathered from this and other excavations, C. W. Bishop[3] derives many interesting facts regarding this Neolithic culture. The types of skeletons and skulls closely resemble those of people living in the same region today. Traces of dwelling places show that the people lived in pits, circular or elliptical in shape, similar to storage pits of the present. They were evidently roofed over with timbers and mud; the entrance was from the top and the floor was covered with reed mats or bark. These pit dwellings were used by the masses well into the historical period. Earthenware cooking stoves were like those in use today.

Hunting, fishing and agriculture were the industries of these early people. There is proof of their hunting in the implements made of antler bones; of their fishing in the fish bones, tortoise shells and shells of fresh-water mollusks. But agriculture seems to have been the leading industry. There are stone leaf-shaped mattocks or foot plows, and small stone hoes. Farther to the south were found polished

ARCHAEOLOGY FINDS THE SHANGS

stone axes, picks, and a tool which reminds one of a sickle. There were numbers of flat stones, mealing stones used for grinding grain. Millet was the chief grain and in one site there appeared signs of giant millet, called *kaoliang* today. The dog and pig seem to have been the only domestic animals.

Pottery fragments were mostly very coarse, some of a gray color, some few pinkish-buff with patterns in a darker shade designed from the impression made by strings or textiles. No textiles have survived but those patterns on the pottery show that weaving was known, probably with hemp thread. The only complete pieces of pottery were found in connection with burial sites. These were three-legged bowls similar to the later bronze sacrificial vessels which are so well known. There was a little painted pottery which may have been brought in from farther west though as a rule the villages show little trace of any connection with other villages or outside regions.

Another very productive site is that of the "Oracle Bones" at An Yang in northern Honan which is a place of a later culture, that of the Bronze Age. The place became known to archaeologists by accident when curio dealers in 1899 brought some inscribed bones to Peking. Some of these fell into the hands of a Chinese scholar and statesman but as he died in the Boxer Rebellion of the next year his collection passed to other Chinese who worked on deciphering the inscriptions. One of these men visited the site and, deciding the find was exhausted, did not attempt any excavating.

Another collection of these bones went to Shantung where it fell into the hands of a local merchant who loaned the collection to an American, Mr. F. H. Chalfant, for inspection. Some of these bones are now in a German collection and some in the possession of the Royal Asiatic Society at

Shanghai. With the bones were also found tortoise shells which, as well as the bones, show cracks and burnings and inscribed characters. Some of the bones are shoulder blades of ox or large deer, and others are tibia bones of deer and goat split lengthwise. As the bones are broken and have been scattered, it is very difficult, generally impossible, to match them together. The characters are archaic, the oldest form of writing yet found in China, and many of them are unintelligible in modern writing. But from the ones that have been deciphered it is clear that the bones were used in divination. It appears that a priest scratched the question of a suppliant on a bone or tortoise shell which was provided with a small round hole. When this was held over a fire by means of a bronze poker run into the hole, there appeared lines and cracks which assumed similarity to written characters. These were interpreted by the augurs or priests who thus announced the answer of the divinity. Out of reverence to the diviner the bones were buried. The rulers depended upon oracles to regulate their affairs even to the minutest details, the taking of a trip, the performing of a sacrifice, going out fishing or hunting, or sending out an expedition. It was obligatory for the ruler to follow the answer found in the cracks as interpreted by the priests. On the bones are recorded the local date, the subject of the query and the oracular answer.

Mr. Chalfant, who has worked on the deciphering of the inscriptions, finds the archaic symbols largely unintelligible. Translation is further impeded owing to the broken condition of the bones and shells and consequent incompleteness of the inscriptions. But he seems to have made considerable progress. One tortoise shell he found almost complete. The upper right-hand row of characters records the local date and an inquiry about the extent of progeny. In the left-hand row appear the characters for "not" and

ARCHAEOLOGY FINDS THE SHANGS

"lucky." On the other side there was a sentence repeated three times, each time with a different date. The date was followed by, "I ask the Serpent Father to inquire." A Chinese student interprets Serpent Father as a mystic title of the soothsayer. Inquiries for divination were made concerning parents, sons, daughters, animals, crops, utensils. Another inscription seems to read, "Ask selection of prime minister. Consultation of the oracle by Royalty."[4]

In 1914 a young man, James Mellon Menzies, went as a missionary to northern China and heard of the Oracle Bones. He visited the site at An Yang and decided that more specimens might be found by digging. Accordingly, he set himself to collecting them from the river banks where he gathered thousands of fragments of bones, some of them as small as a bean. Unfortunately, this material, left in Mr. Menzies' house, was destroyed in 1927 in the civil wars but not before pictures had been taken. The information from these finds is similar to that already translated and is all connected with divination practices.

Still later, Dr. J. H. Ingram made translations of other bones. He found, with the names of the kings, the names of wives and those of two grades of concubines. Hunting was carried on for the purpose of obtaining materials for sacrifice. One inscription read, "On the day *i mao,* inquiry was made if the Emperor should go hunting to the region known as Chéh, would he encounter heavy rain," and the answer, "He would not encounter heavy rain."[5]

On another, "Last month the rain stopped. This month it rained again and we captured an elephant."[6] Characters were used for all the words except elephant which was a pictograph, a very good drawing.

In recent years the Institute of History and Philology under the direction of Dr. C. Li assumed excavation work at An Yang as one of its enterprises. In this undertaking it has been aided by the Freer Gallery of Art of Washington, D. C.

The bones, besides the valuable information they give regarding religious rites, are of great aid in the historical reconstruction of the period. Recorded on some of the bones is a list of kings which is found to be the same as the list of the Shang Dynasty found in the *Bamboo Annals,* a court record written on bamboo strips in the third or fourth century B. C. But as this was a millennium after the names and events chronicled, modern scholars could place little reliance upon them until verified by some archaeological evidence. This the Oracle Bones have furnished, establishing the Shang Dynasty as one that existed in fact as well as in legend.

The other fragments found with the bones are equally useful in working out the culture of the period. Bronze sacrificial vessels, cups and bowls show that the Shangs had developed the art of casting bronze to a high point of beauty and excellence. Utensils, some of stone, some of bone, and others of bronze, indicate that the people had not entirely abandoned the stone tools of the Neolithic Age but possessed a mingled culture of Stone and Bronze Ages. Maybe the supply of metal was small or maybe the people clung to the old familiar stone and bone tools. The pottery fragments included some of a finer texture than is usual in the ancient sites. It was white with an incised pattern. A Japanese scholar, Mr. Hamada, holds the theory that this white pottery was the de luxe pottery of ancient China and that it was used by the nobles and for religious ceremonies.

The bronzes are splendid examples of the artistic ability of the Chinese. These are libation cups and sacrificial vessels of rare beauty of shape and with raised designs in fish and dragon pattern. Besides the pictorial designs there are inscriptions in the archaic characters which also add to the beauty of the vessels. The inscriptions give direct evidence of ancestor worship. They were ritual and sacrificial in character and were evidently ordered cast by some personage on the occasion of an auspicious event or in honor of an ancestor or sometimes a brother. The announcement of the event was made to the recipient's ancestors as in the following inscription: "Hu of Teng ventured to devise and cause to be made (this time in honor of) his late revered father to be placed among the symbols of favor conferred by the ruler of the State, and treasured as a sacred vessel."[7] Another inscription in Shang calligraphy reads: "On the lucky first day of the 8th moon, it being the *i-mao* day, the duke bestowed serfs on Chí: Chí to commemorate the event, made in honor of his illustrious father whose birth fell on an *i* day, this precious sacred vessel for descendants to share."[8] These sacred vessels the descendants were bidden to treasure.

From archaic inscriptions on the Shang sacrificial cups and bowls as well as from the Oracle Bones, Mr. Hu Shih, Chinese modern student of philosophy, concludes that, "it seems clear that the Shang people were devout worshipers of dead ancestors, that they apparently had no worship of a Supreme God, that they believed in divination."[9] Mr. Bishop differs a little from Hu Shih. In the Neolithic Age, he agrees, "they believed in divination, holding a universal belief with other peoples in Southeastern Asia in spirits, ghosts, mythical monsters, and the efficacy of magic. Mountains, rivers, trees, thunder, tempest, rain were all objects of superstitious awe."[10] But at the time of the Bronze Age (Shang Dynasty) he believes that ancestor worship was held by the aristocracy only. Social divisions between "nobles" and "simple" prevailed, he thinks. The "nobles" consisted of rulers, feudal lords, priests, landholders and fighters. "Simple" were the bulk of the population who as serfs in villages tilled the soil for their masters. These lower classes did not share the religious beliefs of the aristocracy who were the only ones practicing ancestor worship and believing in a Supreme Deity called *Shang Ti,* an all powerful god, or *Ti'en,* Heaven.

These archaeological discoveries bring the Shang Dynasty out of the shadowy traditional stage. They place the early Chinese civilization in the Yellow River Basin and show that by 1700 B. C. the people had entered the Bronze Age. Their bronze vessels and weapons were of fine workmanship while the inscriptions on them and on the Oracle Bones are written in a pictorial form but in a style that indicates a long use of the art. The relics of the Neolithic and Shang periods, so far found, bear out the theory of the legendary writings of China that the growth of her civilization had covered many centuries before it had reached this point of development. The Shangs in their turn handed on a rich heritage of culture to the next dynasty, the famous Chou.

CHAPTER V

THE CHOU DYNASTY. THE FIXING OF CUSTOM

THE Chou Dynasty brings us to the period of historical China. Even yet, however, authentic dates are difficult to determine because items are stated in terms of the reigns of the local princes, each principality having its own system of keeping dates as well as its own style of writing. But the practice of ancestor worship has provided an aid to the research workers in Chinese chronology. As each small state preserved very accurate lists of its chieftains, modern scholars by a careful comparison and checking back and forth of the various histories and the local lists of chieftains are able to determine the first authentic date as 841 B. C.[1] In that year the records show Li Wang, the tenth Chou ruler, fled from his capital. Working backward from this date, the historian established the beginning of the dynasty as 1051 B. C. instead of 1122 as had generally been supposed.

In addition to the ancestral lists there are various court annals which give us more information as to events. The *Bamboo Annals,* written by an anonymous writer of the third century B. C., were dug up from a tomb in 281 A. D. and today are considered one of the most authentic of the Chou Annals. The *Spring* and *Autumn Annals,* written late in the dynasty, furnish a chronological record of events in the state of Lu between the years 722 and 484 B. C. These were brief court records, each event being noted according to the year, month, day and season. The Chinese designate the year by two seasons, warm and cold. The *Spring Annals* included events of spring and summer and the *Autumn Annals* included those of autumn and winter. They ran like this: "In the seventh year of Duke Chou, in Spring, the northern Yen state made peace with the Chi state." "In the summer on the Chia Shen day of the fourteenth month (March II, 594 B. C.) the sun was eclipsed."[2]

Piecing together various records and the results of archaeological finds, we glean the main events of the origin of the Chous and the eight hundred years of their dynasty. The Chou people, pressed from behind by barbarous tribes, slowly migrated eastward. They set up a state in the mountainous district which is now the province of Shensi. This new state thrived and in time overshadowed its neighbors lying to the east, the Shangs of the loess land. At last the founder's son, Wu Wang, overcame the Shangs and ruled from his capital, Ch'ang An in Shensi.

In founding this capital the Chous probably followed the custom which we find recorded in an old ode. It is there set down that a town was surrounded by a ring wall of earth within which were built the chieftain's residence, the temple of his ancestors and an altar for his God of the Soil. Such undoubtedly was the beginning of Ch'ang An, destined to become again and again the capital of China and many centuries later one of the most gorgeous cities the country has ever known.

By the time the Chous became a factor in the affairs of China there were in the Yellow River Basin a number of small states vying with one another for supremacy. The tribal chieftains of earlier days had become lords with much power. Each lord commanded charioteers and foot soldiers and horsemen conscripted from the subjects of his state. He called out his followers to the beat of the drum. Then sitting in his chariot, made of leather or wood and drawn by four or eight horses according to his rank, he rode forth to battle. Behind came other war chariots driven by his nobles. Behind these came the foot soldiers bearing shields made of the skins of rhinoceroses, wearing helmets of skin or copper, and carrying bows and arrows, copper spears and knives. For a brief day a state would gain superior power only to arouse the jealousy of another state, which in turn by bribery, treachery or fighting would gain the supremacy.

When the Chous gained this superior power and set up their dynasty, they called their rulers king, *wang,* and conducted the worship of the sky-god, calling themselves "Sons of the Sky." The royal symbol of the Chous was a battle-ax. They proceeded to organize a kind of feudal system for the country as a whole. There is a tradition that outside the king's domain they divided the land into nine regions. Each region contained thirty first-class, sixty second-class, and one hundred and twenty third-class states classified according to size. Though the Chous may not have worked out so regular an organization as this, still we do know that the Chou rulers developed a system of graded nobility and that large fiefs were given to nobles of the king's own clan. According to tradition, the domains of the first class were one hundred *li* square, those of the second were seventy, and those of the third fifty. As a *li* is one-third of a mile these states were not large, the smallest, in fact, being comparable to our counties. There were smaller states but they hardly ranked as such for they sent their tribute through a near-by first-class state. In the beginning of the Chou Dynasty there were seventeen hundred and seventy-three of these states, but by constant warfare among themselves the number was continually reduced. Smaller states were swallowed up by the more powerful ones until in the course of time we read that the number was reduced to one hundred and sixty, then to twelve, and finally to seven.

The heads of the states held sovereign power in their own domains giving to the king homage, tribute and military aid. It became the habit of the king to cultivate the good will of the larger states, since their military strength was necessary to him. In turn the states needed his moral support. Each state was divided among lesser nobles who owed feudal allegiance to the heads of their state. Unruly nobles carried on war with each other and threatened the position of their overlords. Thus each state was as full of war and intrigue as was the empire itself.

For about two hundred years the Chous managed to hold imperial power over their turbulent vassals. Then came a depraved man to the throne whose misgovernment stirred up discontent and the nobles refused to bring presents to the court. It all resulted in the flight of the king, Li Wang—that flight in 841 B. C. already mentioned as the first authentic date in Chinese history. For a time after this there was no king, but after the death of the exiled ruler his son won back the throne. After another seventy years, however, the Chous had again fallen on evil days, and in 771 B. C. Ch'ang An was sacked and captured by the barbarians from the north because the king failed to obtain sufficient military help from his vassals, the heads of the states. However, the Chous were not entirely undone for they moved their capital eastward to Lo Yang in Honan. This event marks a division in the Chou Dynasty—the early part being known as the Western Chou Dynasty and the latter part as the Eastern Chou.

Though the central government of this dynasty was so lacking in unity and stability, the people were fixing the customs of their economic and social life into a mold which has prevailed with little change down to the present era. Accounts of the customs of the people are found in the *Book of Poetry* or *Odes,* a collection of three hundred

THE CHOU DYNASTY

poems, folk songs from the Shang and Chou Dynasties. These songs give an incomparable picture of the customs of the people. They became very popular and formed a basis for learning and correct manners. It is said that Confucius inquired of his son, "Have you read the *Book of Poetry?* You cannot learn to talk without studying it." Another work, the *Chou Li,* reputed to be written by the Duke of Chou, younger brother of the first Chou king, but really not written until several centuries later, sets down explicitly the official and ceremonial ritual of the Chou Government. The *Chou Li* was largely oral at this time and so its tenets when later written down may have given a somewhat idealized picture of the Chous. But the importance in which the *Book of Poetry* and *Chou Li* came to be held resulted in fixing very rigidly the customs of China, until the last few years. Government practices, religious rites, business organization, family customs were all set forth in much detail.

The land of each state was, as we have seen, parceled out to vassals or lesser nobles. These in turn apportioned the land among the peasant families. The story goes that the land was divided into large squares and each large square into nine small ones. The eight outer squares were allotted one to a family. The c e n t r a l square, which contained a well, was cultivated in common by the group. The produce of this common land went to the lord. This plan of land

1	2	3
8	HELD IN COMMON O WELL	4
7	6	5

tenure was called "The Nine Dots." It was a semicommunal system of farming in which the peasants were serfs on the land. However much the scheme may have been idealized in the written accounts that have come down to us, it evidently had a basis of fact as the title to the land was held by the nobles and the people possessed no ownership rights. They owed to the lord produce, labor and military aid.

The people did not live on their apportioned lands, but in villages of twenty-five families which afforded them protection and sociability. You can see these villages today if you visit northern China much as they were centuries ago. Mud houses stand closely together in a long line down the two sides of a road. At harvest time on the flat or rounded brown mud roofs of the brown mud dwellings lay great heaps of yellow corn, or red-brown grains of the giant millet. The villages at such times are empty, for everyone is busy in the harvest fields. In ancient times the people abandoned the villages from spring until after the autumn harvest and lived in groups of three families in huts erected on the fields. There the peasants worked, clad in hempen clothes probably neither bleached nor dyed.

Their dues of produce and service paid, the people were left free to govern themselves. This they did in a very simple and direct way. At night, on the hard packed threshing floor, the men of the peasant families squatted on their haunches around an old—perhaps the oldest—man in the community. This village father discussed with them the problems of the village life. He gave a decision when disputes arose and meted out punishment. This "talk of the people" was the village government and the word of the "old one" of the village was law. Thus, whether there was war or not, the discipline of the villages went on.

There were no laws by which a man was forced to labor

against his will but custom taxed indolence. "If the ground of the homestead is left bald—not sown with hemp or planted with mulberry trees—the owner must pay money tax to his village head man." Wood was scarce in the loess land and each family was allowed to cut just so much from the hillsides. "The furrow, a foot wide and a foot deep bounding the fields, regulated the amount of water that could flow into a man's field. The earth dug out and placed next to the ditch made the path by which man and beast could traverse the country."[3] The village fathers tended to all these matters.

Between the aristocracy and the rural population there seems to have been a great gap. The noble families lived in walled towns and were occupied with court ceremonies and etiquette. Mr. Bishop says there was a "barbaric but brilliant civilization, the nobles delighting in lavish display of gold, bronze, jade, ivory, silks, furs, and bright plumes."[4] In the center of the town was the fortified castle of the lord and around it the houses of his clansmen. These were built of wood, often of bright colors. The nobles engaged in great hunts, they themselves riding in chariots. They also showed much interest in the breeding of cattle and horses. Warfare was another of their concerns, waged among themselves and against the aboriginal tribes on their borders. The nobles practiced polygamy and the Chou rulers maintained harems with eunuch attendants. Quite separate from this grand life was that of the peasants who were mere serfs with all the drudgery the term implies. For the rustics the nobles showed great disdain. "Grouped around their master they chant their contempt for the people of the field, the clownish people."[5]

The family is another important division of the Chinese social system, around which history has woven itself. The great feudal families had much power. In the various states power and wealth were divided among a few families only. By Chou times the descent was from father to eldest son and the patriarchal family became the pattern for all time. Very powerful became the father of the patriarchal family, whose household often numbered a hundred or two hundred members with as many more servants and slave girls. He demanded filial duty of the members be they grown men and women or little children. He had the power to compel obedience—the power even unto life and death. Assuredly this was a real power in the state, probably the strongest in the days of the warring lords of the Chou Dynasty. Until the last few years the family has been the strongest factor in Chinese society. I have known men of sixty who could not move to another part of the country without the consent of their aged parents. A debt contracted by one member of the family is the responsibility of every member.

The *Odes* and the *Book of Rites (Li Ki)* give a definite position to every member of the family. Their relations to one another are carefully described. There was one lawful wife. In these ancient times her position was most distinguished. She is spoken of as the "established," the "acknowledged" or the "proper" wife. According to the *Book of Rites,* three months after her marriage she presented herself in the ancestral hall of the family and was styled "the new wife who has come."[6] Then she sacrificed at the shrine of her father-in-law. These lawful wives and their sons took part in the most solemn ceremonies to ancestors—the funeral rites.

The position of young women and girls was inferior. Sons must be reared to perform the ceremonies to the family ancestors; daughters must go as brides to other men's families and bow before other men's ancestors. Therefore, if a girl died it was no great family disaster. In the homes of the poor it was often a blessing where stress of poverty

THE CHOU DYNASTY

was such that lack of food ground the family down to the point of undernourishment. Female infanticide and the selling of girls was resorted to in order to save the family from starvation. Sons must be kept to worship the ancestors; daughters were not so necessary. An ancient ode runs:

"Sons shall be born to him;—
They will be put to sleep on couches;
They will be clothed in robes;
They will have scepters to play with;
Their cry will be loud;
They will be resplendent with red knee-covers,
The future princes of the land.

"Daughters shall be born to him;—
They will be put to sleep on the ground;
They will be clothed with wrappers;
They will have tiles to play with;
It will be theirs neither to do wrong nor to do good;
Only about the spirits and the food will they have to think,
And to cause no sorrow to their parents."[7]

Great stress was laid upon the relation of children to their elders. The *Li Ki* says:

"Housework is to be performed by the children of inferior wives.

"These at the first crowing of the cock should wash their hands and mouths, gather up their pillows and fine mats, sprinkle and wash out their apartments, hall, and courtyard, and spread the mats, each one doing this proper work.

"When fully dressed they are to go to inquire after the health of their parents, bring them water to wash, and the best of food. They should reverently regard their staffs and shoes but not presume to approach them, nor should they meddle with their food and utensils unless to eat what was left from the parents' meal.

"Sweet, soft, and unctious things left by grandparents should be fed to the little children."[8]

Young married people were subordinated to the old and the very young. Children were to be petted and indulged until the age of eight when they were taught manners and the art of yielding to others. Aside from the mere acts of filial duty, children were taught the greatest reverence and thoughtfulness for their parents. The dead were as great a factor as the living.

"Although your father and mother are dead, if you propose to yourself any good work, only reflect how it will make their names illustrious and your purpose will be fixed. So if you propose to do what is not good, only consider how it will disgrace the names of your father and mother and you will desist from your purpose."[9]

Another institution of the people, the trade guild, grew up in China in the time of the Chous. Undoubtedly it originated in the patriarchal family. When China ceased to be exclusively an agricultural land and began her industrial life all the members of one family worked at one trade and the patriarchal home was the workshop. The strict rules of the patriarchal family were naturally applied to the workers as the workers and the family were synonymous. Gradually as the trades grew, members of other families or an entire other family would be called in to assist. It is easy to see that the rules of the original patriarchal family would control this larger group.

In time the trade group separated from the family and became a guild of workers. These guilds held to the autocratic laws of their patriarchal family and like the family arrogated to themselves many rights which in most countries belong to the state. Punishment of their members for wrongdoing was one of these. These guilds were powerful enough to cause the government to modify or withdraw laws which they did not like. If the feudal lord taxed them too heavily they protested by calling a cessation of all business. Thus the boycott became a favorite tool even in the early days.

The *Chou Li* mentions a hundred different crafts. The entire first book is taken up with the customs and laws of the hundred trades, the workers in wood, stone, metal, jade, ivory, pearls, skins, feathers and others. There was a needle makers' guild. The gold beaters, carpenters, silk weavers, druggists and even the pawnbrokers began their guilds then. The Ningpo Bankers' Guild of today claims to date back to the Chou Dynasty. Some of the forefathers of the members of today were members in the days of the Chou, for membership in guilds is inherited as is a trade.

Thanks to *Chou Li's* enumeration of trades, it is not difficult to see the workers of those far-away days. Along the village street in the mud huts with their dirt floors and open fronts sat the forefathers of the present-day craftsmen, doing the same things in the same way as the workers do today. Even at the time of the Chous many trades had grown to such proportions that they embraced all the families of one village. If you had lived then, in some of these villages you would have heard only the whir of the distaffs twirled by the spinners of silk thread; in others, the click of the looms as the weavers threw their shuttles across the silk warp. In still others, only the tap of the hammers of the gold or copper beaters.

Trade appears to have been well developed by the time of the Chous. Merchants traveled from town to town and from state to state exchanging commodities. In the north transportation was by means of the pack ox or ox cart, while in the south it was by water. Metal money did not appear until the latter part of the dynasty, but various media of exchange were used, cowrie shells, jade and silk. Iron is first mentioned during the Chou period. "In 513 B. C., two officials of China levied 480 catties of iron to cast a tripod on which was inscribed the criminal code."[10] Iron was evidently rare for not until the third century B. C. was it used for making plows or weapons. The sixth century is reckoned as the beginning of the Iron Age in China, several hundred years later than in Egypt or Mesopotamia.

In religion, divination still remained the most powerful influence among all classes but the method had changed since the days of Shang. Besides consulting cracks on burnt bones and tortoise shells they made their prophecies from bamboo sticks upon which were written judgments for every possible set of circumstances. The marked sticks were shaken up in a quiver. The one which fell out told the fate of the person seeking knowledge of his future. The most elaborate system was based on the *I Ching (Book of Change)* supposedly written by the Duke of Chou, used by Confucius and later reckoned as one of the Sacred Books. There are sixty-four hexagrams made from whole and dotted lines. Each individual could read from his hexagram his own destiny. How was each to know his own hexagram? The answers to that differ, but by chance apparently. Sixty-four sticks bore the number of the hexagrams and the last stick in a person's quiver determined his hexagram. Because of so much dependence on divination the priests held a very important position. They deciphered the characters on the Oracle Bones and bamboo sticks and finally became readers of the stars. They thus became a group learned in the intricate ideographic writing and the art of astrology. To them fell the task of declaring lucky and unlucky days and of reforming the calendar.

Around their belief in spirits—heavenly spirits, earthly spirits, spirits of dead men—there grew up worship ceremonies and set rituals which consisted chiefly in the offering of sacrifices. The priest-king (the Son of Heaven) as representative of the people worshiped the Spirits of Heaven and Earth. At the beginning of the winter solstice, after fasting and purification he went alone at daybreak, clad in a sky-blue gown, and bowed and prayed before the "deep blue jade tablet to *Ti'en,* Heaven," while a young ox and twelve rolls of blue silk were burned as a sacrificial offering. Incense was burned and there were music and dancing. A similar ceremony was performed in the summer solstice but to Earth rather than Heaven. Then the king wore a yellow gown, suggestive of the yellow clay of the soil. The lesser ranks of officials worshiped the elements of Nature, mountains and streams, a hierarchy of gods,—among them the Fire God, the God of Waters (the Dragon King), the God of Thunder, and the Goddess of Wind.

The spirits of the ancestors also had by this time come to be worshiped most assiduously by the people as well as by the nobility. Such spirits might come back to the house and bring disaster if not well treated. The worship of ancestors developed elaborate ritual. The spirits of the dead were supposed to descend into wooden tablets. These were inscribed with the name of the dead person and set up in the ancestral hall of the family or, in the case of the poor, in the honorable end (opposite the entrance) of the main room of the house. On certain festival days cereals, fruit and burning incense were placed before the tablets. Observation of the rites of ancestor worship was the duty of the sons of the family, the chief wife of the eldest son, and his sons. Thus sons became the most important thing in life. "Death without an heir is sin unpardonable," the Chinese have believed from earliest times. This necessity of having sons is given by Li Ung Bing as the reason for polygamy.

In the *Odes* and *Book of Rites* were written the habits of worship and many mourning and sacrificial customs which had through the past centuries slowly taken shape among the people. Even small matters concerning the dead were punctiliously set down. "In a house of mourning one should not laugh. When there is a body shrouded in the village one should not sing in the lanes."

The superior man must observe his period of mourning consistently at whatever cost. "It is not proper for a man to take office while in mourning for his parents." And the period of mourning in China was long—three years for one's parents. The *Chou Li* adds that if his services are needed by the state during that time he may give them gratuitously. And "a man though poor will not sell his vessels of sacrifice, though suffering from cold he will not sell his sacrificial robes, though he wants wood to build a house he will not cut down trees on his grave mounds."

The people worshiped the spirits of land and grains by burning incense and offering bowls of cereals before the tablet of the Gods of the Soil. But chiefly were they engaged with the spirits, good and evil, which inhabited every nook and cranny of their universe. To avert disaster, the evil spirits must be appeased and the protection of the good spirits must be elicited by sacrifices and burning incense at stated times before the household tablets.

Thus do we see a "cake of custom" hard baked by the time of the Chous. Reverence for ancestors and the Ancients, observance of propriety, duty to the overlord, learning as the entrance to officialdom—all these became fixed in an indelible pattern. There was a proper procedure, *li*, for every minute phase of life whether family practices, religious rites, business methods or official decorum.

CHAPTER VI

THE EASTERN CHOU DYNASTY. AN AGE OF CREATIVE THOUGHT AND LITERATURE

WHEN the Chous fled eastward in 771 B. C. they set up their capital in Lo Yang, but there they never attained the political power and glory that they had in Ch'ang An. War followed war, whole principalities were destroyed and others changed allegiance. Several states became large and powerful, contending among themselves for more political and economic advantages. This condition is reflected in the name of the early part of the era, "the independent and contending states," and after 403 B. C., "the warring states." Scant allegiance did these states pay to the ruling emperor, who became more and more a shadowy figure. Much suffering prevailed among the people who began to complain of their wrongs and to wonder if it were not time for "a new incumbent to mount the Dragon Throne."

The amalgamation of states caused social as well as political changes. Many petty chieftains and nobles became of little importance when fused into a larger state. This condition tended to break down the prestige of the higher classes and to take away many privileges which hitherto had been considered as belonging exclusively to the nobles and priests, who must be well versed in the rituals of government and religion. With the breakdown and shifting of social classes a more general spread of education followed. Education was now permitted to others than the nobles and priests and these new groups of students became the poets and philosophers of the age.

Another cause for the diffusion of learning is to be found in the invention of more convenient writing materials. The Shangs had cut the characters of their inscriptions on bone, and cast them on bronze, but now a great improvement came with the use of bamboo strips pared thin. As each strip or slip was only seven-sixteenths to five-eighths of an inch wide and nine inches long, only a single line of characters was written down the slip. Each slip admitted of from twenty to thirty characters only. They were strung together with silk or leather thongs. Imagine the size of the books! One of China's philosophers when he traveled from state to state carried with him three cartloads of these bamboo books. Writing was done with a sharp stick or bronze stylus. For ink they used a kind of lacquer. A little later the hair brush and ink were invented and that brought another change—the writing on silk. But as silk was expensive it is probable that most of the writing of the time was done on bamboo.

The improvement in writing materials was accompanied by another step in intellectual progress and the development of the simple language of the Shangs into one more elaborate and better suited to the expression of complicated ideas. The Shang characters were derived from natural objects—crude pictures for the sun, moon, hills, animals, parts of the body, etc. In time, these became symbolic and thus less like the original pictures. The strokes made by the stylus on bamboo were circular but, with the hair pen, angular strokes and square forms superseded the earlier round and curved ones. Thus ⊂⊃ (eye) became 目 *muh* and ⌒⌒ (hill) became 山 *shan*. But these characters were too simple for the writing of abstract ideas. So pictures of related objects were combined. Sun and moon ☉ ☽ combined to express brightness 明 *ming*, and woman plus child became the character 好 *hao* meaning

THE EASTERN CHOU DYNASTY

good. The style of writing of the Chou period is known as the "Big Seal" because first used on stone and jade seals. The language thus enriched became adequate in the time of Confucius for the expression of philosophical ideas but only in the form of simple dialogue.

While these means for the expression of the people's thought were being perfected, the subject matter of their thinking was also being enriched. Perhaps it was the stimulus of change, the breakdown of old customs and conditions that set men to thinking—particularly groups of the newly educated. They felt an urge to voice the wrongs and oppression of the people, thus becoming the first social reformers of China. They began a period of writing that resulted in a literature which today is considered one of the most creative in Chinese thought.

First came the poets. They told the story of the toils and hardships of the people thus:

> "Shoes thinly woven of the dolichos fibre
> May be used to walk on the hoar frost
> And the delicate fingers of women
> May be used to make clothes
> Sew the waist band and sew the collar
> And the good man wears them."[1]

Failure of the government to help the people in their distress is also mirrored for us by the poets:

> "I look up to great Heaven
> But it shows no kindness
> It has long disquieted us
> And now great calamities befall us
> There is no peace in the country
> And the people are in distress."[2]

and again:

> "The sun and moon announce evil,
> Not keeping to their proper paths.
> All through the Kingdom there is no proper government,
> Because the good are not employed.
> For the moon to be eclipsed
> Is but an ordinary matter.
> Now that the sun has been eclipsed,
> How bad it is!"[3]

Evidently this skeptical spirit of the poets gave rise to the age of Chinese philosophers. They vented their feelings even more strongly than the poets in writings of protest and criticism. The age of the philosophers began in the latter part of the sixth century B. C., and the greatest names are those of Lao-tzŭ, Confucius and Mo-ti. These three may be called the fathers of Chinese philosophy.

Lao-tzŭ, if traditional stories are true, was first in point of time. We know little of his life—some scholars even doubt that he ever existed, but there remains a set of teachings and a school of philosophy which are attributed to him. He mirrored to an extreme degree the critical and doubting tendencies of the age, revolting against the old religion and voicing the cry of the people against tyranny of the great lords. This critic and seer emerged from the Chinese people in the same century that Buddha, in India, was beginning to see visions and to teach a new religion and one hundred years before Socrates began teaching in Athens. Born about 600 B. C. in the Province of Honan, he early held a high position at the court of Chou. Here he became very much disgusted with the prevalent lawlessness, and well he might, for the country of China had fallen into disorder.

By now the Chou Dynasty existed in name only and was at the mercy of the strong nobles, heads of the seven powerful states. It is said that the imperial power extended over only seven cities around the capital. The barbarians just without the empire, taking advantage of the confusion within, increased their raids upon the country. In the general disorder moral standards declined to a very low ebb. Constant warfare and desire for supremacy led to intrigues among the states. Sons of nobles, anxious for power, killed their fathers, and brothers murdered brothers. These family intrigues were enhanced because polygamy had become the practice of the nobility.

It was in the midst of this confusion and moral decline that Lao-tzŭ came to the royal court. Becoming more and more disgusted with the lawlessness and seeing no hope for reform, he retired from office and began teaching the people that happiness consisted in spiritual things. *Tao,* the true road, or way, was the nucleus of his thought. It was a method which led along the way of peace. True peace, he taught, came from ceasing to strive. *"Tao* always does nothing and yet it achieves everything." All things come from being and being from non-being. His Utopia was a small country with few people and perfect contentment. In this country people were to return to Nature and to an exaltation of the non-being. One of his maxims runs, "Put yourself behind and you shall be put in front."[4]

Lao-tzŭ had his interpreter in a famous disciple, Chuang-tzŭ, who was born in the fourth century B. C. His writings glorify Lao-tzŭ and his teachings. Of the *Tao* he wrote, *"Tao* cannot be heard. Heard, it is not *Tao*. It cannot be seen. Seen, it is not *Tao*. It cannot be spoken. Spoken, it is not *Tao*. That which imparts form to forms is itself formless; therefore *Tao* cannot have a name. What there was before the universe was *Tao*. *Tao* makes things what they are, but is not itself a thing."[5]

Apparently, this mystical teaching of Lao-tzŭ and Chuang-tzǔ was not understood for it dropped into the background. In time it became associated with superstitious practices of the people and became involved with magical arts and a search for the elixir of immortality. This mixture gradually came to be known as Taoism and grew into a very popular religion of China but one with little connection except in name with the high-minded philosophers, Lao-tzǔ and Chuang-tzǔ.

The philosopher whose teachings have come to be most widely followed was Confucius. He was a teacher who taught the Chinese people doctrines of a more practical character than those of Lao-tzǔ. To be sure, like Christ, Confucius was not during his lifetime generally accepted as a great teacher, but later generations of Chinese claimed him as such and all down through the ages his teachings have controlled the Chinese. He did not create a spiritual philosophy of life; he did not say that peace lay in giving up the things of this world. But he taught that peace and order lay in imitating the ways of the past. He went back to the Ancients for examples of goodness and order. He took the lives of Yao and Shun of the Golden Age and built his teachings around the accounts of their doings.

Confucius was born in 551 B. C. in the state of Lu. There is a myth surrounding the story of his birth. His father was an old soldier, tall and strong. At the age of seventy, because he had no son to carry on the religious rites at his ancestral shrine, he married a young woman. This young wife, Ching Tsai by name, went up on a mountain to pray for a son. That night a spirit appeared to her saying, "You shall have a son, wise beyond other men." The words of the spirit seem to have been a prophecy, for Confucius from boyhood up was a lover of knowledge. He told his disciples that at fifteen the acquisition of knowledge was the one object that engrossed his thoughts. But he was not too one-sided in his growth, for he diligently performed the gymnasium exercises, loved the chase and practiced on the lute. We read that he was passionately fond of music. When he was three his father died; at fifteen he gathered together his first disciples; at seventeen he received a subordinate appointment in the state of Lu; at nineteen he married; at twenty he had a son; and at twenty-four his mother died. He strictly obeyed the ancient custom concerning mourning and for three years after her death retired from public life.

When he returned to his duties, such confusion prevailed in the state of Lu that Confucius took some of his disciples and wandered into the near-by states hoping to find some princes who would take up with his ideas. Failing this, he spent time editing ancient works and compiling them. Matters went from bad to worse in the state of Lu, so that in a few years in desperation they recalled Confucius. Upon his return he filled various offices: first, Chief Magistrate of the town of Chung-Tu, then, State Assistant Superintendent of Works, and finally Minister of Crime or Justice.

Confucius held the opinion that the ruler should be like a father in the family and that nothing, however small, was too insignificant for his notice. First in the town and then in the state he proved his theory. The state of Lu under Confucius' guidance became peaceful and orderly and prosperous. In fact, it became too prosperous for the good of Confucius. The neighboring state of Ch'i became so jealous of its rival that its prince set out to bring about the downfall of the great teacher. Failing in other methods, he at last sent to the ruler of Lu a present of eighty beautiful women skilled in music and the dance. These women so poisoned the mind of the ruler against Confucius that he was forced to leave the state.

So at the age of fifty-six, Confucius started out with his disciples to wander for fourteen years from state to state. They were sorrowful years, for he felt that his work in Lu was all in vain. And in his wanderings he found no one who had the interest or the bravery to come out for him and his teachings. Like Christ, in his lifetime, he was forsaken by all but a few chosen disciples. He was enabled to go back to Lu to die, but even this return was saddened by the fact that his two best beloved disciples died before he did. His son also had died, but a grandson was left to carry on the family. The son apparently never understood his father's teachings, but the grandson was worthy of the sage and later compiled some of the classical writings.

Much of the written literature which has been attributed to Confucius was probably not actually written by him. He was a teacher rather than a writer. But his disciples took the pains to write down his ideas and teachings. Chief of these is the *Analects,* the sayings of Confucius, which came to be one of the first books studied by every Chinese student. Confucius sought to inculcate the principles of morality and good government; he exalted the three great virtues, propriety, filial duty and reverence for tradition. As he sat talking with his disciples he would say:

"Respectfulness without the rules of propriety becomes laborious bustle! Carefulness without the rules of propriety becomes timidity: Boldness without the rules of propriety becomes insubordination: Straightforwardness without the rules of propriety becomes rudeness; Meticulous adherence to the rules and customs long established brings peace."[6]

Filial piety, he taught, embodied first filial reverence for father and grandfather and then for the eldest brother. A later development of filial piety went so far as to teach that the body was a sacred inheritance from one's parents; therefore it is a sin against one's parents to live carelessly, to be disloyal, dishonest or faithless. In state matters he taught that filial piety applied to the state and the ruler. He says:

> "From the loving example of one family a whole state becomes loving and from its courtesies the whole state becomes courteous."[7]

Tsze asked about government. The Master said,

> "Go before the people with your example and be laborious in their affairs."[8]

Confucius' teachings are colored with love of tradition. To his disciples he said:

> "I am not one who was born in the possession of knowledge: I am one who is fond of antiquity and earnest in seeking it. A transmitter and not a maker, believing in and loving the Ancients, I venture to compare myself with old P'ang."[9]

These teachings have produced a very formal and punctiliously ethical people.

Of personal virtues, the Master said, "I do not know how a man without truthfulness is to get on."[10]

Tzu Kung asked, "Is there some single word which I may take as the rule of conduct throughout life?" The Master said, "Is not 'consideration' the word? What you would not wish done to yourself never do to others."[11]

Confucius must be considered one of the greatest teachers the world has ever known in that his teaching has made some universal appeal to millions of people for thousands of years. However, his teachings have never taken hold of the hearts or imaginations of other peoples than the Chinese, as have the teachings of Mohammed, Buddha and Christ. They are teachings indigenous to the soil of China, unique to the national life, and have not spread except to Japan.

Confucius lived to be a man of seventy-three. Though his teaching had never been of a religious nature still in the course of a few centuries, in the great Han Dynasty, his teachings, somewhat modified and known as Confucianism, were set up as the state religion. Temples were erected to his memory and until the last few years twice a year, at dawn, the officials of the government have offered sacrifices before his tablet. Every year many pilgrims visit his birthplace and many more go up the mountain, sacred to him, the mountain Tái Shan, near the little hamlet where Confucius was born and where he lived.

Like Lao-tzŭ Confucius had his disciple to go on with his work. Mencius, born about a hundred years after his Master, was educated by a grandson of Confucius. Following in the footsteps of his Master, he held several official positions and then retired to teach and write. His chief interest was in the science of government and his books on political economy have formed part of the Confucian classics. He says, "The people are of the greatest importance; the gods come second; the sovereign is of lesser weight." And again, "Chieh and Chou lost the empire because they lost the people, which means that they lost the confidence of the people. The way to gain the people is to gain their confidence and the way to do that is to provide them with what they like and not with what they loathe."[12]

Mo-ti, the last of the three great philosophers of the age, born in 490 B. C., thus appeared about sixty years after Confucius. He was not so much interested in morals and

THE EASTERN CHOU DYNASTY

government as Confucius but rather in religion. His teaching was of a universal god who was a god of love. *Ti'en,* Heaven, he said is good and watches over the world with boundless love. "The will of God is love, love for all and without distinction."[13] Apparently he practiced his teachings, for his critics admit that Mo-ti was willing to wear out himself "from head to heel" for the benefit of mankind. Another of his teachings was against offensive warfare. He developed a method of logic to prove his beliefs which, carried on by later scholars, came to be known as the Mo school of thought. The philosophers of this school became more interested in logic than religion; thus China failed to develop a monotheistic religion.

China's modern philosopher, Hu Shih, says that the three great leaders, Lao-tzŭ, Confucius and Mo-ti laid the foundations of Chinese philosophy for all the centuries to come.[14] He characterizes Lao-tzŭ as a rebel in religion and a revolutionary in philosophy, Confucius as a humanist and an agnostic, and Mo-ti as a religious leader who sought to reform the ancient religion and to purify it. The teachings of Lao-tzŭ became corrupted and the religious outgrowth, Taoism, is not worthy of the name of the revolutionary thinker, Lao-tzŭ. Mo-ti's reforms, as we have seen, became involved in methods of logic. Of the three, Confucius came to hold the most exalted place in the history of his country. His and his followers' teachings became embodied in the classics, which served until 1905 as the basis for the civil service examinations. As such it has been the core of learning throughout the ages.

In art as well as literature the Chous have gained much fame. The art objects that are left from the dynasty are largely in the form of bronze pieces similar to those of the Shangs and of the same sacrificial character. In every museum in America where there are exhibits from the Far

East these may be seen. Because of the fragile housing of Chinese antiquities much had been discovered and scattered by curio dealers before the arrival of archaeologists. One particularly interesting and significant find occurred in 1923 when a grave in northern Honan was accidentally opened. Mr. Bishop, who was not far from the place at the time, was notified and arrived on the spot before the articles were all scattered. There was unearthed part of a skeleton with accompanying articles of cowrie shells, mother-of-pearl beads, laminae of jade, a small carved jade tiger, bones of horse, ox and sheep, pottery and bronzes. The grave appeared to be "a regular Bronze Age chariot burial," though there were only fragments of the chariot. Other bronzes were in the shape of large and small bells, three-legged vessels, and two beautifully wrought cranes. From the forms of the characters in the inscriptions the grave is dated somewhere between 400 and 250 B. C.[15]

In the museums we find numerous specimens of jade ornaments and weapons from this period. Many of the jade ornaments are cut in flat round-shaped disks with a hole in the middle, called *pi,* which the emperor used in worship. The *Chou Li* says: "With the round *pi* of green and blue color the Emperor worships Heaven." There are also sword-like pieces, insignia of office and rank. Except for these ornaments in jade and the elaborate bronzes we have almost nothing to prove the accounts found in the *Book of History* of numerous art objects made in the early Chou period. Apparently the only relics are the "Ten Stone Drums," now in Peking, which some say were made in the ninth century, others in the third century B. C. They are mountain boulders roughly chiseled and bearing inscriptions. The inscriptions are in Seal characters, in the style of the *Odes.* They are significant as being their oldest extant writings on stone.

Some of them read thus:

"Our chariots were solid and strong
Our teams of well matched steeds
Our chariots were shining and bright
Our horses all lusty and sleek.

"The nobles gathered round for the hunt
And hunted as they closed in the ring
The hinds and stags bounded on
With the nobles in close pursuit."

In the writings of the day there are many references to mural decorations on buildings and tombs. Confucius left an account of a visit he made in 517 B. C. to the court of Chou at Lo Yang. He saw on the walls of the Hall of Light, where the feudal princes were received, portraits of Yao and Shun and a picture of Chou Kung attending his infant nephew.

Chiseled in stone, another record tells of a vast enclosure surrounded by a high mud and brick wall, inside of which stood the palaces of the emperor, the empress, the concubines, the offices of ministers, reception halls and temples, shops for weaving silks and hemp for the court, buildings for all things necessary for the emperor and his family. The palace where the emperor dwelt was reputed to be a work of magnificent grandeur and has since often been portrayed in paintings and on porcelain and praised in poetry. But nothing of this palace has survived the ravages of the winds and the floods. It has vanished as completely as the dragons of that day. We can only trust that the literature and the painting of later dates portray a real building.

Before we plunge into China's story of expansion and intercourse, let us take one brief glance backward over this dynasty. The civilization of the Chou period is spoken of as the Shang-Chou culture as it is a mingling of Shang and Chou elements. The Shangs contributed divination practices, ancestor worship, writing, the art of bronze casting, and the beautiful fabric, silk. During the eight hundred years of the Chou period we have already seen that certain of these contributions were improved.

Writing became more adequate for the expression of abstract ideas and writing materials more convenient. In religion, whether the Chous brought the idea or not, at least the worship of a Supreme Being, *Shang Ti,* was accepted, and ancestor worship, which had been practiced by the Shang nobles, now filtered down to the masses.

But the most glorious achievement of the Chou Dynasty was the great advancement of literature and philosophy. P. C. Hsu says: "There appeared a galaxy of thinkers particularly between the sixth and third centuries B. C., such thinkers as Lao-tzŭ, Confucius, Mo-ti, Mencius, Kwang-tzu."[16] Is it not these men who have brought fame to China?

PART TWO
THE PERIOD OF EXPANSION AND INTERCOURSE

CHAPTER VII

THE CH'IN DYNASTY. A UNIFIED EMPIRE

ALTHOUGH China had experienced the sufferings of war as the loosely hung together states fought among themselves for supremacy, she had so far never felt the iron hand of an autocratic ruler. The former emperors were little more than priest-kings who left the feudal states pretty much to themselves. If taxes had been paid the people would cry: "What is the strength of the Emperor to us?"

But now China was to know a new kind of ruler. The Prince of the state of Ch'in had conquered the other six states and set himself up as emperor. This Ch'in Emperor was not to be satisfied with mere feudal allegiance. He wished to be a power in the country regulating government, religion and the social life of the people. It is no mere happening that the Ch'in Emperor espoused the cause of a strong central government. Before his time there had lived a strong man, Lord Shang, Minister of the state of Ch'in, who advocated the strengthening of the power of the ruler of the state at the expense of the feudal vassals. He believed in the use of law to curtail wickedness and promote centralization. In time there appeared a group of thinkers called legalists and a body of law called the Shang Law. The legalists claimed that orderly government rested on law, good faith and right standards. They showed that it was not enough simply to point to a good standard as the scholars did when they admonished rulers and people to follow the example of the Ancients. Most rulers as well as people, they claimed, needed standards, law, and severity to keep them in order. The growth of this school of thought in the state of Ch'in made it a powerfully governed state and the one which gave to China a centralized government.

The Ch'in Emperor styled himself Shih Huang Ti, which means "First Emperor." His ambition was so overweening that he desired that Chinese history should know nothing earlier than himself. Emperors coming after should be called Erh Huang Ti, San Huang Ti (Second Emperor, Third Emperor, etc.) To make his power unlimited he did away with the old feudal states. In their place he organized thirty-six provinces which were further divided into districts, but the officials of all these were directly responsible to the Emperor. There was to be one empire, one emperor and one set of customs and beliefs.

The Literati, the men steeped in the glory of tradition as taught by Confucius, objected to the abolition of feudalism on the ground that the government which was good enough for their fathers was good enough for them. They criticized the Emperor and quoted from the classics to prove that he was wrong.

Opposed to the group of Literati was the leading statesman of the day, Li Ssu. He criticized the scholars vehemently for believing only in the Ancients and the good old ways and proposed to the Emperor the destruction of all books owned by private individuals. The Emperor acted on this suggestion and in time issued an order directing every subject in the empire to send to the nearest official all the literature he possessed, except works on agriculture, medicine and divination. Then these great piles of bamboo books were burned. Only a pitifully few books were saved, buried in the ground or sealed up in the walls of the houses by some brave scholars. Next, the Literati themselves felt

THE CH'IN DYNASTY

the weight of the Emperor's displeasure. Some four hundred and sixty were killed with great cruelty. Thus did the Emperor Shih Huang Ti seek to rid China of the scholar and the old methods of government.

Shih Huang Ti, after his bold thrust at feudalism and the scholars went on with his work of consolidating and unifying the empire and then of enlarging its borders. After much fighting he extended his borders east to the Yellow Sea and along the sea to Cochin China; west into the fertile red basin of Szechuen; south into the rich and fertile Yangtse Valley. What gracious and rich land he acquired for China! He called his dynasty Ch'in, from his own native state of Ch'in, and some authors claim that this is the origin of the word China. To Westerners the Chinese were early known as the people of Ch'in, from which the words China and Chinese were perhaps derived.

None too soon had Shih Huang Ti strengthened the country, for there appeared on the north a much-dreaded foe, the Hsiung-nu, or Huns as they are called in the West. They were nomadic tribes with their wealth in flocks and herds. In the ways of civilization they were far inferior to the Chinese. Much of their livelihood came from hunting; they used the skins of animals for clothing; they worshiped the Dragon God; they had no knowledge of writing. They fought with bows and arrows from horseback, and were very skillful archers. The Chinese had constantly to defend themselves against them.

To defend his empire better against these barbarians, Shih Huang Ti built the Great Wall of China, across China's northern frontier—"ten thousand *li* wall" it was called. A stupendous task! Today it extends for fifteen hundred miles across the northern border of China, dividing her from Mongolia and Manchuria. It is a fit memorial of its fierce creator. Boldly it tops the hills, and extends across the lowlands and salt marshes to the Gulf of Chihli (an arm of the Yellow Sea).

When he who styled himself the First Emperor built it, it was but a crudely thrown up earthwork, formed by uniting short stretches of wall already built by various of the states. But little by little, successive emperors rebuilt it in greater strength, until at last it became a wall thirty feet thick, flanked with towers which accommodated small garrisons. For a thousand years men worked on it before it reached its final form—a perpendicular precipice forty to fifty feet high, faced with gray bricks and topped with high battlements.

What the Pyramids are to Egypt, the Great Wall is to China. It was not built as early as the Pyramids. The date of the Great Pyramid of Cheops is 2900 B. C. and that of the Wall is 214 B. C., about twenty-seven hundred years later than the Pyramids. But it is the oldest distinctive monument in China, comparable to the great monuments in other countries. Some consider it the greatest of Oriental enterprises in building. It is a great feat—fifteen hundred miles of wall, forty to fifty feet high, broken every few miles with turrets and towers, arched gateways and huge doors, done without machinery.

One can scarcely conceive of the toil and the hardship that went into its building. Here and there in an old poem or fragment of history we pick up bits of the picture. We see thousands of men digging stones from quarries, carrying them up the steep slopes, cementing them into place. Among them move the overseers, driving the laborers on with their scourges. Some of the stones, historians tell us, still have the stains of blood upon them. They also tell us that the work was done by forced labor. He who called himself the First Emperor commanded that all criminals, then merchants

THE CH'IN DYNASTY 79

should be used, and lastly that all the Literati who were found with books should be branded and then put to labor on the Wall.

You can stand today on the Great Wall stretching away as far as you can see, and think of those thousands upon thousands of men who built it, toiling and struggling against weakness, even dying as they labored; men shaping the lofty arches of the gateways, often and often pausing to fight back the barbarian hordes sweeping down upon them from the North. Moving swiftly across the plains, the mounted hordes would sweep toward the wall. And from behind a half-built turret or a gateway, perhaps still without its heavy gates, but hastily blocked with stones, the men of China would rain down arrows upon them.

The Ch'in Dynasty is the story, not of a dynasty, but of one man, Shih Huang Ti, the burner of the classics, the destroyer of feudalism, the unifier of China, the builder of the Great Wall. As a conqueror and expansionist, and as an administrator of a great empire, he stands in the first rank. He was a builder and a ruthless creator. Not only does the Great Wall testify to this, but there are records of several palaces he built, the grandest one, *A Fang Kung*, near Hsien Yang. Seven hundred thousand forced laborers worked upon it. The central hall could accommodate ten thousand persons and banners sixty feet in height could be unfurled and hung upon its wall.

And yet this conceited man, trying by violence to destroy all memory of other great men, this bold fighter and creator, was ruled by fear. The hugeness of the palace was dictated to him by fear. He was so afraid that he would be murdered in his bed that he changed his sleeping apartment every night. He was afraid to die. The *Fang Shih,* or magicians, were very strong in China at this time and had gained power over him because they claimed to be able to drive out the demons and evil spirits to which the Chinese attributed the causes of disease and death.

In addition to their power over disease and death, the *Fang Shih* claimed to have discovered the elixir of life. To strengthen their prestige they went back to Lao-tzŭ, claiming him to be the founder of their sect saying that he had overcome death and become one of the genii. The discovery of the abode of the genii, reputed to have a garden of plants of medicinal value, was one of their greatest desires. In the search for this abode they were aided by the Emperor who commanded expeditions to be sent to the Yellow Sea to find the home of the genii. There is a story that one of these expeditions, made up of boys and girls, never returned but drifted to the shores of Japan and there settled.

In religion the Ch'ins made numerous changes from that of the Shangs and Chous. They brought with them their own tribal religion which was animistic and polytheistic. To their four highest gods they added a fifth to correspond to the five elements, metal, fire, wood, water, earth; and to the five directions, north, south, east, west and center; and to the five colors. This group of five was installed instead of the one god, *Shang Ti,* and became the state religion.

The tomb in which Shih Huang Ti was buried bears testimony to the ideas and superstitions of the man and the times. Ssu-ma Ch'ien, a Chinese historian, gives a description of the building of the tomb:[1]

> "In the ninth moon the First Emperor was buried in Mount Li which in the early days of his reign he had caused to be tunnelled and prepared with that view. Then, when he had consolidated the Empire, he employed his soldiery, to the number of 700,000, to bore down to the Three Springs (that is, until water was reached) and there a foundation of bronze was laid and the sarcophagus placed thereon. Rare objects and

costly jewels were collected from the palaces and from the various officials, and were carried thither and stored in vast quantities. Artificers were ordered to construct mechanical cross bows, which, if anyone were to enter, would immediately discharge their arrows. With the aid of quicksilver, rivers were made, the Yangtze and the Huang Ho and the great ocean, the metal being poured from one into the other by machinery. On the roof were delineated the constellations of the sky; on the floor the geographical divisions of the earth. Candles were made from the fat of the man-fish (walrus) calculated to last for a long time.

"The Second Emperor said, 'It is not fitting that the concubines of my late father who are without children should leave him now' and accordingly he ordered them to accompany the dead monarch to the next world, those who thus perished being many in number.

"When the interment was completed, some one suggested that the workmen who had made the machinery and concealed the treasure knew the great value of the latter and that the secret would leak out. Therefore, so soon as the ceremony was over, and the path giving access to the sarcophagus had been blocked up at its innermost end, the outside gate at the entrance to this gate was let fall, and the mausoleum was effectually closed, so that not one of the workmen escaped. Trees and grass were then planted around, that the spot might look like the rest of the mountain."

With Shih Huang Ti's death, the Ch'in Dynasty virtually passed away. His eldest son had been banished because he had dared to question the policy of his father and was not present when his father died. Unfortunately, the direction of affairs fell into the hands of a depraved eunuch, who issued a false decree of succession. By it the banished first son was put to death and the throne went to the second son who was known as Erh Shih, Second Emperor. He was tyrannical and under the influence of the eunuch who had put him on the throne. Taking advantage of this moment of weakness in the Ch'in State, the other six of the great states rebelled; Erh Shih was murdered and a grandson of the First Emperor was put upon the throne. This grandson, evidently feeling no security in the court, put himself under the power of the first of the rebellious generals who entered the pass which guarded the capital. This was Liu Pang, who after four years of fighting against his rivals founded the next dynasty, the great Han.

CHAPTER VIII

The Hans

THE iron rule of their despotic Ch'in Emperors had not suited the Chinese, who were accustomed to the leniency of the old priest-emperors. The scholar class hated Shih Huang Ti and his house for "burning the books" and searching out and killing learned men who had tried to hide the ancient literature, and the people detested strict laws. So as soon as the successors of the First Emperor showed signs of weakness the whole country, as we have seen, was thrown into active turmoil and war. The general, Liu Pang, who first entered the pass and became custodian of the grandson of Shih Huang Ti, carried on warfare for four years with the other powerful states. It resolved itself into a war between the two states of Ch'u and Han which was Liu Pang's state. Liu Pang finally triumphed and set up a dynasty in 206 B. C., called Han after his native state. The Hans ruled China for four hundred years and so successfully that the Chinese feel honored to call themselves "the sons of Han."

In revolt against everything the new dynasty abandoned the autocratic policies of their immediate predecessors. Then, too, the Hans were plebeian in origin, uneducated, and unaccustomed to the ways of government, which perhaps helps to explain why they adopted the old Chinese policy of non-interference. In this they were aided by a prime minister, Ts'ao Ts'an, whom they appointed in the early days of their rule. Ts'ao Ts'an had previously been advised by a philosopher of the school of Lao-tzŭ that the best policy in government was to let the people alone. This policy he had tried out in the state of Ch'i where it had been eminently successful.

Naturally, when he became prime minister of the empire he adopted the same course. Here also it proved beneficial. So much so that the Han Emperors, for the first seventy years of their rule, followed this policy. The prosperous condition of the country at the end of the period is thus described by a Chinese historian, Ssu-ma Ch'ien: "The empire was then at peace, the public granaries were stocked, the government treasuries were full. In the capital strings of cash were piled in myriads until the very strings rotted and their tale could no longer be told. The grain in the imperial storehouses grew moldy year by year. It burst from the crammed granaries. The streets were thronged with horses belonging to the people. Village elders ate meat and drank wine."[1]

In 140 B. C., after this seventy years of non-interference in government, there came to the Dragon Throne the first strong ruler of the Hans. His name was Wu Ti. He was evidently something of a tyrant, for the old records tell of the heavy taxes under which the people groaned, and of the confiscation of their property if they did not rightly value it. But the records grant that he was a strong ruler.

Like his predecessor of an earlier dynasty, the First Emperor, Wu Ti was an empire-builder, and he led his people farther and farther in the pursuit of more territory. Beyond the eastern end of the Great Wall they went and brought southern Manchuria and Korea under their control. To the southwest they worked over all but impassable mountains and finished the conquest which the First Emperor had begun, thus making the fertile plateau of Chengtu Chinese territory. But most significant of all were the additions to the empire of Chinese Turkestan and the great region south of the Yangtse.

Now the addition of this country south of the Yangtse changed China from a rather poor country into a rich one. No longer was China to be held down by the rigorous demands of the loess land. A nation entirely cradled in the valley of the Yellow River could never hope for a great future, but a country also drawing sustenance from the rich basin of the Yangtse had every chance for continued prosperity. By this addition China was augmented and made powerful much in the same way that the United States was when she secured the Louisiana Territory and settled the trans-Mississippi country. This great Yangtse Valley had a splendid rainfall, and the rich earth produced, in some parts, two and three crops a year. Here the mulberry trees would grow better than they had ever grown in the bleaker country of the north. Later, bamboo, rice and tea were all to flourish here. Here also were found iron and forests which gave a supply of charcoal for smelting purposes. Rivers traversed this fertile land in all directions, making communication easy. Truly did Wu Ti do a great thing for China when he grafted this rich tract on to his own less productive territory.

We know little of how closely Wu Ti governed this vast empire of his. We can scarcely believe that in many places he exerted more than a nominal rule for many of these countries were very far from the capital city of Ch'ang An situated in the Yellow River basin. Travel was slow and arduous, done on foot, on horseback, or in crude and slow-moving carts. Horseback riding, learned from the Tartars in the third and fourth centuries B. C. had greatly improved the art of warfare and made possible the movement of troops to distant territories. The generals of these troops governed these far-away districts.

Wu Ti did much for his people by strengthening China's

northern frontier against the Huns. From the writings of the contemporary historian, Ssu-ma Ch'ien, we get a glimpse of how devastating to China had been the invasions of these terrible Huns:

"At this period the Huns were harassing our northern frontier, and soldiers were massed there in large bodies. In consequence of which food became so scarce that the authorities offered certain rank and titles of honor to those who could supply a given quantity of grain."[2]

This historian tells his story very simply but how vivid he makes the picture of distress: the men who should have been farming used in defense, the neglected land producing less and less, money growing scarcer and scarcer, until at last, "not even the Son of Heaven had carriage horses of the same color."

This condition meant constant campaigning against these horsemen, the Huns, who continually swept down from the north. Simultaneously with the fighting the work on the Great Wall went on as they turned it gradually from a crude earthwork into a brick-faced, splendid structure. Sir Aurel Stein, in his recent excavations, has found old manuscripts telling of its defense, and out of the sand where they had been buried for two thousand years he dug bundles of straw, which the sentinels had evidently planned to use as signals if the Huns attacked. The northern frontier and its defense was ever in the minds of the ruler and the people. They put it into their writings of the day. There is an old poem translated by Chavannes:

"Every ten *li* a horse starts;
Every five *li* a whip is raised high;"[3]

THE HANS

Wu Ti hoped to lessen the power of the Huns by making an alliance with a tribe, Yüeh Chih by name. Although they were a kindred tribe of the Huns, they had been the Huns' arch enemies ever since the time, many years before, when the Huns had expelled them. They had migrated to the west and set up a strong state in Bokhara, source of the Oxus River. Wu Ti determined to send a general, Chang Ch'ien, to visit this tribe and enlist them in an alliance against the Huns.

He started out with a hundred comrades, traveling to the northwest through the Tien Shan (Tien Mountains) region. Past the western end of the Great Wall they went in a northwest direction until they reached the town of Hami, then south and west to Bokhara, a journey of two thousand miles through the most difficult kind of country. The region is very high and dry with cold dry winds—a land of sifting sands and little vegetation. Even the Tarim River Valley is a sandy desert. On foot and on camel-back they made the slow and arduous journey.

Chang Ch'ien, the general, was captured by the Huns and held for ten years, after which he proceeded on his errand. He tried to return by a more southern route, Khotan-Lobnor; was again captured, but finally after thirteen years returned to China with only two of his hundred companions. He failed to make the alliance, for the Yüeh Chih were no longer interested in China. They were looking toward the West. Later they became the vanguard of the Hun invasions into Europe.

Though Chang Ch'ien failed in his mission, he did a great thing for China. He interested the vigorous Wu Ti in foreign trade. In the market place in Bactria he had come across bamboo staves, cloth, and other goods which he recognized as coming from Szechuen. They were said to have been brought there from India, which meant that there was some road from Szechuen to the southwest. On his return he reported this matter to Wu Ti and also much interesting news of Central Asia; of the people, of their products and industries. He told of the trade of Kashgar and Yarkand and the products he saw there: gold, copper, jade and cotton stuffs.

Chang Ch'ien's return must have been to Wu Ti something like Columbus' return to Queen Isabella. It awakened in Wu Ti and the Chinese their first vital interest in foreign lands.

And now begins China's thousand years of intercourse with the West. In consequence, the caravan routes across the great expanse of Asia became busy thoroughfares during the Han Dynasty. Chang Ch'ien's reports of desirable products in the West stimulated China's interest and the desire for silk aroused the merchants of the West. History gives us no record of how long there had been a desultory traffic in silks but now in the time of the Hans this route, possibly started hundreds of years before, became a bustling highway of trade.

It is too bad that no one wrote down the daily happenings of the long caravan trail, but those traders, traveling back and forth, never dreamed what an important thing they were doing and left no records.

We can only imagine the Chinese camel drivers starting forth from Turfan, plunging into the desert. First came the driver, his head muffled against the dust, then the head camel, a hempen rope fastened to his saddle, running back to the nose of the next camel. From saddle to nose, back to the last camel in the train, went the rope. Heaped high on the back of each camel were the packs containing the precious rolls of silk. Thus the caravans moved off in brown heaving lines across the desert sands, and the silk started on its long, long journey to Rome. Relayed from

THE HANS

caravan to caravan, at last the silk reached Parthia, thence it was carried to the Tigris River or to the Persian Gulf, and finally to Rome. Often it was two or even three years in getting there.

Rome was greatly interested in China. In the Roman writings there are many allusions to the connections between East and West. According to them, actual trade existed between China and the Roman Empire as early as 36 B. C. when Marcus Antonius was governing Egypt. Horace speaks of Chinese arrows, and Virgil, Ptolemy, and Pliny, the Elder, all refer to Chinese products,—silks and fur. This is an interesting picture: the great Roman Empire in the West—the great Han Empire in the East! Between these lay the sandy and arid regions of Middle Asia, and Parthia the middleman in this traffic. It may have been the middleman's jealousy and determination to hold such position which kept these two great empires from coming closer together.

Often they reached out to know each other more intimately, but something always prevented their coming into close contact. We know that the Chinese respected this other great state, the Roman Empire. They spoke of it as both great and flourishing.

Along the trade route prosperous cities grew up and although the men at the two ends of the route never saw one another, the culture of East and West mingled and each enriched the other. "The peach and the apricot, silk and tea, porcelain and paper, playing cards and probably gun powder, went to Europe over that route. The grape and alfalfa, the carrot, glass manufacture, Nestorian Christianity and Mohammedanism, and some impulses of Greek art were a few of the things that the countries of the Far East received in exchange."[4]

Gradually, after the Han Dynasty, because of the migration of barbarian tribes, this route between these two empires of the East and West fell into disuse. Twice more it became the highway of trade between Europe and Asia, but now the sea route has taken its place. Sir Aurel Stein, while excavating a few years ago along this road, unearthed a roll of yellow silk dropped from some caravan, which the shifting sand had buried for two thousand years. Mute testimony to the rich caravans and the men of all races and creeds who used to pass across the now solitary waste.

Sea communication also began for the Chinese nation in the time of the Hans, but not by their own initiative. The Chinese, although so far advanced in other inventions, were content with barges and ferries for use on the river. Their only skill with boats was the skill of river sailors. In the north this was almost nil, as navigable streams were scarce. The proverb of ancient times, still true today, runs, "A Northerner to ride a horse, a Southerner to sail a boat."

The restless, eager spirit of this age did not lead the Chinese to build boats and investigate the ocean which bordered their territory on the East. They were content with the glimpse of the ocean which could be seen from the mouth of the Yellow River. Possibly they had sailed out a little way from the mouth of the Yangtse.

For the ocean routes connecting China with other countries the Chinese must thank the Arabs and Romans. It was they who first explored the high seas and at last reached the shores of China. Ptolemy, writing from Alexandria in the second century A. D., gives their farthest eastern point of navigation as Kattijara, the Malay Peninsula, or possibly Cochin China. In 166 A. D., it is reported that Syrian merchants (claiming to be envoys of the Roman Emperor, Marcus Aurelius) landed on the cost of Cochin China, seeking the court of the Emperor of China. Roman envoys are reported in Canton in 226 and 284 A. D.

THE HANS

The Arabs were intrepid seafarers and very early sailed their ships through to the Persian Gulf, then to India and Ceylon, through the Straits (Malacca between the Malay Peninsula and Sumatra) and up the coast of Cochin China to China proper. It is thought that the Arabs reached some part of China as early as the second century A. D. The Javanese also sent envoys to the court of China during the Han Dynasty.

It was in this dynasty that another great religion, Buddhism, entered China. Buddhism was supposed to have been introduced from India about 67 A. D. However, there are various stories: In some, the date is placed much earlier, even as early as 123 B. C. in the reign of Wu Ti. It is said that Chang Ch'ien knew the name of Buddha and that one of his generals brought home as a part of his booty a golden image which is said to be that of Buddha.

In another legend the Emperor, Ming Ti (58-76 A. D.), dreamed of a golden image standing in the palace court holding two arrows in his right hand. Ming Ti, thus directed by heaven, sent envoys to India who brought back with them two Indian priests and some Buddhist classics written in Sanskrit. A temple known as the White Horse Temple (named from the white pony that carried them from India) was built to house the priests and here they lived and translated Buddhist literature into Chinese.

Buddhism took little hold on the people during the Han Dynasty but a little later this religion flamed into popularity and became one of the leading religions in the country.

During the Han Dynasty there were any number of worships and religious beliefs. The Han emperors were quite as much under the influence of magicians and superstitions as was Shih Huang Ti. Wu Ti, the great Emperor, was credulous and a patron of all superstitions. He traveled much and performed rites at various places of worship, to *Shang Ti* (Supreme Deity), to the Earth Mother, and to lesser gods. When he traveled to the east coast it is said that ten thousand methods of magic and alchemy were presented to him and he was friendly to them all. Instead of sending expeditions to find the home of the genii, he built towers from which he believed communication might be had with them.

Toward the end of his reign he made Confucianism the religious and moral teaching of the empire, but this state religion was quite a different teaching from that of its founder. To the ceremonial rites and the maxims taught by Confucius were added the practices of alchemists and magicians. The so-called "Science of Catastrophes" was in great vogue. When the government was guilty of ruinous acts, *Shang Ti* gave warning in the form of fire, famine, flood, earthquake or some like disaster. Around this idea there developed a literature devised to interpret the meaning of these signs from Heaven. These interpretations were embodied in the classical writings.

In the latter part of the Han Dynasty a scholar, Wang Ch'ung, from the south, wrote some essays as a protest against the new superstitious Confucianism of the time. He said, "Right is made to appear wrong and falsehood is regarded as truth. How can I remain silent?"[5] He pointed out that the Science of Catastrophes did not coincide with astronomical knowledge, that eclipses occurred at more or less regular intervals and had nothing to do with the political acts of the government. He showed that they erred in their whole conception of nature. Wang Ch'ung started a movement to revive the old naturalistic philosophy of Lao-tzŭ which was gradually accepted by the scholars. "All things are produced naturally. Individuals only are real. Men should live as freely as possible."[6] The philosophers wished to cast aside rituals and institutions but this was not easy.

THE HANS

But this tendency toward naturalism and nihilism in thought paved the way for the intellectuals to grasp Buddhism and this they did, a few at first and finally the scholar class as a whole. By 300 A. D., the intellectuals talked about Buddhism as the greatest system of philosophy ever invented by man.

The acceptance of Buddhism did not mean that China gave up her old religions. Like the Athenians, who begged Paul to tell them of his God, so they might worship him also, the Chinese have never been averse to accepting several religions at a time. The Chinese today worship at many altars. Even the scholar, who is primarily a Confucianist, is also a Buddhist, and he calls in both Buddhist and Taoist priests to perform the funeral rites, which in turn are a part of ancestral worship.

The new religion robbed China of none of her time-honored customs and supplied some long-felt wants. It had in it many things that the humble people could take to their hearts. Thoroughly to enjoy the teachings of Confucius one must live in the high, rarified atmosphere of the scholar. And for the uneducated, the Spirits were most terrifying and threatening, if any little ceremony had been left undone. But this new religion gave something concrete, something tangible, something hopeful. The calm-faced Buddha, sitting on the Lotus bud, was a man in his own image, but a man who had found how to live without too much pain. He taught that all life is suffering, and the common people of China, the men who were forced to labor on the Great Wall or engage in the campaigns against the Huns or travel long weary miles across the desert in the camel trains; the women left alone in their little huts to tend the children and the silkworms, understood that this Buddha-man knew about life. He taught them that suffering was caused by desire and that to gain peace and happiness they must overcome desire. This, too, at least in part, they could understand. He spoke to them of mercy and patience and kindness to all men, humble virtues which they knew a little about. And as long as this kind being allowed them to go on worshiping their ancestors they were quite happy in the double worship.

And then the religion delighted their hearts by adding display and color to their worship. Before this new god they could place candles and incense and there were priests who added mystery to religion, priests who would act as mediators between them and their god. In time the temples grew very big and beautiful and the people thronged them to watch the yellow-robed priests offer sacrifices and prayers. Thus Buddhism became the religion of the people, for it offered them gorgeous ritual and an image to help them visualize the presence of their deity.

In literature the Han period was not a creative one but one largely spent in an attempt to restore the writings lost in the burning of the books by Shih Huang Ti.

The scholar class, long incensed over the loss of the ancient Confucian literature, seized its earliest opportunity, which came under the leniency of the Hans, to start a search for any books that might have escaped the general destruction. Various people claimed that they had found copies sealed up in the walls of houses of scholars. Fu Sheng, an old man of ninety, vouchsafed to recite from memory the *Book of History* and the *Book of Poetry* and scribes wrote down his recital. After many years, in 100 B. C., Kung An-kuo, a descendant of Confucius, brought forth a copy which he claimed was written in the old script of the time of his illustrious ancestor. He claimed that as his copy was written in the old script it was more authentic than the earlier versions written in the new script, the style of writing of the Han period. Schools grew up around each one of these

THE HANS

texts, writing treatises, setting forth fine points of argument to support the authenticity of their own particular versions. Some of these were probably forgeries. The question has never been settled and today there are scholars working on the problem, trying to find out which are the spurious and which the authentic versions of the old Confucian literature. The text to which the Han Government gave its approval was known as the Standard Text, or Confucian Canon, and in 175 A. D. it was cut in stone on the outside gates of the State Academy. Each succeeding dynasty followed this custom of cutting its authentic version in stone.

A very natural outgrowth of this frenzy to reconstruct the literature of the past and, through it, the history of former centuries was the interest of the Han scholars in history writing. Ssu-ma Ch'ien, the so-called father of Chinese history, leads in this work. Born in 145 B. C., he was a good scholar by the age of ten; by twenty he had begun a pilgrimage which took him over the empire; and by thirty-five, he inherited his father's position of Grand Astrologer. In addition to his work on reforming the calendar he wrote a history which covered the period from the earliest ages to 100 B. C., called the *Shih Chi* (Historical Record). Since his writing, each Chinese dynasty has had its historian whose work has been modeled after that of Ssu-ma Ch'ien.

The history of the first half of the Han period was written by the Pan family. A scholar, Pan Piao, father of the General, Pan Chiao, was anxious to do the work but died while still collecting material. His son, Pan Ku, who was well qualified was chosen to proceed with the history but was imprisoned on charges that he had altered the records. He was released only to be imprisoned again through a political intrigue. During the second imprisonment he died. Then the Emperor ordered his sister, Pan Chao, who had been assisting him, to finish the work, which she carried up to the Christian era. She was a brilliant woman, a poet as well as an historian.

Today there are no remains of the early Han literature except a number of fragments of wooden books discovered by Sir Aurel Stein and Sven Hedin in their excavations in Chinese Turkestan. These wood books are similar to the bamboo ones, the slips being somewhat longer and accommodating about one hundred characters.

The next material to be used for the writing of literature was paper. In the official history of the Han Dynasty we find an account of the invention of paper. It was written by Fan Yeh in the fifth century and was found in a collection of biographies of famous eunuchs. He writes, "In ancient times writing was generally on bamboo or on pieces of silk which were then called *chih*. But silk being expensive and bamboo heavy, these two materials were not convenient. Then Ts'ai Lun thought of using tree bark, hemp, rags and fish nets. In the first year of the Yüan-hsing period (A. D. 105) he made a report to the Emperor on the process of paper making and received high praise for his ability. From this time on paper has been in use everywhere and is called the paper of Marquis Ts'ai."[7] Mr. Carter adds: "The examination of paper fragments found in Turkestan dating from the second to the eighth centuries A. D. shows that the materials from which they were made were bark of the mulberry tree, hemp (both raw fibres and fabricated such as fish nets) and plant fibres, especially Chinese grass, not in raw form, but taken from rags."[8]

The archaeological finds referred to by Mr. Carter are those found by Sir Aurel Stein and Sven Hedin. In 1907 the former dug from a spur of the Great Wall a fragment of pure rag paper made about 150 A. D., thus proving that the Chinese were right when they claimed to have invented paper by the beginning of the second century A. D. The earliest dated paper was found by Sven Hedin bearing a date comparable in our reckoning to 264 A. D.

Calligraphy and painting go hand in hand in China for every writer is something of an artist. The tools of writing are substantially the tools of the painter—the brush pen of various sizes and ink not like ours but more like painting material. It comes in the form of a small brick or stick made of soot combined with glue and oil dried. This moistened with water and rubbed out on a small slate or stone slab makes a mixture much like paint. Then also the Chinese characters are ideographs and drawn rather than written. The writer with his brush strokes may acquire great skill—a skill which would easily lead him to draw the form of a leaf, flower, tree or mountain. Little wonder that the Chinese have become masters in painting. Painting was done on silk and later on paper stretched tight over a heavier substance. In shape paintings are either narrow and long in hanging scroll form, or wide and short, designed to be rolled from side to side like papyrus rolls. Chinese writings tell of paintings as early as 114 B. C., but none of these are today in existence. However, one great painter, Ku K'ai-chih, of the next century after the Han, exemplifies the style of the early-Chinese painting which was in vogue until the seventh century. The British Museum claims the only survival of his work. This particular picture portrays scenes from court life. "The striking characteristics of these compositions are the lightness and delicacy of style, the poetry of the attitudes and the supreme elegance of the forms. Heavy black tresses frame the ivory faces with refined and subtle charm. The voluptuous caprice of garments in long floating folds, the extreme perfection of the figures and the grace of gestures make this painting a thing of unique beauty."[9] The style of Ku K'ai-chih is that of the earliest Chinese painting, before any foreign influence had touched it.

In the bas-reliefs on the walls of caves in Shantung and Honan we have examples of the sculpture of the Hans, dating back to the first and second centuries B. C. Petrucci finds the technique primitive and of unequal artistic merit but maybe the greatest value lies in the knowledge of these early times which the carvings portray. There are scenes of war, the chase, processions bearing tribute, scenes of agriculture and engineering. Some of the reliefs are pictures of historical events; the visit of the Chou conqueror to the Queen of the West, the early deeds of Han itself. In a more imaginative mood the artists pictured "a whole menagerie of animal forms, frequently representing spiritual beings, flying horses with wings and serpent tails, monkeys and imps, beings half-human half-animal with interlacing tails, forming in places net-works of design with added whirls of cloud, of hundreds of figures caught into an interlaced wriggling pattern."[10] In front of the more elaborate tombs are sculptured beasts and animals which gradually developed into avenues of animals and men. At this time they were huge and solid down to the ground. In western Han there is a scene of a horse trampling on a barbarian, the horse with short legs and solid elongated body.

In the tombs are found sacrificial vessels similar in shape to those of the Chous but with some differences in decoration. The designs of the raised ornamentation tend to the simple and austere rather than to the elaborate style of the Chous. Some of the vessels are made of pottery instead of bronze. They are heavy, like jars, covered over with a dark greenish glaze, very evidently copies of the earlier bronze ones. A new pattern in the decoration consists of the curving ranges of mountains seeming to symbolize that wonderful Pamir, roof of the world, which adventuresome generals and merchants were at that time absorbed in crossing.

Groups of pottery objects found by archaeologists in old

THE HANS

graves in Shensi, though giving some information regarding the art of the period, are more useful in the knowledge they give of the customs of the people. This mortuary pottery is composed of miniature models of buildings and utensils. The pottery farm sheds and granary urns dug from these graves have tiled roofs or mud ones with tile ribs and thickened ridge pole, the method of tiling being the same as that of today but the corners of the roof are not turned up at the corners. The granary urns, used for holding five kinds of grains for the subsistence of the departed ancestors, were modeled like the square and round public granaries which have been in vogue since the days of the Ancients. Another favorite mortuary object of all classes was the cooking stove. In the bottom part of the clay box-like shaped stove is a hole for feeding the fuel and on the top are round holes for holding the shallow copper kettles. In bas-relief by the side of the holes for kettles are brush, knife and spoons almost identical to those in use today.

The Dynasty of the Hans ended in weakness, intrigue and wars. They have much to be proud of in achievements of consolidation and expansion of the empire, the development of the silk routes and the knowledge of the West, tolerance of Buddhism, the invention of paper, the history writing of Ssu-ma Ch'ien and the Pan family. But the glory of the Hans, conquerors, empire builders, traders and patrons of art came to an end. Ssu-ma Ch'ien says:[11]

"At length under lax laws, the wealthy began to use their riches for evil purposes of pride and self-aggrandizement and oppression of the weak. Members of the imperial family received grants of land while from the highest to the lowest every one vied with his neighbor in lavishing money on houses and appointments and apparel altogether beyond the limits of his means. Such is the everlasting law of the sequence of prosperity and decay."

CHAPTER IX

THE DARK AGES IN CHINA

THE Han Dynasty has come to an end in 220 A. D. The high tide of its culture and trade recedes. Like the tolling of the knell we hear the word of the historian, Ssu-ma Ch'ien, "Such is the everlasting law of the sequence of prosperity and decay."

Under the Hans the empire had grown nominally to be as big as the United States of today. The Dragon Throne at the end of the dynasty was situated in Lo Yang, in Honan, hundreds of miles removed from the west and south of the empire. But the size of the empire was a source of weakness rather than strength. These far-away regions could only be reached after months of travel for in the north the fastest means of transportation was a two-wheeled cart pulled by an ox and in the south a slow-moving boat. So communications from the capital reached these distant parts of the empire sometimes a half year after they had been written. National government in any true sense was impossible. There was not even the tie of a common language.

In various parts of the empire there was a great variety of spoken dialects. The official language was by now unintelligible to the masses of the people and even so badly understood by many officials that they could not explain to the people the laws and the imperial edicts. Therefore the government decided to give public office only to those who had studied the Confucianist classic literature. This system grew into the famous one of literary examinations for public

THE DARK AGES IN CHINA

office which lasted until 1905 and kept this dead language the official language of the country and the pride of the scholars.

Instead of the strong emperor that the times called for, each new ruler seemed weaker than the last, all of them grown soft with luxury. Too often they were engrossed with pleasures of the court and with the fascinations of the latest beautiful royal concubine. Thus the generals in the west and the south had ample opportunity to grow strong in their own power. Seeing the central authority grow lax they began to dream dreams of thrones of their own which finally became realities and China was broken into three parts: north, south and west, the three kingdoms of Wei, Wu and Shu, respectively. This period is known as the period of the Three Kingdoms.

And now did China go down into her dark ages of struggle and suffering, dark ages which have cast their shadow down through the centuries, even on the China of today, for the habit of strife between north and south then established has persisted. Times without number, south has fought north and often refused to be dictated to by the Dragon Throne. And the west of China, with its fierce and proud fighters has always been difficult to hold in leash.

But to go back to that far away time—three or four hundred years after Christ: Not for the good of the people but for the aggrandizement of men, seeking power, were these three parts of China pitted against one another. Back and forth across the country moved the armies of the three kingdoms, trampling down the crops, taking the harvest grain, demanding of men that they abandon their fields and become soldiers. Famine stalked the land and often whole villages and cities were burned and men, women and children put to death. The generals who so despoiled the people were living in luxury and grandeur. "Eat, drink, and be merry for tomorrow we die" was their slogan. Indeed short were their lives; often they met death at the hands of a rival general; at best they lasted only for a few short years until some other man stronger than they took their kingdoms and luxury away from them. But no matter who were the rulers, and it would be impossible to name all the rulers of the Dark Ages, so quickly did they rise and so quickly did they fall, the people suffered, ground under the heel of the military. Made weak by so much internal strife China was an easy prey too for the Tartars or Huns who might have completely conquered China at this time had not one branch of them, headed by Attila, the Hun, "the Scourge of God" as he was called in Europe, turned westward and despoiled Europe.

But China was to know even darker days than those of the Three Kingdoms. She entered into what she herself calls the "Period of Utter Darkness." North China was now broken into sixteen kingdoms. The south no longer acknowledged any allegiance to the capital in the north, but had set up her own dynasty, the Tsin, with its capital first at Wuchang and then at Nanking on the Yangtse. There was no law or order anywhere, and bandits, always China's curse, augmented by peace-loving farmers who were hungry because their crops and villages had been destroyed and by unpaid soldiers also hungry who furthermore had learned to love violence, ravaged the country at will.

No man in all China was safe. The ring wall of earth which the early Chous built around their cities was not now sufficient protection. To make them stronger they threw up the earth ramparts thicker and higher and then faced the sides and top with large sun-dried bricks. These brick-faced walls, ten or fifteen feet thick and forty or fifty feet high, were provided with gates where the roads or canals ran into the cities. The gates were massive, made of heavy wood overlaid on the edges with metal and fitted with powerful locks. But locks were not enough to keep out the invader, so when the gates were closed huge beams, extending the entire width of the gates, were pushed into heavy sockets. At sundown the people retreated behind these walls and barred the massive gates. Even some of the farm lands lay within the great walls but for the most part the peasants went out each day to till their lands, returning at night. But all day as they worked they watched for a cloud of dust on the horizon which meant a marauding lot of bandits or an army from some neighboring state.

Even in so chaotic a period, literature was not entirely forgotten. In the capital, scholars continued to busy themselves in writing commentaries on the classics. They began collecting libraries, and other groups of philosophers, revolting against these commentaries and all social and political institutions, "longed for a free life in the ideal or idealized world of the Taoist Immortals who move about in the clouds and on the winds and who are never subject to the limitation of matter or of man-made institutions."[1] And poetry flourished, a poetry of folk songs bearing the wild undisciplined spirit of the age, a swashbuckling daredevil age with poets a care-free, drunken lot, who drank and wrote poetry. Their philosophy of life seems to have been in the words of one of them, "Let me always be followed by two servants, one with a bottle of wine, the other with a spade to bury me when I fall."

A strange picture in the sober land where since Confucius all forms of exuberance had been discountenanced and a man was counseled to live with his eyes reverently fixed on the Golden Age, when Yao and Shun ate lentil broth.

The Chinese have often gone back to this roistering age for the theme of their dramatic tales. Ever since men, women and children have sat breathless in the theaters watching the dramatic, harebrained exploits of their "Robin Hood." It is to this period also that the first great novelist of China, centuries later, went for his theme when writing his three-volumed novel entitled, *The Romance of the Three Kingdoms*.

Both in the north and in the south this is the time when Buddhism got its real hold on the Chinese people. Perhaps the Chinese turned to Buddhism much as the Europeans turned to the Christian Church during Europe's Dark Ages. In its mysticism the people seemed to find something to sustain them in their distress. Even the court neglected the teaching of Confucius and Lao-Tzŭ and embraced the tenets of Buddhism. A decree was sent out saying that Chinese could enter the Buddhist priesthood and millions deserted their homes to become priests and nuns and millions of acres were given to Buddhist monasteries. Toward the end of the Dark Ages, so a story goes, there is even a monarch who dedicated himself as a Buddhist priest. His imagination had been fired by an Indian Buddhist priest named Buddhidharma, who had made a pilgrimage to China. The monarch gave him a grottoed cave in which to live and became his chief student. Sitting day after day in the seclusion of this grotto, listening to the priest picturing the spiritual blessing of abnegation, the monarch decides he will lay aside his kingly robes of comely yellow silk, deny himself the dainty foods deemed fit for a monarch, put from him the unctuous adulation of the court eunuchs, the court ladies, the princes and the nobles, and humble himself to the coarse garb, the shaven head, the vegetable diet, the unattended life of a priest. Monarch and people are filled with religious zeal. China became fanatically religious for we read that it became a fashion for Buddhist priests to burn a finger, an arm or the whole body as a sacrifice to Buddha. Monks would wrap their bodies with cloths soaked in oil, seat themselves

THE DARK AGES IN CHINA

on platforms, light the fire, and slowly burn before thousands of wailing men, women and children. This seems doubly fanatical when we remember that this is a land where filial piety had taught for centuries that every hair of the body was a sacred heritage from one's parents.

Now hundreds of Chinese priests took the perilous journey to India to make first-hand contacts with Buddhism. One, Fa Hsien, the greatest of these pilgrims, made the long weary journey on foot to Ch'ang An and thence along the trade routes of the Hans. It is he who says of the road, "no sign of life in the sky, nor any on the vast expanse of sand, no pathway marked except by the bones of those who had perished." He went across northern India through the valley of the Ganges, stopping at the holy places of Buddha. From there he went by sea to the Island of Ceylon of which he gives an account. On his return he traveled by sea on a merchant ship between the islands of Sumatra and Java and up the coast to Shantung. He had gathered copies of the Buddhist canon, statutes and relics and was gone fifteen years, 399-414 A. D.

The narrative of Fa Hsien's travels is still in existence and in a translation we find a description of the Desert of Gobi through which he passed.

"In this desert there are a great many evil spirits and hot winds. Those who encounter the latter perish to a man. There are neither birds above nor beasts below. Gazing on all sides as far as the eye can reach, in order to mark the track, it would be impossible to succeed but for the rotting bones of dead men which point the way."[2]

Again after he had reached India, he writes of the manifestation of the veneration in which all pertaining to Buddha was held.

"The pilgrims arrived at the cave where the Bodhisattva, having entered, sat down cross-legged with his face to the west and reflected as follows, 'If I attain perfect wisdom there should be some miracle in token thereof.' Whereupon the silhouette of Buddha appeared upon the stone, over three feet in length and is plainly visible to this day."[3]

Of Buddha's alms bowl he says:

"The four joinings (of the four bowls fused by Buddha into one) are clearly distinguishable. It is about one-fifth of an inch thick and of a glossy lustre. Poor people throw in a few flowers and it is full, very rich people wishing to make offering of a large quantity of flowers may throw in a hundred or a thousand bushels without ever filling it."[4]

"In the city Hiro there is a shrine which contains Buddha's skull-bone entirely covered with gold leaf and ornamented with the seven preciosities. The king of the country deeply venerates this skull-bone, and fearing lest it should be stolen has appointed eight men of the leading families in the kingdom to hold each of them a seal with which to seal and guard the shrine and bone."[5]

"Entering the valley and traveling west for four days Fa Hsien reached a shrine where one of Buddha's robes is the object of worship. When there is a great drought in this country, the officials gather together, bring out the robe, pray, and make offerings; rain then falls in great abundance."[6]

One of the chief purposes of these pilgrims was to find authentic texts of the Sutras (Buddhist canons) for translation into Chinese. On their return they translated thou-

THE DARK AGES IN CHINA 107

sands of these for use in Buddhist temples and monasteries.

As is so often the case a new religion finds expression in art forms and so it was when Buddhism took hold upon China. Painting, while holding to the technique of Ku K'ai-chih, developed into religious painting. Now instead of court ladies we have gods wrapped in contemplation of Nirvana with smiling mouth and half-closed eyes and priests with harsh features and wrinkled face of the Hindu. "Chinese painters took up the new subjects and treated them with a freedom, an ease, and a vitality which at once added an admirable chapter in the history of art."[7]

Sculpture also was influenced by the new religion, especially in that northern of the Three Kingdoms, the state of Wei. In earlier days the people of Wei had worshiped their ancestors in caves and now after they had become converted to Buddhism they made Buddhist temples in the caves, lining the walls with sculptured images of gods and saints. In our museums we find many of these pieces that were sculptured in the sixth and seventh centuries. Some of these are of a single figure of Buddha Guatama Sakyamuni and others of the Buddha with two attendant figures, one on each side. All the figures have long flowing robes and faces of serenity. By some critics this Wei sculpture is considered the most beautiful of all Chinese sculpture.

The growth of Buddhism stimulated yet another art form, that of architecture. The monarch priest ordered hundreds upon hundreds of temples to be built high up on the mountain sides where the priests might live and meditate in perfect seclusion. Pagodas were erected by the Buddhists as depositaries of religious relics. At a later period the building of pagodas became involved with a superstition called *Feng Shui*. *Feng Shui* attempts to explain how the location of a house or a grave or the like affects the destinies of an individual, a city or even the whole country. The site for many pagodas came to be chosen in order to bring good luck to a person, a family or the people as a whole.

The pagodas form a fascinating part of the landscape, perched on the mountain sides, along the rivers or in the courtyards of temples or monasteries.

At last we draw toward the end of the cycle of decay; new forces are stirring. Toward the end of the Dark Ages came a strong man, the Duke of Sui (589 A. D.) who set up the short-lived Sui Dynasty of less than thirty years. He was a soldier by profession; he gained the throne by seizing it from a weaker ruler but, unlike the former rulers, he was strong and humane. First he stopped the petty lords of the north from warring among themselves and brought peace to that much ravaged land. Then he started south, crushing dissolute rulers and rebellious generals alike and united China under his rule, which was good. But his second son murdered him and lived luxuriously. Out of his luxury, however, grew one good thing. In order that he might travel south in comfort he commanded a great canal to be made between his capital and the Yangtse. He built four main canals which connected cities in Shantung with the Hwai River and with the Yangtse. One canal extended south of the Yangtse to Hangchow. Such a gigantic work was done without regard for his people and with cruelty. Men were forced to carry the heavy stones for embankments and bridges. Even the women served as pack animals to carry away the earth out of the road that was to be a canal. Like the Great Wall, the Grand Canal (of which this was the beginning) was built out of the sweat and the blood of the people.

Nevertheless, it was a great blessing. Never before had there been any direct communication between north and south. The Yellow River and the Yangtse, flowing as they do east and west, divide China into compartments of thought, rather than mingle the modes of thought and habits. Furthermore, troops could not be moved easily, so the canal helped in the unification of the empire. And it guarded against famine, for if the Yellow River, "China's Sorrow," overflowed her banks and destroyed the crops, foodstuffs raised in the fertile south and east could be packed in barges and sent north. This marks the beginning of the great system of canals.

In foreign affairs the Emperor was quite as aggressive as at home. He sent expeditions to the south and to the northwest where he was successful in forcing tribute. Then he tried Korea but it took three expeditions to bring the Koreans to the point of even granting a small tribute. His fame spread to Japan whose Emperor sent an embassy of peace and good will to the Emperor of China.

When there were no wars he set out on pleasure trips whose expeditions were quite as imposing as military ones. He insisted on taking his whole harem. On one of these journeys the line of boats which carried his retinue was one hundred miles in length. As the districts through which he passed were forced to feed and clothe his huge family and retainers the burden fell heavily upon the people. On his last trip to the south rebellions broke out in the northern part of the empire and seven usurpers to the throne appeared. The Emperor, hearing of the rebellion, decided to remain safely in the south, but this precaution proved to be a false hope for he was assassinated in his southern retreat. One of his strong generals got control of affairs in the north and set up a new dynasty known as the T'ang, one of the most famous and brilliant in Chinese history.

CHAPTER X

The Golden Age of the T'ang Dynasty

AGAIN a great line of emperors holds power over the entire empire, the famous and brilliant T'ang Dynasty which ruled for three hundred years (618-907). The T'angs rank with the Han Dynasty in the veneration of the people who linked them together in the phrase, "The sons of Han and the men of T'ang."

Though they ultimately attained to such honor, the T'angs came to the throne by force and usurpation. In the last years of the Sui regime the Emperor sent one of his generals, Li Yuan, against the Turkie, one of the most troublesome tribes on the northwest border. Li, unable to defeat the Turkie and knowing that to surrender would mean his own death, finally decided to follow the dangerous course of allying with the enemy against the Emperor. With the help of the Turkie he was able to march on Ch'ang An and put a regent on the throne. The next year the regent was forced to resign in favor of Li himself. There were eleven rivals who contested his right to the throne but he succeeded in 618 in bringing the empire under his power with the aid of his able son, Shih Min.

The Li family were ashamed of their lack of royal blood but hit upon an effective way of overcoming this handicap. It chanced that their surname was the same as that of Lao-Tzŭ, the famous sage. Blandly they claimed descent from him and thus buttressed their official position with religious prestige. Naturally the followers of Taoism were ready to

GOLDEN AGE OF T'ANG DYNASTY

lend their support since it brought them and their religion both into the highest official position in the period of the T'angs.

Li Yuan himself did not reign long. Dissension in the family resulted in a plot against the enterprising son, Shih Min. When he detected it he organized a counterplot against his two rebellious brothers. Soon thereafter the father abdicated and Shih Min became emperor under the name of T'ai Tsung.

T'ai Tsung, known as "The Great," was the most powerful of the T'ang rulers and upon his ascension to the Dragon Throne began the work of expansion which was continued during the reign of his successor, the Empress Wu or Wu Fu. The rule of these two extended for eighty years and they expanded the bounds of China far beyond those attained by the Hans. To the northeast they added northern Manchuria and an adjoining section of Mongolia. They brought Tibet under their control and thus extended the southwest corner of China down to the borders of India. On the northwestern boundary of the empire they overpowered the Turkie and flung out the boundaries toward the Aral Sea. By these additions they were able to revive and to guard the old Han trade routes which spread out like fan ribs across the desert sands of Turkestan.

This T'ai Tsung is one of the great men of China, perhaps we might say the man responsible for this brilliant age which is known as "The Golden Age of the T'angs." He not only expanded the empire but ruled wisely at home, giving the people a breathing spell in which to recover their resources, depleted during the Dark Ages. He was a humane man as things went then and, although he, like all the others, really thought little of the mass of the people, he set an example to his representatives to live simply and not oppress the people. Immediately he became ruler, he sent three thousand of the palace ladies to their homes, thus lessening the luxury and the expense of the court.

One of the first tasks that he undertook was the removal of corruption from official appointments. The system by this time provided for a permanent commissioner in each district who arranged candidates in nine classes, but no appointment was made except by personal recommendation of the commissioner alone. Sons of the highest ranking families were put in the highest grade of offices and the plebeians in the lowest. Now the T'angs revived the old system of examination based on the Confucian classics but made it obligatory and open to all classes of society. This system of appointment was for civil service only, military offices being excluded. Opportunity was thrown open to the young men of each little hamlet by providing a preliminary examination to be given in the candidate's home town. Those who were successful in this examination and the graduates of government schools then went to the capital, Ch'ang An, to try for the degrees *Hsiu Ts'ai, Ming Ching* and *Chin Shih*. The holders of degrees were put on the lists for appointment to civil office. Ch'ang An became a sort of center of higher education for the sons of officials. There was a school accommodating three hundred men for sons of officials above the third grade, another of five hundred for sons of those above the fifth grade, and four other schools for the sons of the lesser officials.

In many phases of social life we find marked improvement by the time of the T'angs. Much of it is due to a gradual development, but the T'angs seem to have accelerated the progress of this slow-moving change. The condition of the serfs had been gradually improving. A system of free holding had been begun under the First Emperor, but the peasants were still liable to civil labor and military service and the land was still considered the property of the state. In

GOLDEN AGE OF T'ANG DYNASTY

the early part of the T'ang Dynasty private ownership was established and a system of taxation inaugurated which lessened the amount of forced labor. In 623 the compulsory military service of twenty days was abolished and in its stead was substituted a tax paid in silk. A hundred years later the creation of a standing army freed the peasants from compulsory military service.

With the development of a system of taxation the problems of a medium of exchange became a pressing one. Copper coins had been in use since the sixth century B. C. Silk also, since it was the leading article of export became the commodity in which most of the taxes were levied and came also to be used freely as a medium of exchange. The national budget of the T'angs was made out in terms of copper coins and silk pieces. In 815, for example, there were appropriated fifty million pieces of silk for military expenditures. Several experiments were apparently made in trying to find a material to eke out the limited supply of copper coins. The copper mines opened by the Hans had already been exhausted and new ones opened by the T'angs lacked a sufficient supply for the demands of coinage. Deerskin was once attempted and in 807 negotiable certificates were tried but not continued. Soon after the T'ang period silver began to be used and we find that tribute was paid in silver and silk.

Changes in utensils and furnishings also show the advancement that was being made in China's civilization. The bronze and horn cups had been succeeded in the Han Dynasty by earthenware cups of a bright green monochrome. But these were crude affairs beside the T'ang wine cups of gold, chiseled silver and carved rock crystal. Toward the end of the dynasty the colored porcelain cup came into use. Colors were selected to enhance the natural tints of wine and tea. In Chou and Han times the furniture had been most simple. There were no chairs but only the "sitting mat" of rushes and bamboo upon which even the highest dignitaries squatted. Laufer has remarked that today the Chinese are the only ones in Asia who use chairs and high tables. He believes that they came to China through contact with the Turks on the northwest border. Stein in his excavations found a decorated armchair in a ruined dwelling of Chinese Turkestan. The Han Emperor, Ling, was fond of the Turkish costume, and in 320 A. D. a Turkish couch is recorded in China. Wherever the influence came from, by T'ang times the Chinese were using the chair and high table and today the custom of sitting on chairs is one which marks a difference between the Chinese and Japanese for the Japanese still use the sitting mat.

The ancient tools, such as the sickle and flail were practically unchanged; two flat stones used for grinding were not improved upon. Dress remained much as it had been in Han days. The gowns were long and flowing. Among the official class the color of the garments denoted the rank of the wearer; yellow for the imperial family, purple, crimson, green and black for princes and lesser officials. In warfare there was an advance. To the earlier weapons were added the battering-ram and scaling bridge.

Tea, in the time of the T'angs, became a common beverage in China. Sometime earlier, about 270 A. D., in the reign of Sun Hao, the Chinese of the south had discovered the use of this plant. Like so many other refinements of living (silk, for instance), it made its appearance unheralded. It is not until well into the T'ang Dynasty, about 800 A. D., that it is mentioned first as a taxable commodity. Whether this tea bush with its small dark green leaves had been growing wild for a long time and the Chinese suddenly discovered its value as a drink or whether it was imported we do not know. When tea was first used the people

GOLDEN AGE OF T'ANG DYNASTY 115

steamed the leaves, then crushed them in a mortar and made them into a cake. Then with rice, ginger, spices, orange peel, salt, onions and whatnot, the tea was boiled as the Mongolians and Tibetans boil it today. The Russian custom of using lemons with tea is a survival of this method and tea in bricks is still the kind most generally sent to Russia. In the T'ang Dynasty the popular use of tea as a beverage powerfully influenced the ceramic art. More and more beautiful became the handleless teacup, more fragile, more delicately glazed.

In the T'ang Dynasty many extravagances began to creep into the daily life of the upper class. Dice, cards, horse racing filled their days. The rich had their own bands of dancing girls to entertain them, military men took them on their military expeditions. Wine, made from rice, was used in excess. Foot-binding was begun, a practice which still persists except in the most modern communities.

We find in the old records of this period the first mention of the poppy. It appears to have been introduced by the Arabs as early as the eighth century. It was prized as a beautiful flower second only to the peony. By the tenth century, during the decline of the T'ang Dynasty, its medicinal qualities were known and it began to be used as a drug. Still later, after tobacco was introduced from the Philippines, opium and tobacco were mixed and smoked. This mixture was introduced from Formosa where it was used to neutralize the dread malarial fever. Gradually ill effects were noticed among the young men of China who got together at night and smoked, first this mixture and later opium by itself.

In the province of Shensi, at Ch'ang An, that ancient capital of the Chous and the Hans, the T'angs established their court renaming it Sian—West Pacified. Little remains of the city today except the foundations of some of the walls and two pagodas, but from the writings of the poets of the times and from paintings, porcelains, jades and bronzes, relics of that day, we can build up a picture of the once beautiful city. It stood high above the clear Wei River surrounded on all sides by mountains and cliffs of loess cut through by deep ravines. The approaches to the city were difficult. "To the north the Chin Ling Range with its steep rocks, perpendicular paths, rushing torrents, and gloomy forests creates a barrier difficult to surmount."[1] Heavy laden were the men and donkeys climbing the passes to the mountain-perched capital bearing tea, silks and porcelains from the south, rice and fruit from Shu in the southwest, jade and bronze from the northwest. In this mountain seclusion the T'ang Emperors lived lavishly, spending time and money in the building of beautiful palaces and parks. Within the city walls they built the palace city with its forbidden parks. To the south of the palace city they placed the Imperial City entered by the Red Bird Gate. To the east stood the Prosperous Felicity Palace and the Palace of Intense Brilliance. Brilliant indeed was the life as officials, eunuchs, ladies of the imperial household, clad in royal yellow or princely purple, red and green silks and satins, roamed through the parks and open courts of the various palaces, sipping tea and wine from gold or thin porcelain cups or gathering in the palaces, painting or writing poetry on silken scrolls.

Far and wide spread the fame of the beautiful capital and magnificent life in China. The Japanese, China's nearest neighbors, were perhaps the most impressed. In fact, so much impressed were they that there grew up in Japan in this period a cult for all things Chinese. They slavishly copied the culture of China. The new capital of Japan at Nara, not far from present Kyoto, was modeled after the Chinese capital; their painting and works of art followed

Chinese patterns; Chinese written characters were adopted, and Chinese literature became the fashion. In matters of government too, they were influenced by China. They created a hierarchy of officials like that in China and a system of civil service in which the examination consisted of the writing of a Chinese essay on some subject from the Confucian classics. Even in matters of dress they were influenced by their enthusiasm for things Chinese for they took the kimono, an adaptation of the ancient Han style of dress, as their native costume, and, too, soon after the Chinese discovered it, they adopted tea as their national drink.

In Europe curiosity over this country of China, from whence for centuries had come the mysterious silk, could no longer be restrained. Not only did the traders talk of China, but at the courts of the Italian cities this great empire of Cathay, as they called it, which lay far to the east of them, was discussed. They decided to appoint envoys to go to the court of China to carry official greetings to Cathay's monarch. These envoys made the long journey along the "silken way" which led across the deserts of Turkestan around the western extremity of the Great Wall to the city of Sian. We know little of the reception of these envoys except that it was gracious.

From the Near East envoys came too, from Persia and from Turkey. The ambassador from Turkey wanted advice about building a temple and China graciously gave it; Persia wanted aid against the growing power of the Mohammedans and received it.

Not only were the political envoys of other countries welcome. Humbler men, the missionaries of various religions, found a like hospitality awaiting them. The Emperor, T'ai Tsung, though leaning toward Taoism, received them all.

And now traveling along the Silken Way from Europe come the first Christian missionaries, the Nestorian priests.

The record of the first journey of Christianity to China was lost until an old tablet was discovered at the capital, Sian, proving that Nestorian Christianity entered China during the T'ang Dynasty. Inscriptions on this tablet in both Syrian and Chinese state that Nestorian priests arrived in China in 635 and that the Emperor, T'ai Tsung, examined the scriptures they brought and blessed the coming of the new doctrine. "This stone," concluded the inscription, "was prepared and raised in the second year of the reign of T'ai Tsung." By 781 the Nestorians had evidently attained a position of power. "At that time the priest, Niu Chou, Lord of the Law (that is to say Pontiff of the Religion) governed the whole body of the Christians in the Oriental countries. Lü Hsin-yen, counselor of the palace and formerly member of the council of war, wrote this inscription."[2]

For two hundred years, all through the fifth and sixth centuries, in the old records both in Europe and China we find references here and there to the journeys of these priests. Abbe Huc, Christian priest, himself of a later day, says, "These apostles wandered on foot, their staves in their hands, along banks of rivers, through forests and deserts, amid privations and sufferings of every kind, to carry the tidings of salvation to the rest of the world."[3]

In the seventh century the traditional perfidy of the trader must have entered a little the Christian missionary for it seems that some of these Nestorian missionaries, returning from China to Constantinople, took with them the secret of silk making. At the time of their departure for home they secreted silkworms in their hollow staffs. That these silkworms ever managed to survive the long journey is almost a miracle, but somehow they did. Thus started the great silk industry of Europe.

China in those days of her religious tolerance became

GOLDEN AGE OF T'ANG DYNASTY

temporarily an asylum for the oppressed. Both the Nestorians and Zoroastrians fled before the Mohammedan sword as the Mohammedans advanced across Bodhar and central Asia. Buddhist priests persecuted in India fled to southern China where they were more than given asylum; they were enthusiastically received by members of their own faith.

Most, if not all, of the great faiths of the world were represented in China under the broad-minded monarch, T'ai Tsung. There is another that must be mentioned and that is Mohammedanism. By the seventh century, the second of the T'ang Dynasty, the Arabs had trading centers and even settlements in four of the southern cities of China. In these merchant colonies the tolerant Chinese by the eighth century allowed them to teach their faith to their Chinese neighbors.

But Mohammedans also sought to enter China by the sword. Early in the T'ang Dynasty the Mohammedans carried their conquests to the frontiers of China. "The world for Mohammed" was the cry of these religious zealots. "The Dragon Throne to the first general who shall reach China," cried the twelfth caliph, little dreaming how powerful was the China which he thus so nonchalantly gave away before he possessed it. Driven on by religious zeal, a general named Kataba moved his victorious host right up to the city of Yarkand on the borders of China. And there the story ends. Why did he withdraw? We do not know. Perhaps he saw that the vast empire of the T'angs was too powerful for him to conquer. Perhaps he grew panicky when he realized how far he was from his base of supplies. Whatever the reason, Mohammedanism did not conquer China at the point of the sword.

Mohammedanism in China has always remained just one religion among many, its distinguishing features changed to fit the Chinese scene. In general the mosques are very like the Buddhist temples and the ancestral halls, except that the Koran occupies the honored position within them in place of the Buddha or the family tablet. The Chinese Mohammedan of today differs very little in his way of life from his countrymen of other faiths. But he is not friendly toward other religions. In the northwest where, as a result of Turkish and Tartar colonization, there is a greater per cent of Mohammedans than elsewhere in the country there has been and still is hatred between the Mohammedan and the Chinese of other beliefs. Massacres of Chinese by Mohammedans and retaliating massacres of Mohammedans by Chinese have continued common even until today.

Buddhism, in spite of the leaning of the T'angs toward Taoism, continued to flourish and to influence Chinese civilization. The Taoists entered into a period of imitating everything Buddhist. They developed a canon with hundreds of volumes of sutras. They adopted the doctrine of the transmigration of the soul and the idea of heaven and hell as places of dwelling after death. The Hindu's thirty-three heavens and eighteen hells were given Chinese names and Chinese deities were chosen to preside over them. Today in Taoist temples one may see representations done in miniature, picturing very graphically the joys of the thirty-three heavens and the tortures of the eighteen hells. The Taoists took over the institutions of priesthood and monasticism but without the most offending feature to the Chinese, that of celibacy. If the Taoists had hoped by their adoption of Buddhist elements to draw people from Buddhism to their own ranks they failed.

Though many scholars were devout followers of Buddhism there were some who felt keenly this defection to a foreign religion. One, Han Yü, became greatly incensed when the Emperor was preparing to receive with great ceremony and reverence a bone of Buddha and he wrote a

GOLDEN AGE OF T'ANG DYNASTY 121

scathing rebuke of the Emperor and a challenge to the country to do away with this imported religion. He urged the Chinese "to secularize their people, burn their books, and use their dwellings."[4] This growing feeling here and there of protest came to a climax in 845 in a terrific persecution of Buddhism, when forty-six hundred large monasteries and over four thousand smaller ones were destroyed and over two hundred sixty thousand monks and nuns were forced to return to ordinary walks of life and millions of acres of monastic property were confiscated. But even so drastic a persecution did not weed out this faith with its gorgeous ritual and its mediators, the priests. It did succeed, though, in driving out the less popular foreign religions such as Nestorian Christianity and Zoroastrianism.

Buddhism, though not driven out, was continually undergoing changes. Chinese leaders of Buddhism decided that the essence of Buddha lay in the double road to salvation, meditation and insight and that both roads must be sought within one's self. This doctrine came to be known as Ch'an or Zen. In the beginning it was dominated by the Indian practice of meditation which included a technique starting with breath control and rising to high states of spiritual joy and peace. Supernatural powers were supposed to be attained through such processes of meditation. These Indian practices, however, were not universally accepted by the Chinese. In 700 a monk in Canton discarded all such methods, declaring that "Buddhahood is within you," and when one recognizes the Buddha within him he will have attained salvation. Likewise Ma Tsu in the ninth century declared there was no Buddha to attain. "Allow your good self to take a rest and set the mind free."[5] The Zen Buddhists evolved a method of teaching, the essence of which seems to be never to tell anything in too plain language. If a novice asked a question he was not to be given an answer but only a box on the ear or told to hide his shame or to go to some other Zen school. So he traveled from school to school seeking various masters. From them he got no further teaching but gradually acquired a rich store of experience derived from admiring nature, suffering hardships, befriending fellow travelers like himself. Then suddenly some day in the chirping of a bird or a stray remark he would understand. His insight was deepened; he had attained! He traveled back to his first teacher and thanked him for never having told him anything. "This is Chinese Zen," as Hu Shih says, "a highly sophisticated method of intellectual discipline. If it teaches anything it teaches the emancipation of the mind from unfruitful seeking after Buddha; that there is no salvation to achieve, no Buddhahood to attain, and no magical powers to acquire."[6]

Buddhism continued to play a very important rôle in the development of Chinese art both in sculpture and painting. Although the sculpture of the Chinese may have reached its height in the Wei Dynasty, still the T'angs continued a high excellence and have left some beautiful pieces. But in painting, probably, the greatest development came in the days of the T'angs.

Archaeological research has again come to the rescue of Chinese history and given us a number of paintings of the T'ang period. Sir Aurel Stein (1906-1908), on one of his expeditions to the frontiers of northwest China, came to Tun Huang, a walled town in a prosperous oasis near which is located the cave of the "Thousand Buddhas." The story is that a monk in attempting to repair one of the shrines came upon a room filled with manuscripts. The manuscripts were left undisturbed and a wood and later a brick wall was put up to protect them. Sir Aurel Stein, hearing of this discovery went to the cave and persuaded the monk first to let him see the manuscripts and later to carry off some of

GOLDEN AGE OF T'ANG DYNASTY 123

them and most of the paintings which were found with them.

The paintings were done on fine silk and when found were rolled up in crumpled little packages weighed down by the manuscripts under which they lay. The room had been sealed in the tenth century and evidently was done suddenly on the advent of some Tartar tribe. One of the pictures substantiates this theory for on it is an inscription, a prayer to *Kuan Yin,* Goddess of Mercy, for help against the Tartars and Tibetans.

Many of the paintings were taken to the British Museum where they have been cleaned and mended. The collection consists of votive paintings of various sizes, mostly on silk, banners some on silk and others on linen, one or two specimens of embroidery, outline drawings and woodcuts. One carries a date corresponding to our 864 A. D., others of the ninth and tenth centuries, most of them falling in the second half of the T'ang Dynasty. The paintings are of Buddhist inspiration; single figures of Bodhisattvas, saints, scenes from the life of Buddha and representatives of the Western Paradise. The prevailing colors are crimson, dull green enlivened by white and orange, pale blue and purple in the halos.

One of the paintings, a very large one, of the Paradise of Bhaisajyaguru is described by Sir Aurel Stein, "His heaven represents itself as in all the huge paradise paintings of Tun Huang as a great assemblage of celestial beings, elaborately staged on richly decorated terraces and courts which rise above a lotus lake. On the sides and above the terraces are seen pavilions and elaborate structures of characteristically Chinese style representing the heavenly mansions. It is in this sumptuous setting that Chinese Buddhism has visualized, from an early period, the idea of a paradise where the souls of believers in the law may be reborn free from all taint in the buds of the lotus lake to enjoy thereafter for aeons, or in popular belief forever, blissful rest and pleasures in the company of Bodhisattvas, Arhats and other beatified personalities."[7] Buddha presides in the middle of the picture with folded legs, wearing a crimson mantle over a green under robe, his right hand raised, his left holding a begging bowl in his lap.

One of the most famous painters was Wu Tao-tzu. Petrucci says that he was the creator of a Chinese type of *Kuan Yin,* Goddess of Mercy. Drapery covers the high drawn hair and the harmonious folds of her garments express authority and the sublimity of divine love. Chinese written accounts of Wu Tao-tzu's painting state, "That the lines from his brush fairly vibrated; all united in marveling at the spirituality emanating from forms thus defined."[8] He used no color but depended upon powerful ink lines which gave his painting a sense of authority and magnificence. There is an account of his being summoned by the Emperor, who was about to build a temple, to paint all the frescoes. He was ordered to represent with consummate skill human beings, religious figures, spirits and demons, hills and streams, terraces and lakes as well as plants and trees. His work has probably all been destroyed but written accounts of his paintings and copies confirm the high opinion of his art.

During the T'ang Dynasty painting was separated into two schools known as the northern and southern; the style of the northern was strong, vehement and bold, and that of the southern, dreamy and melancholy. The foundation of the southern school is attributed to Wang Wei of the eighth century who was a great landscape painter. Landscape painters were in the habit of using a predominating color called *luo-ts'ing,* a mineral color ranging from malachite green to lapis-lazuli blue, using the bluish tints for the distant expanses of the landscape and azure tints for mountains forming screens in the background. Wang Wei took another step from this monochrome painting in one color to monochrome painting in Chinese ink. With black and white and with gradations from white to black, he produced the same effects that he had produced with the blue-green *luo-ts'ing*. This has come to be known as the literary man's painting as it is so closely allied to calligraphy.

Besides religious and landscape painting there was that of flowers and birds, plants and insects, and animals, the horse in particular. The Chinese painters of horses exerted a strong influence upon the painters of horses in the following Mongol period.

The T'ang Golden Age saw Chinese poetry reach its height although the writing of poetry had been increasing for several centuries. Since 200 A. D., court musicians had been accumulating many of the folk songs, which though written in the colloquial dialects came to be recognized by the classical poets. These heroic and warlike songs of the north and plaintive love lyrics of the lower Yangtse region furnished inspiration for the great T'ang poets. Under very strict rules did the Chinese poets work. They must consider not only rhyme but also tone. For purposes of poetry all characters had two tones as flats and sharps which held fixed positions so the natural order of the words had to be sacrificed to the tones.

Long poems did not appeal to the Chinese. The most desired length was twelve lines, although eight was popular and even that of four lines, called "stop-short," was frequently used.

One is amazed at the mere volume of poetry produced in this age. Later publications of the T'ang poetry contain nearly fifty thousand poems. The poets were nearly as numerous as the poems; but there are two who stand out above the rest. These two the Chinese love to honor, Li Po and Tu Fu.

Of Li Po, Mr. Giles says in his *Gems of Chinese Literature* "he is the best known of China's host of lyric poets, famous for exquisite imagery, for his wealth of words, his telling allusions to the past, and for the musical cadences of his verse."

Tu Fu is considered the finest craftsman of all the poets, but translators seem to agree that his work is almost untranslatable. Cranmer-Byng in his *Lute of Jade* says, "He seeks after simplicity and its effects as a diver seeks after gold. He is possessed of a continual sadness because he is forever haunted. He is haunted by the vast shadow of a past without historians that is legendary, unmapped and unbounded. He is haunted from the crumbled palaces of vanished kings. He is haunted by the traditional voices of the old masters of his craft, and lastly more than all by the dead women and men of his race, the ancestors that count in the making of his composite soul, and have their silent say in every action, thought and impulse of his life."[9]

Tu Fu (712-770) had failed at the public examinations but held a high regard for his own poetry, in fact so high that he prescribed it as a cure for malarial fever. He felt great resentment over his failure at the examinations, but finally obtained a post at court which he later lost in the rebellion of 755 about which he wrote in allegorical form.

He was a man of unusual grace and charm, tall, thin and elegant, and in his youth he lived to the full in the beautiful city of Sian. This youth in his saffron silk robes danced with other courtiers to the jeweled lutes, in the palace of a thousand rooms, with birds and beasts painted upon the walls in gold, and with ceilings of lacquer. He strolled with other dandies along the roads and sat in the taverns drinking precious Thunder Tea. If it was warm they had Snow Bubble wine with flowers floating upon it, served in beaten silver cups. Later in these same taverns Tu Fu, poor and an outcast with an assumed name, paid for his food with a song or a poem. For thus ran the fortunes of the day. One moment a man was in favor and the next he was an outcast, for intrigue ran riot, and the court was suspicious of all, even its favorites.

Li Po (705-762) led a wild, wandering life until at length with five other poets as wild as himself he retired to the mountains where they wrote poetry to their hearts' content. Finally he reached the capital where he wrote poetry for the Emperor to celebrate all occasions and became the darling of the court. The ladies in waiting held a screen of pink silk upon which he wrote his poems. He wrote often of wine and debauchery. Later intrigue expelled him in disgrace. He died by drowning, so the story goes, as in a drunken sentimental mood he leaned too far over the side of the boat to embrace the moon mirrored in the river.

Tu Fu and Li Po lived in the days of the Emperor Hsuan Tsung or Ming Huang and his famous concubine, Yang Kuei-fei, said to be the most beautiful woman of all China. These poets' lives mirror the romance, the gaiety, the extravagance, the dissipation, the frivolity, even the dandyism of the later T'ang days, when luxury had gained a momentum. Evidently men lived far beyond their means in their effort to keep up to the style of the day. It was said that you could not tell a rich man when you saw him because all a man had he might be wearing on his back. A hundred thousand men worked in the silk factories outside the capital of Sian in order to supply the needs of the courtiers. The atmosphere of an extravagant age had enveloped these poets. Luxury and extravagance had gained a momentum that was driving the nation to her doom. It was Hsuan Tsung's fate to stand at the peak of her greatness and in his old age bring about her downfall.

In his youth he strove to follow the principles of T'ai Tsung, his grandfather, and live soberly. He founded the famous Hanlin Academy, the Forest of Pencils. To the Hanlin Academy only the best scholars of the land were admitted. Examinations took place in the Emperor's palace once in three years and from among the candidates six only were chosen at each examination for membership in the Academy. The necessary qualifications of a successful candidate were Physique, Oratory, Penmanship, and Knowledge of Official Documents. The Academy was a sort of research institution engaging itself in the preparation of historical and literary works. As the civil service examinations were based on a knowledge of the classics the works of the Academy were in great demand.

But the Emperor lived in the midst of luxury and as he grew older he abandoned his austere life patterned after the classics. In his sixtieth year he became enamored with the beauty of Yang Kuei-fei and although she was his son's concubine, he took her for himself. From then on to the end of his reign the fate of the empire hung on the whims of Yang Kuei-fei and those of her brother whom she had managed to install as high minister to the aged Emperor. All sobriety of living, all thought for the good of the empire, seemed to have been crowded out of the monarch's head. In the palace of a thousand rooms with its barbaric splendor the Emperor gave himself up to the life that Yang Kuei-fei decreed. Intoxicated with her power, she led the monarch into more and more extravagant living. She and her brother, insolent and careless in their success, intrigued for greater and greater power until at last they overplayed their hands and their enemy minister, An Lu Shan, succeeded in starting a revolt. The monarch with his beautiful concubine and her brother were forced to flee the palace.

On the road, as the fugitives fled from the indignant people, their last hope was taken from them. Their bodyguard, on whom they depended, mutinied and demanded first the head of the brother, then that of Yang Kuei-fei herself. And now, in his extremity the faithless old monarch, in order to save himself, surrendered the woman on whom he had lavished the riches and strength of the empire. Thus, in ignominy and flight, ended the reign of the Emperor who had once stood at the peak of China's glory.

Swiftly on the heels of China's period of prosperity followed her decline. The son in whose favor the fleeing monarch abdicated was weak; the court life was decadent. There was no strong hand to hold the country together. The lack of sympathy between north and south which lay just below the surface again became open. War was the order of the day. The glories of the T'ang Dynasty, its toleration, its culture, its learning, its splendor fade quickly. Its poets, painters, philosophers, pass from the scene.

CHAPTER XI

THE "FIVE LITTLE AGES" AND THE SUNG DYNASTY

WE ARE not surprised that the T'angs' kingdom of luxury, built upon the shaky foundation of peasant poverty and discontent of merchants and peasants, toppled and broke. From 907 to 960 five little dynasties, "Five Little Ages" as the Chinese call them, came and went.

To understand how the seeds of discord sown by the T'angs were reaped in the chaos of the fifty years of the Five Little Ages, we shall need to glance back for a moment over some of the unhappy developments that had been taking place under the surface. The later T'ang rulers in their demand for luxury had forgotten the precepts of Confucius, the example of the Emperors, Yao and Shun, who affected simple garb and ate their lentil broth from a clay dish, and had put a heavier and heavier burden of taxes upon the people. But even when the people groaned under a well-nigh unbearable taxation, a still heavier tax was levied—upon the merchants a tax which was called "borrowing money" or a tax on shelves; from the farmers too an extra tax. Then a tax was levied on each family: silk, salt or flax must be contributed according to the product of that section. Lastly, there was a tax upon the individual man. Forced labor was revived. Each was obliged to give from twenty to fifty days' labor a year.

The plight of the masses had grown worse and worse. As the centuries had gone on, the belief in ancestor worship had increased the population to such an extent that in many

THE "FIVE LITTLE AGES" 131

places the country was crowded so full of people that there was really not enough for them to eat. The soil in the days of the Chous was new and rich. Now in the days of the T'angs it was much depleted. The farmers had to conserve every resource. They worked early and late. They wasted nothing. They used the night soil as fertilizer; they burned in their little clay stoves the chaff from their rice, and in winter in the north, flues from the kitchen stove led under the brick beds and heated them. In these larger stoves they used shrubs and the dry grass from the hills. There is every evidence that even at this time the large timber of the country had been cut. If the officials had lived simply and not bled the people of their resources all might have been well, for the Chinese peasant has always been industrious, but the heavy taxation left many a farmer and petty merchant in debt.

And the famines became a common occurrence. Every few years drought or the flooding of the Yellow River would bring famines to a district already poor from over-taxation. In the earlier days of the T'angs the government had, in such emergencies, provided relief in the form of tax exemption or the opening of the public granaries. But as time went on, the ruler left the people to their miseries, and often the poor wandered away from the farms leaving the land unplanted and barren.

But as the poverty of the peasant was China's danger, the democratic life of the peasant was China's safeguard and during all the fighting and disintegration, the town fathers or village elders continued to control the people. This was all that kept the nation from complete ruin, ravished as it was by bandits, ambitious military men, a series of civil wars, and constant change of dynasties with continuously diminishing power, and a frequent shifting of capitals.

However, there is a bright spot in this period of the Five

Little Ages for there occurred a great invention—the block printing of entire books. Printing had had its beginnings long before this but not until now had the art been sufficiently developed to permit of the printing of books. In tracing the history of printing we find it had had a slow growth. There were many contributors—Buddhist monks and Confucian scholars. In the Han period, as we have seen, the Confucian scholars began cutting the classics in stone in order to preserve them. From these characters cut into the stone they later, after the invention of paper, learned to take rubbings. Impressions were taken by laying felt next to the stone and then a tough piece of cohesive paper already moistened. The paper with felt behind it was brushed and rubbed until it fitted into the depressions of the cut-in characters. Then the paper was inked all over which left a black background with the characters white. This reproduction is called an "ink rubbing," a method still used.

The Buddhist monks became interested in printing when they began cutting the raised figure of the Buddha in wood. These blocks were inked and pressed on paper and then used as charms. Desiring to duplicate the sacred books and texts they came upon the next step in the evolution of printing. To some inventive genius there occurred the idea that he might turn his stamp upside down, lay the paper on it and wet it with a brush. Rubbing from stone, seal and stamp, cutting raised characters, inverting them, all these devices advanced the art to the stage of block printing, the exact date of which is uncertain. Even the difficulty of finding the date of the printing of entire books is enhanced by the fact that the evolution of the art was so gradual as to be almost imperceptible. The nearest approximation of a date for its beginning would be during the early days of the Five Little Ages, or possibly in the end of the T'ang Dynasty.

The first official printing of the classics was made in the

THE "FIVE LITTLE AGES"   133

ninth century, in the state of Shu, now called Szechuen, in the western part of China. Shu, remaining independent for all but five years of the period of the Five Little Ages, became the most prosperous and cultured part of China. When it had acquired its independence at the very beginning of the period one of the first acts of its new ruler was to have a corrected text of the classics engraved on stone in imitation of work done by the great Han and T'ang Emperors. Besides this a noted statesman petitioned the Shu ruler to have the nine classics printed by means of the new block printing in order that books might be within reach of all scholars.

Meanwhile back nearer the center of the country, with their capital first at Sian, that beautiful but ravished city of the T'angs, and after 904 at Lo Yang, one little dynasty was succeeding another little dynasty. Only one person remained constant, a prime minister by the name of Feng Tao (881-954). Under four of the five dynasties and under seven of the emperors he managed to retain his place. When one of these little emperors conquered the state of Shu and held it for that five years, Feng Tao was quick to seize the new and as yet little known process of block printing which the Shus had been using. But Feng Tao resented the Shu state printing various versions of the classics. He wanted an orthodox edition so he petitioned the throne thus: "If the classics could be revised and thus cut in wood and published it would be a great boon to the study of literature. . . ."[1] The Emperor answered his plea by ordering the National Academy to proceed with such an enterprise. This gave a national standing to block printing.

Among the manuscripts found in the Cave of the Thousand Buddhas is the oldest printed book yet discovered. It is in the form of a roll sixteen feet long made up of seven sheets, each two and a half feet long and one foot wide.

It bears "the statement that the book was printed March 11, 868 by Wang Chich for free general distribution in order, in deep reverence, to perpetuate the memory of his parents."[2]

It is a strange story—this persistent work of scholars in the midst of chaos. Carter remarks, "To those who are acquainted with China of our own day and have seen government education steadily pushing forward in spite of governmental anarchy, it is not hard to understand how the National Academy and the various commissions appointed to revise texts of the classics for printing went their way unruffled by the storm that was beating about them."[3]

The invention of printing came to be used by the Chinese at least five centuries earlier than in Europe. But the Chinese in the centuries that intervened before Europe discovered the art never learned to use movable type. They made some attempts to do away with the cumbersome page printing, for the Chinese method was to cut the whole page on one block and not the characters separately. They tried various experiments in making single characters, using clay, wood and metal before Gutenberg's invention, but none of their attempts to invent a system of casting type was practiced for general usage.

Mr. Carter sums up the matter when he says, "The invention of block printing is the truly significant form of the invention of China" and "there are three important features which contributed to make the work of Gutenberg a success but which was lacking in the Chinese method, the type mold, alphabetic type and the press."[4] Even so China has to her credit the earliest printing of a book.

The chaos of the Five Little Ages was only the beginning of the disunion that was to come to China. How powerful the soldier of fortune had become and how weak the ruling house is seen in the passing of the Dragon Throne to a general of the army. Some soldiers, securing the yellow robe

THE "FIVE LITTLE AGES" 135

of royalty, threw it over their drunken general, declaring him emperor. Thus nonchalantly, a new ruling house, the Sungs, came into power, remaining nominally on the throne for some three hundred years from 960 to 1279, three hundred years of terrible strife and dismemberment of the empire.

The Sungs ruled over all China for only a brief period. Tartar tribes were overrunning North China and Chinese military skill could not cope with the vigorous barbarians who charged wildly into battle on horseback.

The first menace came from the Khitans whom the Chinese alternately fought and made peace with by paying tribute. This was a fatal mistake for larger and larger tribute was always demanded. After the Khitan invasion of 1004 China agreed to a yearly payment of one hundred thousand ounces of silver and two hundred thousand pieces of silk. The Chinese Emperor was to be addressed as Elder Brother and the Khitan chief as Younger Brother. Another tribe, the Tanguts, added their incursions to those of the Khitans and again the Sungs were forced to pay tribute and this time a larger one, two hundred fifty thousand ounces of silver, two hundred fifty thousand pieces of silk, two hundred fifty thousand catties of tea. So by 1044 the Sungs were being drained by these two yearly tributes. These are recorded in Chinese annals as presents to the Khitans and gifts to the Tanguts.

At this stage when the country was being drained of her richest resources and threatened with bankruptcy there appeared a great reformer who tried to rehabilitate the empire. This man, Wang An-shih (1021-1085), did not believe in the large landowners escaping taxation and the small ones bearing more than their share. He saw that the farmers lived from hand to mouth and that their income, coming only after harvest. was used to pay for the needs of the past year. He saw that the rich took advantage of them, forcing down the price of grain when the farmers sold their crops and forcing it up later when the farmers had to buy for their own needs. The farmer borrowed from the rich at an exorbitant rate, several hundred per cent. Wang wanted the state to lend them money at a low rate, forty per cent.

Wang An-shih was a most interesting figure, a scholar, a social philosopher and a statesman, a man who never washed his face. At an early age he distinguished himself in the examinations and because of this obtained many official advances, holding the offices of magistrate, judge, expositor in the Hanlin College and finally State Counselor to the Emperor. He was a devoted student of the ancient classics but was also a reformer and a radical. In the reform of education he advocated the introduction into the village schools of primers of history, geography and political economy and suggested a compounding of characters to simplify the written language.

Wang An-shih wanted to change and regenerate social conditions. One emperor allowed the reformer to put some of his ideas into practice. The fundamental principle underlying his reforms lay in the idea that it was the duty of the Emperor to provide the necessities of life for all his people. The State should take entire management of commerce, industry and agriculture with a view to succoring the working classes and preventing them from being ground into the dust by the rich. The land taxes were lowered and were made payable in grain or other produce. The government made loans to the farmers at an interest of two and a half per cent per month, and these loans were to be repaid after the harvest. These were called the "Green Sprout Law" and the "Grain Loans." In order to keep the price of grain from rising and falling, the government was to buy up grain when the price began to fall and sell it when prices rose. Instead of using forced labor to carry out all the government's public works, Wang proposed to pay for this labor by the levying of a graduated tax. For this purpose the people were divided into five groups according to their wealth. These reforms did not meet with the approval of the conservative element, the scholars, who, of course, felt this was too big a departure from the teachings of Confucius. The people also saw danger in these changes as they gave so much power to the central authority and so, though Wang held office for eight years more, he was at last dismissed and died in disgrace.

A contemporary of Wang An-shih, and one who opposed him in his reforms, was the historian, Ssu-ma Kuang, comparable only with the Han historian Ssu-ma Ch'ien. His famous work is the *T'ung Chien,* or *Mirror of History,* socalled by the Emperor because, "To view antiquity as it were in a mirror is an aid in the administration of government." The *Mirror of History* covers the period from the fifth century B. C. until 960, the beginning of the Sung Dynasty.

These conservative traditions of Ssu-ma Kuang were reinforced by Neo-Confucianism, a movement among the philosophers of the day. The scholars, rising in revolt against Zen Buddhism, turned to the Confucian classics and commentaries much as the Humanists of Europe went back to Greek and early Roman literature. Hu Shih says, "The significance of the Neo-Confucianist movement lies in this attempt to reconstruct the classical past as a new foundation for a secular philosophy, a secular education, and a secular civilization to take the place of the Buddhist-Taoist civilization of Mediaeval China."[5] And yet as P. C. Hsu points out they were all imbued from their birth up with Buddhist and Taoist ideas, so that Neo-Confucianism is at least tinged with these other philosophies from which they were trying to escape.

Under leaders Ch'eng I and Chu Hsi, they repudiated the Han commentaries, reinterpreted the Confucian texts, and made these new commentaries easily accessible. Because of the invention of printing this was possible and large numbers of books were printed and distributed. Schools were founded and learning encouraged.

The Neo-Confucianists came near to adopting a scientific method. They held that in every human mind is the knowing faculty, and in everything there is reason, and that the incompleteness of knowledge is due to the lack of investigating the reason of things. But things they interpreted as "affairs," and more and more they relied on the old Buddhist methods of long meditation leading to sudden insight. They came to no scientific investigation resting on experiment nor did they try to find the laws governing Nature. They went back to the ethical realism of Confucius and Mencius. The universe and man they thought are real and running through the universe and all life is an ethical principle, *li,* reason. The Neo-Confucianists hoped by a return to Confucian teaching to bring about political and social reform.

But neither Wang An-shih nor the philosophers could revitalize the Sung Dynasty. It was harder and harder pressed by the Khitans and the Tanguts. In order to cope with them the Chinese decided to league themselves with another Tartar tribe, the Chins or Kins who were growing powerful to the northeast in what is now Manchukuo. Their territory was known as the Golden enclosure and called by the Chinese, *Chin Kuo,* Gold Country. By the agreement between the Chinese and Kins the Chinese were to have given back to them the territory which had been lost to the Khitans, and the Kins were to have the yearly tribute or present that the Khitans had been receiving. The Kins did as they had promised, defeated the Khitans, but it was the old story of the camel's head within the tent. The Kins in a short time boldly entered Chinese territory and the Chinese found they had a more formidable enemy than the one just expelled.

The Kins advanced on the Sung capital in the province of Honan. We can imagine the terror of the capital as this ruthless band marched upon it, many thousand strong, a great horde on horseback, enveloped in a cloud of dust raised by the hoofs of many horses, the thud of many horses' hoofs beating against the earth, the war cry of the soldiers filling the air.

There followed a succession of fighting, evacuation of the capital, flight of the Emperor, paying of tribute. Then the Kins retired and went home for a short time, but in a few years the whole thing was repeated with ever bigger losses to the Chinese. Finally, the court was forced south to the Yangtse where they set up a capital at Yangchow. The Kins, fortunately for the Chinese, were horsemen and knew nothing of boats and fighting on water so they gave up the struggle over the river.

China was again divided in two parts. The north was now ruled by the Kins but not entirely conquered. In the one hundred and fifty years that they ruled northern China they gradually were dominated by the Chinese culture. They accepted the Chinese written language and literature. Culturally, the Chinese conquered them. But this did not satisfy the Chinese. They wanted to be the material rulers of the north.

So decade after decade they harried the Kins, and generation after generation they expended themselves and their wealth in campaigns and tribute. The Yangtse became a busy thoroughfare, not so much of trade as of war. Better and finer junks were built as transports to carry the troops. The river presented a busy scene. Hundreds of junks spread their great sails and set forth up and down the Yangtse, landing troops here and there to advance upon the Kins.

At last both the Chinese and the Kins were becoming worn out by the long struggle. Another Tartar tribe, the Mongol, was growing strong and harrying the Kins on their northern frontier. The Chinese repeated their former mistake and now allied themselves with the Mongols to drive out the Kins. This paved the way for their conquest by the Mongols and the setting up of the Mongol Dynasty in China.

In spite of all this turmoil and disaster the Sungs have left visible signs of their ability in the works of art which today may be seen in the museums of the world. In this realm the Sung period has left a record of high excellence. Painting followed the tendencies of Wang Wei of the T'ang Dynasty. Monochrome was generally used and landscape was the favorite theme. The painters lived with nature, the nature of South China as it appears today. The effect of their pictures is of mysticism and extreme delicacy. A fairy boat rises out of a sea of mist or a pagoda's faint lines show above the misty vapors of the valley.

The Sungs are also famous for their pottery and porcelains. Vases remain today, beautiful in line and shape with monochrome glazes in soft pastel shades; light green, creamy white or pale yellow. It is possible that this type of art is a result of the chaotic conditions of the Sung Dynasty. Scholars and artists retired to monasteries and lonely nooks to escape the turmoil of the times. In long meditation and dreamy mood they evolved these delicate imaginative productions.

CHAPTER XII

THE MONGOL RULE

THE original home of the Mongols is believed to be in what is now Siberia in a region southeast of Lake Baikal, and the Mongols are thought to be descendants of the Huns and thus related to Attila, the Hun, devastater of North Europe in the fifth century. Certainly, Attila, "the scourge of God" and Jenghis Khan, the first of the Mongols to rule a part of China, held in common the ruthless and cruel traits of the barbarian.

At the age of thirteen Jenghis succeeded his father as head of all the Mongols. His extreme youth caused some of the tribes to refuse to acknowledge him, but his mother, displaying the ensign of the Mongols (the ox-tail), rallied half of the tribes to his support. As he manifested royal qualities and distinguished himself in many battles, a confederacy of the Mongol tribes met on the Onon River in 1206 and declared him ruler over them all and gave him the title "Khan"—most mighty ruler.

Jenghis Khan promptly entered on a campaign of wide and ruthless conquest. He conquered the northern part of China, that part held by the Kins, Korea and Kharezm, a region lying to the southwest of Lake Baikal and between it and the Caspian Sea. With Russia, which was then made up of many states, he tried to make treaties. When his overtures were not cordially received, he forced some of these states to pay him tribute. Now an old man, but with his heart still set on the conquest of the Sungs, he returned to Mongolia. There he died in 1227 at the age of sixty-five with his desire for defeat of the Sungs still unfulfilled.

All accounts agree that Jenghis Khan was cruel and destructive. The cities in his path he razed to the ground and boasted that "he could ride over their sites without meeting an obstacle large enough to make his horse stumble." It is difficult to estimate such a man or his work. His destruction of lives and property for the mere love of destroying places him among the barbarians, but his skill in military strategy and in the direction of large armies over long distances ranks him with Alexander the Great, Hannibal, Julius Cæsar. By some he is considered the greatest conqueror in history and at the same time the most horrible and destructive. Boulger says, "He is remembered as a relentless and irresistible conqueror, a human scourge, but he was much more. He was one of the greatest instruments of destiny, one of the most remarkable molders of the fate of nations to be met with in the history of the world."[1]

Although Jenghis' conquests extended far, the final and complete conquest of China was left to his grandson, known as Kublai Khan. Kublai Khan fixed his capital at Cambuluc, "City of the Great Khan," situated on the present site of Peking. From here he sent out generals who conquered southwestern China. There they worked east down the Yangtse River toward Hangchow which the southern Sungs had made their last capital, capturing the young Emperor, Kung Ti, and sending him and his mother to Cambuluc in 1279.

But even yet the conquest was not complete. Loyal members of the court fled from the capital taking with them the two younger brothers of the captured Emperor, hoping thus to save the dynasty. From city to city they fled, finding no sanctuary for the boys, the older of whom they had quickly proclaimed emperor. Hurriedly, on a seagoing junk, they started on the last lap of their flight southward, only to have their sailing vessel wrecked on an island off the coast of Kuangtung. The boys were rescued but the one who had been so newly appointed emperor died. Thereupon his brother, a mere child, was put in his place. At last the party took refuge on an island off the southeastern coast and made a final desperate stand against their enemies. But what could a handful of men, soft with years of self-indulgence at court, do against a race every man of which was equipped with four horses and followed the life of a soldier from fifteen years to seventy, a race of soldiers who, on the march, when food was unattainable, sucked the blood of their horses and went on?

When the Chinese saw they could no longer hold out, the proud commander determined on a final flight from his enemies: this time beyond all possible reach of the advancing hordes. Taking the newly made child-Emperor upon his back, the commander drove his own family into the sea, then plunged after them, carrying the Emperor down with him. Around the island where the last stand was taken a hundred thousand corpses strewed the water—testimony to a last but futile protest against becoming a subject race. Thus ends the series of flights of the royal house of China, beginning with the craven old Emperor of the T'ang Dynasty who gave up his adored concubine to save his own skin, ending in this jump into the sea of the proud and brave commander. The swift decline of the empire is accomplished. China is completely conquered. The Mongols now hold both North and South China and all of the Chinese people are their subjects.

Kublai Khan was not content even now that he had conquered China but looked farther east, farther south. From Korea he sent out an expedition by sea toward Japan.

This sea campaign was a dangerous experiment. The nomad Mongols, accustomed to fighting on horseback, knew nothing of boats and seamanship. Kublai's large force—fifteen thousand men in three hundred vessels, many of whom were Koreans and Chinese who had been captured on the Island Tsushima—was overcome by the Japanese. Not to be daunted, however, Kublai sent a still larger fleet to invade Kiusiu, but the major part was destroyed by storm and the remainder captured by the Japanese, who were used to the sea. Japanese accounts say the fleet was wrecked by the divine wind of Ise. It is said that the Japanese killed all the Mongols, but spared the Chinese and Koreans. Another story says that thirty thousand were taken prisoners and three only were sent back to tell the story. Whatever the correct details may be, it is certain that the Japanese repelled the Mongols.

In the south of Asia, however, the Mongols were more successful; they defeated the Burmese, Annam they brought into semi-dependence on them, forcing her to pay tribute. They invaded Tibet and as a result adopted Lamanism, the type of Buddhism which prevailed there, as the state religion of the Mongols, but Kublai as Emperor of China performed the Confucian state ceremonies. The Lama priests occupied a position of temporal as well as spiritual power in Tibet. Kublai recognized this fact and appointed a Lama as king of Tibet with himself as overlord of the country. This custom has prevailed to the present though the overlordship today is exceedingly weak.

But the nature of the Mongol rule in China is what interests us most. In spite of the Mongols' savagery when at war, they were surprisingly humane to their conquered peoples. They displayed admiration for the very culture they destroyed in war. Now that China was conquered and in their power, they were not only willing but desirous that her cultural life should continue. In fact they adopted her culture.

The great Khans, like the great Han and T'ang rules, sensed the value of foreign intercourse. Chinese engineers are said to have been employed during this period as far west as the Euphrates Valley. At the Mongol court representatives from many nations were welcomed. Many monks, Italian, French, Flemish, were charged with diplomatic missions to the great Khan, and Mongols of distinction went to the capitals of Europe.

Toward the end of Kublai's reign, a Franciscan of the Kingdom of Naples, John de Monte Corvino, was sent by Pope Nicholes IV to Cambuluc. His missionary labors in China extended over forty-two years, during nine of which he was without fellow countrymen. Later, the Pope sent him seven colleagues with authority to consecrate him (Corvino) as archbishop. He made thirty thousand converts, translated the New Testament and Psalms into Mongolian.

The most celebrated by far of all the Europeans who came to China during the Mongol reign were Marco Polo, his father and uncle. The elder Polos made their first trip to China by accident because of a Tartar war. Unable to return from the Crimea, where they had been on a business trip, they went forward and at last landed at the court of Kublai Khan. He received them kindly, as was his custom with all travelers. He inquired much about Europe and finally sent them back to ask the Pope for a hundred missionaries.

The Polos reached their home in Venice, and after many vicissitudes started again for China, accompanied by Marco, who was then seventeen years of age. But instead of the one hundred missionaries the Khan had asked for, only two accompanied them. Despite this fact the Khan received them graciously making much of the young Marco. The boy learned the language, obtained the confidence of the Khan, who sent him all over the country on trips of inspection and even gave him Yangchow, in the Yangtse region, as an official post.

In all, the Polos spent seventeen years in the service of the Khan and at the end of that time when they wished to return home the Kahn demurred. But chance was with them. The Khan of Persia had sent to Kublai Khan for a wife, a Mongolian princess, but when all was ready for the journey to Persia it was discovered that the land routes were blocked because of war among the Tartars. The envoys who were accompanying the bride begged that the Polos, skilled navigators, be sent with them on the sea voyage now necessary. Kublai consented and after the Polos had reached Persia they went on to Venice, arriving there three years after they had left Peking.

Marvelous were the stories they told to their countrymen, so marvelous that everywhere there was a renewed interest in the East, in the far-away Cathay. It was while Marco Polo was in prison in Genoa (taken prisoner in a war between Venice and Genoa) that he dictated in French his famous account of his travels and his stay at the court of Kublai. He pictures a country possessing a material culture superior to that of Europe. Undoubtedly, the Orient with its spices, jades, silks seemed luxurious to a man from Mediaeval Europe. It must have been exciting to the Venetians to read of a land of such wonders.

Marco Polo's description of the great Khan's palace in the city of Cambuluc runs as follows:

> "The Grand Khan usually resides during three months of the year, namely December, January and February, in the great city of Kambalu, situated near

the north-eastern extremity of the province of Cathay: and here on the southern side of the new city is the site of his vast palace, the form and dimensions of which are as follows: in the first place is a square enclosed with a wall and deep ditch; each side of the square being eight miles in length, and having at an equal distance from each extremity an entrance gate, for the concourse of people resorting thither from all quarters. Within this enclosure there is on the four sides an open space one mile in breadth where the troops are stationed, and this is bounded by a second wall, enclosing a square of six miles having three gates on the south side, and three on the north, the middle portal of each being larger than the other two and always kept shut excepting on the occasion of the Emperor's entrance or departure. Those on each side always remain open for the use of common passengers. . . . Within these walls which constitute the boundary of four miles stands the palace of the Grand Khan, the most extensive that has ever been known. It reaches from the northern to the southern wall, leaving only a vacant space (or court) where persons of rank and the military guards pass and repass. It has no upper floor, but the roof is very lofty. . . . The sides of the great halls and the apartments are ornamented with dragons in carved work and gilt, figures of warriors, of birds, and of beasts with representations of battles. The inside of the roof is contrived in such a manner that nothing besides gilding and painting presents itself to the eye. On each of the four sides of the palace there is a grand flight of marble steps by which you ascend from the level of the ground to the wall of marble which surrounds the building. . . . The exterior of the roof is adorned with a variety of colors, red, green, azure and violet and the sort of covering is so strong as to last many years. The glazing of the windows is so well wrought and so delicate as to have the transparency of crystal."[2]

The great Khan's power is further revealed as we read of the White Feast held at the New Year.

"On this occasion great numbers of white horses are presented to the great Khan. . . . His majesty receives at this festival no fewer than a hundred thousand horses. On this day it is that all his elephants amounting to five thousand are exhibited in a procession covered with housings of cloth. . . . Each of these supports upon its shoulders two coffers filled with vessels. . . . On the morning of the festival before the tables are spread, all the princes, the nobility of various rank, the cavaliers, the astrologers, physicians, and falconers, with many others holding public offices, the prefects of the people and the land, together with the officers of the army, make their way into the grand hall in front of the Emperor. . . . When all have been disposed in the places appointed for them . . . a high dignitary says with a loud voice, 'Bow down and do reverence,' when instantly all bend their bodies until their foreheads touch the floor. . . . This being done, the prelate advances to an altar richly adorned, upon which is placed a red tablet inscribed with the name of the Great Khan. Near to this stands a censor of burning incense with which the prelate, on behalf of all who are present, perfumes the tablet and the altar with great reverence; when every one present humbly prostrates himself before the tablet."[3]

Marco Polo tells us also how the Khan kept open his communications with all parts of his vast empire and of the eternal vigilance kept over the subjected but restive Chinese people. Always we feel the grandeur and now and then we catch a glimpse of the strain on the resources of the people.

"In his dominions no fewer than two hundred thousand horses are thus employed in the department of the post, and ten thousand buildings, with suitable furniture, are kept up. It is indeed so wonderful a system, and so effective in its operation, as it is scarcely possible to describe. If it be questioned how the population of the country can supply sufficient numbers for

THE MONGOL RULE

these duties, and by what means they can be victualled, we may answer, that all the idolaters, and likewise the Saracens, keep six, eight, or ten women, according to their circumstances, by whom they have a prodigious number of children; some of them as many as thirty sons capable of following their fathers in arms; whereas with us a man has only one wife and even although she should prove barren, he is obliged to pass his life with her, and is by that means deprived of the chance of raising a family. Hence it is that our population is so much inferior to theirs. With regard to food, there is no deficiency of it, for these people, especially the Tartars, Cathaians, and inhabitants of the province of Manji (or Southern China), subsist, for the most part upon rice, panicum, and millet; which three grains yield, in their soil, an hundred measures for one. Wheat, indeed, does not yield a similar increase, and bread not being in use with them, it is eaten only in the form of vermicelli or of pastry. The former grains they boil in milk or stew with their meat. With them no spot of earth is suffered to lie idle, that can possibly be cultivated; and their cattle of different kinds multiply exceedingly, insomuch that when they take the field, there is scarcely an individual that does not carry with him, six, eight, or more horses, for his own personal use. From all this may be seen the causes of so large a population, and the circumstances that enable them to provide so abundantly for their subsistence."[4]

Polo also shows us the strength of the Yangtse, and its importance to the Chinese people and the greatness of the junk trade.

"Leaving the city of Sa Yan Fu and proceeding fifteen days' journey towards the south-east, you reach the city of Sin-gui (Kiu kiang) which although not large is a place of great commerce. The number of vessels that belong to it is prodigious, in consequence of its being situated near the Kiang which is the largest river of the world, its width being in some places ten, in others eight, in others six miles. Its length, to the place where it discharges itself into the sea, is upwards of one hundred days' journey. . . . A great number of cities and large towns are situated upon its banks and more than two hundred with sixteen provinces partake of the advantages of its navigation by which the transport of merchandise is to an extent that might appear incredible to those who have not had an idea of witnessing it. . . . The principal commodity, however, is salt. On one occasion when Marco Polo was in the vincinity of Sin-gui he saw there not fewer than fifteen thousand vessels and yet there are other towns along the river where the number is still more considerable. All these vessels are covered with a kind of deck, and have a mast with one sail. . . . With these ropes the vessels are tracked along the rivers by means of ten or twelve horses."[5]

If by mile he means the Chinese *li* which is about one-third of our mile, the river in Polo's time was the same as it is today. He speaks of the boats being tracked by horses. Today on the rivers of China a like method is used but the trackers are men.

Marco Polo says little of two of the great things the Khans did for China. First the rebuilding of the Grand Canal, which had been begun in the time of the Sui Dynasty (589-618 A. D.), was a great public work, although it was done for a personal reason. It was deepened and extended in order that the rice destined for the palace in Cambuluc might be loaded at the city of Hangchow and without transshipment be carried by canal to Tientsin, where the boats could pass directly into a small river which took them to Peking. There is very little rise and fall in the land through which the canal is built. Where such rises and falls did occur the Chinese used a very simple device: a sluice embankment of stones and dirt was built across the canal and

THE MONGOL RULE

boats were pulled up and let down this slimy incline by ropes which were fastened from the boat to windlasses on either side of the canal. These ropes were wound up by men walking round and round the windlass, chanting as they walked.

This method is still used. The boat in which I first traveled from Shanghai to Hangchow was hauled from one level to another in this fashion. The canal was simply a well-cut ditch; stone masonry faced the sides. Built in the days of the Khan it is still in use. The stone bridges over the main canal and the lesser ones that enter it have one, three or five arches depending on the width of the canal. They add very materially to the attractiveness of the landscape. In the days of the Mongols and until the latter part of the nineteenth century the canal was the only line of communication uniting north and south.

The second contribution of the Mongols was a cultural one, their patronage of the drama and the novel. These two types of literature in China had been largely spontaneous outbursts of the people and as such were frowned upon by the classical scholars who felt that no literature could be written except in the highly polished classical language and style of the classics. The Mongols were free from any such restrictions. Then too they had already developed dramatic performances before coming to China. So it was natural that they should lend their support to these hitherto unrecognized arts. It has been claimed that the Mongols introduced the drama and novel into China, but it seems more likely that they brought into the open the Chinese beginnings and allowed them to flourish while undoubtedly contributing some elements of their own.

The first traces of drama are found in the pre-Confucian era when solemn dances were held on festival days and at times of great ceremony. A remnant of this has been handed down in the ceremonies at the Confucian temples held twice a year until the establishment of the republic. On these occasions groups of boys sixty-four in number, and sometimes one hundred and twenty-eight, performed a stately dance in the open portion of the temple. Dressed in long gowns with Mandarin squares on front and back, with tasseled Mandarin hats and with long stiff feathers in their hands they swayed their bodies and kept time to the music of flutes and drums.

A more jovial type of entertainment was in existence in the time of Confucius when entertainers or actors amused the courtiers and officials with stories and jokes, dances and acrobatic feats. One of the T'ang Emperors developed a school known as the Pear Garden for training some three hundred boys and girls in singing and dancing preparing them for court entertainers. From 900 to 1300 there appeared various kinds of the dancing girls and public entertainers; these furnished the tunes for the singing parts of the first dramas.

These various beginnings welded together under the patronage and freedom given by the Mongols firmly established the drama in forms which have come down to modern times.

Plays are a very popular form of entertainment both in the large cities and throughout the rural districts. Today all through the country plays are given in temple enclosures or on temporary platforms erected in empty spaces in the villages. As you travel through the country, especially on festival or market days, you will see huge crowds of men standing around these stages gaping at the actors, who in worn and dirty, but very elaborate costumes, ride imaginary horses, cross imaginary rivers and stop in the midst of the most thrilling adventures to drink tea from the spout of a teapot.

In cities such as Peking one sees the selfsame play and

the same mode of acting it that the Chinese saw in the Mongol Dynasty. Much of the play is sung in a high falsetto and the musicians sit on the stage. There is very little in the way of scenery but as a rule the actors wear elaborate costumes. There are many devices to make up for the lack of stage setting: a backward kick and a lifting high of the foot indicate that the person has crossed the high threshold of a Chinese house. A large piece of stiff cardboard with a wheel painted on it shows that the person holding it is riding in a cart. The actors for women's as well as for men's parts are men. Actors had to undergo a vigorous training for with so little stage scenery much depended upon the acting. Socially the actor was looked down upon and he brought hardship on his family since for three generations no one in the family might compete in the literary examinations.

Chinese plays are not long but follow one after the other in quick succession. The plays fall into two groups: the military and the civil. The military plays are based on historical fact, usually the rivalry of two small kingdoms, their military chieftains appearing in fine array and indulging in considerable acrobatic work. The civil plays concern themselves with rather simple things of everyday life and are generally farcical. The names of some of the well-known plays are *The Orphan of Chow,* which appears in the hundred plays of the Yuan Dynasty, *The Sorrows of Han,* a historical play, and *The Story of the Western Pavilion,* a drama of passion and intrigue in sixteen scenes.

The novel, too, came into prominence in the time of the Mongols. The origin of the novel is found with the story-tellers who by the eighth century wrote down the tales substantially as they were recited. The professional story-tellers who recited their stories in the teahouse to the masses prepared "spoken texts" which were written in the spoken language of the people, the only one they could understand. Many of the historical tales they told were very long so they developed a kind of continued story. In the middle of a breath-taking episode they would suddenly stop, promising the audience to continue the next day. These stories at first crudely written by public reciters of little education were gradually added to, until finally during the Mongol Dynasty they appeared as the first real novels. The art of story writing continued to progress, the finished products appearing in the sixteenth and seventeenth centuries.

Schoolmasters and parents forbade the reading of novels, insisting on the study of the classics, but nevertheless, as in every country, they were read and enjoyed by the people. Two of the most popular novels were the *San Kuo* (Romance of the Three Kingdoms) and the *Shui Hu* (The Heroes of Liang Shan). The *San Kuo* consists chiefly of scenes of warfare and cunning schemes of military chieftains of the time of the famous Three Kingdoms in the third and fourth centuries.

The *Shui Hu* is one of the stories that developed through the centuries though it is said to have been written by Shih Nai-an during the Mongol Dynasty.[6] The story is laid in the late Sung period when society was in disorder and chaos. A group of one hundred and eight men seeking refuge from the oppressive government took refuge on a mountain and became brigands and robbers. But they had a moral code of their own, attacking the rich men and oppressive officials but showing mercy to the poor and desolate. Naturally such a book gained great popularity among the people.

One of the episodes is of a huge brigand who was befriended by a man of influence and the patron of a monastery who in order to gain protection for the brigand induced the abbot to admit him as a novice. The robber stood the rules of the monastery as long as he could and then

THE MONGOL RULE

escaped and got drunk, returning to the monastery and making a great riot. He was reinstated at the request of his benefactor but repeated the performance. This time on returning to the monastery he was refused admittance by the gatekeeper, whereupon he knocked to pieces a huge idol at the gate for not aiding him. By threat of fire he succeeded in getting the monks to open the gate "through which no wine or meat might pass," and as he fell through it out rolled from his gown a half-eaten dog's leg. This he tore to pieces and forced into the mouth of one of his fellow priests. The book consists of escapades of his and the exploits of other ruffians.

Although the Mongol Emperors gave peace to China, increased the trade and fostered the Chinese culture, the Chinese were not satisfied under their rule. A proud people, they felt the humiliation of having become a subject people. They hated the Mongol garrisons stationed in each city and town; they hated the military administration which the Mongols had introduced in the place of their scholar administration. They hated to see their blood mixed with the blood of the conquerors. For many years there was nothing they could do. Kublai held the highest position in the world— ruler over most of Asia, all powerful. But at last the opportunity of the Chinese people came.

Kublai Khan, like so many strong emperors all over the world, before and since, left no strong successor. That there was no great man may be attributed to the fact that the Mongols, coming more and more under the influence of Chinese civilization and luxury, had lost much of their native vigor. At court the Mongols had adopted the fatal Chinese custom of employing eunuchs to watch over the concubines. Weak ruler followed weak ruler, made weaker still by the enervating influence of the eunuchs.

As disasters, floods, famines and earthquakes impoverished

the land, the people became discontented and rebellious. The military expeditions of the Khans, the building of Cambuluc and public works such as the Grand Canal, and the expense of the imperial court made large demands on the treasury. The policy tried by the T'angs and Sungs of using paper money was revised and three kinds of notes were issued, based respectively on silk, silver and copper. In Kublai's reign of thirty-five years it is said that over six hundred million dollars' worth of these notes were issued but without sufficient, if any, reserve. Metals, always scarce in China, had in this period been augmented by gold and silver which came from Europe in payment for silk. But instead of keeping it as a reserve for their paper currency they foolishly wasted it in large gifts to the imperial family and to victorious generals.

During the last days of the Dynasty, many rebellious secret societies flourished, one known as the "White Lily Society." Pirates infested the southern coast of China. The government was too weak to do anything but offer bribes which finally, as the bandits became stronger, they refused. Among the leaders of rebellious bands was one Chu-Yuan-chang, whose ancestral home was in An-hwei Province, just north of the Yangtse. When he was a young man, all his family had been carried off by a pestilence. After this he had retired to a Buddhist monastery where he had remained several years. Finally he became so sympathetic with the rebellion of his own people against the Mongols that he left the monastery and entered the ranks of the rebels. His power of leadership soon made him chief of one of the bands. Chu in time placed himself at the head of a union of several bands, seized Nanking, and declared it his capital. The people accepted him as their deliverer from the foreign Mongols. Even the pirate chiefs to the south allied themselves with him.

THE MONGOL RULE

The Mongolian Emperor, threatened by Tartar bands on the north, even as the Chinese in the past had been threatened by the Mongols, was too weak to resist Chu's advancing, victorious hosts. One of his generals got as far north as Kai-feng fu. Then in 1368 Chu declared himself emperor of a new dynasty, called Ming, Bright, or Brilliant Dynasty and took for himself the imperial title of Tai Tsu. The Mongol Emperor, in order to avoid capture by the Chinese, fled to his ancestral home and thus ended the Mongol Dynasty in China.

With the passing of the Mongols went China's free intercourse with the rest of the world. The hospitality of the T'angs and the Mongols when China invited all the world to come to her court has never been repeated. "The Silken Way," that long route across central Asia linking China with Europe, was closed forever by the Saracens; Europeans turned westward for their routes and China's old northwest gateway sank to decay. When the rest of the world, advancing in their explorations, reappeared in China they came by the water-gateway of the Arabs on China's southeast corner. But by this time China did not invite them, as in the days of the T'angs, to enter. She closed her doors and shut herself within her own borders.

PART THREE

THE SHUT-IN PERIOD

CHAPTER XIII

The Ming or Bright Dynasty

Chu Yuan-chang, the conqueror of the Mongols, established his capital at Nanking. He took the reigning name of Hung Wu for himself and Ming, or Bright, for the dynasty which he founded (1368). Although the Chinese welcomed him as their deliverer from a foreign rule, there were still large parts of the empire to be brought under his control. The most difficult were the mountainous districts in the west and southwest, but these in the course of a few years he was able to pacify. A worse menace was to be found in the Mongols who, after they left their capital, Cambuluc, continued to make raids on the northern border. Hung Wu decided that the best policy was to carry the war boldly into the territory of the enemy. In a decisive battle he was victorious and the Mongols were forced to give up Manchuria and the part of Mongolia itself which lay south of the desert. Toward the close of his reign he further enlarged his power by forcing tribute from Korea on the northeastern border and from Burmah on the south.

In addition to consolidating his territory Hung Wu set about organizing the government of the empire. He inaugurated the provincial system which has prevailed ever since. In China proper, instead of the eighteen provinces of today, he established thirteen and two metropolitan districts. At first the treasurer was the highest officer in a province but toward the end of the dynasty, in the northern provinces and where military operations were taking place, the offices of governor or viceroy were created. Maybe the purpose in this change was to forestall any attempt at a revival of the old states so long a menace to any unified government or maybe it was a conscious patterning after the autocratic ways of Kublai Khan. At any rate from this time on we hear no more of states warring against one another, struggling for supremacy. The empire was not always strongly centralized, but in name at least it became a unit. The provinces at times had considerable autonomy but they were recognized as subsidiary parts of the empire.

The Ming Dynasty began most auspiciously. The Chinese people welcomed this return to native rule and held high hopes for the restoration of peace. Both among the people and the rulers there was a great reaction from all foreign ways and things. Hung Wu himself led in this pro-Chinese policy and set an example to the people by reviving ancient customs. He followed the practices of ancient emperors by performing the annual ceremonial of planting and caused the Empress to offer the annual sacrifice to the spirits of the mulberry trees. It is interesting to note that this first Ming Emperor immediately brought the emphasis back to agricultural pursuits, reviving the annual ceremonies of the seasons, the planting of the crops and the fostering of silk culture. In dress he put a ban on the high riding boots and military attire of the Mongol type and restored the slipper-like shoe and long gown of the Hans and T'angs.

Last and maybe most significant he laid emphasis on the time honored provincial and national civil service examinations. But Hung Wu, in his revival of the competitive examination system brought it down to a very rigid form by the introduction of a certain style for the essay called the "Eight Legs." A theme was given the candidates, always chosen from the Confucian Four Books or Five Classics and this must be treated in four paragraphs, each consisting of two members of an equal number of sentences and words. The writer was to express no opinions of his own but simply to put the few words of Confucius or his disciple Mencius given in the theme into an essay following the prescribed rules. Those who were successful obtained degrees which entitled them to official appointment.

The examinations were held at Peking and at the provincial capitals in halls especially built for the purpose; those at Nanking have only recently been demolished. The Examination Halls consisted of acres upon acres of stalls arranged in long rows, each stall just large enough for a man. In each of these tiny compartments stone ledges of different heights were built. A board laid on the top of the lower two of these ledges made the competitor's seat and another laid on the higher ledge made his table. Food was brought to them by servants. From high lookout towers officials watched that none left the cells or received help. In these tiny cells the men stayed for three days writing continuously.

The preparation of the examination required close study of the classics and gave no chance for independent thought or for any knowledge of practical affairs. Even more it hampered creative efforts in literature. But at least it was a rigid mental discipline. It cost the men almost a lifetime of close study and the men who took the degrees were marked with the attributes of real scholars. They were marked also physically, for the stooped shoulder, emaciated face and delicate hand of the scholar became revered and envied in all the land. The system bound them to the past, left them without curiosity or knowledge about the things of their own day or the outside world. The high peak of Chinese culture was caught or frozen into form before the Modern Era.

Literature seems to have been stifled by the spirit of conventionality and tradition typical of the age. Poetry did not reach the high pitch of the T'angs, nor did drama and novel writing flourish as during the Mongol Dynasty. The most creditable accomplishments in literature were in the form of compilations of information. The Great Encyclopedia was produced—a work of five hundred thousand pages. Two thousand scholars labored for three years over it. Only three manuscript copies were made, two of which perished at the downfall of the Mings. The other was kept in the Hanlin Academy, but was largely destroyed when the Academy was burned to the ground during the Boxer troubles in 1900. Another work, similar in character, was an encyclopedia of agriculture. This is in ninety volumes. And there is also the *Materia Medica* written by Li Shih-chen after twenty-six years of work.

The first Ming Emperor inspired confidence among the people by his acts of magnanimity and benevolence. He moved farmers from densely populated regions to those more sparsely inhabited; he opened waste fields to agriculture; planted more mulberry trees; and ordered lakes and reservoirs to be put in condition for irrigation. But the evils left from former days were great. The soil was depleted and it was no easy task to restore it. "Land-gobbling" families were on the increase and thus it was hard for the farmers to hold their small farms. To alleviate immediate distress the Emperor established granaries in which to store food, and at various times and in various localities he exempted the farmers from taxes.

But all this emphasis on agriculture and learning did not do away with strife. At the end of thirty years of kind and humane rule this first Ming Emperor placed his grandson on the throne, deeming his sons unfit to carry on his just rule. In thus passing over his sons he followed the old custom of the ancient rulers, Yao and Shun. But this revival of

THE MING OR BRIGHT DYNASTY 165

the procedure was not so successful, as one of the new Emperor's uncles, the fourth son of Hung Wu, began warring on the boy king, and again Nanking was the scene of fighting and bloodshed. The boy king was conquered and fled, it is thought, to a Buddhist monastery. His uncle, the new Emperor, proved a very capable sovereign, but the beginning of his reign was marked by great cruelty. He slaughtered in cold blood the ministers of state who had obeyed the decree of the old Emperor and remained loyal to the grandson he had appointed. Not only the ministers but their whole families were murdered.

Whether this new Emperor tired of Nanking or whether he felt that a northern location for his capital was a more advantageous place from which to combat China's most persistent enemies, the barbarian hordes, we do not know. At any rate, he moved his capital in 1421 to the site of the Mongol Cambuluc, naming it Peking, "northern capital." Over and over have the capitals of China been built, destroyed and rebuilt. Ch'ang An, Lo Yang, Nanking all had their day. Now Peking, first made the national capital under the Mongols, was to reach its zenith.

Since the days of the Mongols some fifty years had elapsed before the Mings moved their capital to Peking—time enough for rain and wind to destroy much. Wanton destruction had done the rest. Some remains of the old Mongol wall are visible today, one bit two miles to the north and another to the southwest of the present walls, testify to the fact that the city of the Mongols enclosed a territory several miles greater in extent than that of the Mings. The Mings did not use a new architectural design but, true to the ideas of Hung Wu, went back to the plans of the old capitals and palaces described in the ancient literature. These they perfected and elaborated, making a city of far-famed beauty. Unfortunately, by the end of the dynasty much of the capital was destroyed by fire but as the succeeding dynasty proceeded to rebuild it on the same foundations and in the same style, in some instances even employing the same architects and artists, Peking today is essentially the city of the Mings.

In design it is really a series of four cities set one within the other, each surrounded by its own wall. The innermost of all is the Forbidden City, so-called because no one except the Emperor's family and the princes were allowed to live in it. A red wall, now dimmed to pink, topped with imperial yellow tiles, surrounds it. Then comes the second city, called the Imperial City, also surrounded by a red wall. The third or Tartar City has a gray brick wall only, but over its twelve gateways rise a succession of curving roofs covered with green glazed tiles. One of the finest of these gateways is to the south of the Forbidden City and is the gateway (Chien Men) which the Emperors passed through to the fourth city, where stand the Temple of Heaven and the Temple of Agriculture. This last city, called the Chinese City, is surrounded by a gray brick wall, in some places sixty feet high, but it is not topped with beautiful tiling as are the walls surrounding the two inner cities.

Let us go back now through the two outer cities to the Forbidden City, the architectural achievement of the Mings. We find the palaces arranged after the conventional Chinese pattern. Within the pink outer wall you pass from court to court, each court a unit in itself—a vast central square bounded on four sides by one-story, lofty buildings, usually but one room deep with doors on the court side only. Imperial yellow tiles cover the roofs, and figures of dragon and phoenix in the same yellow glaze are mounted on the curved points of the roofs. Gleaming white marble balustrades carved with dragons surround the shallow verandas. The windows and doors of the buildings are of wood, intricately carved in a pierced design.

As one passes from court to court toward the innermost part of the palaces one's sense of the grandeur and magnificence of the place increases. In the brilliant sunlight of northern China the acres of glazed yellow tiles shimmer and throw gleams of yellow light dazzling one's eyes. The vast empty spaces of the courts create within one a satisfied sense of balance and symmetry.

And then if one turns his back on the Forbidden City and goes out to the Chinese City he finds the Temple of Heaven and the Altar of Heaven. The Temple is a small building not over fifty feet in diameter, exquisite in form and coloring. The perfectly circular wall of the building, made of beautiful faun-colored brick, fine and delicate in texture, is surmounted by a circular, convex roof of blue tiles crowned at the apex with one large blue tile shaped something like the button the mandarins used to wear on their hats. The roof extends beyond the wall of the building a foot or more in an upward curve. Close under this flaring eave on the circular wall are a series of frescoes exquisitely done in soft pastel colors.

The Altar of Heaven stands in the same great enclosure with the Temple. It is a huge marble platform built in three tiers, each tier set back from the one below, surrounded by a white marble balustrade covered with dragons. The highest and smallest of these platforms is the altar proper. One can hardly fail to be profoundly impressed in coming upon this vast white altar set among the dark cypress trees. All other places of worship in the world shut the worshiper away from the deity they worship. It was for the Chinese to build this altar to Heaven with no other roof than the great blue vault of the sky. There is grandeur and solemn beauty in this simple, three-tiered marble altar where the Emperor came once a year to worship Heaven.

At the winter solstice, the south gate of the Forbidden City and the gate of the Imperial City directly opposite were thrown open. The street connecting the two gates and all the streets of the Imperial City were deserted. No ordinary folk went about their daily business. By royal edict the subjects of the Son of Heaven remained within their houses lest they look upon their divine ruler.

Slowly the procession moved forth from the Forbidden City. Hundreds of men, nobles, princes and mandarins, dressed in high pointed boots, silk robes of state, each with the insignia of his rank embroidered upon his breast, mushroom hats with the peacock plumes of officialdom upon their heads, rode ahead on ponies. At last came the imperial sedan hung with yellow trappings, carried upon the shoulders of sixteen men. Within it, closely curtained from a chance profane gaze, sat the Son of Heaven, the perfect man. Through the Chien Gate with its succession of green tiled roofs moved the cavalcade along the deserted streets of the outer city of the vast enclosure where stood the Altar of Heaven.

At night the Emperor went alone into the little rounded building of the Temple of Heaven and under its blue roof he prayed. As he knelt there alone, much activity was going on in the slaughter houses near the altar, where the ram, the bull and the boar were being made ready for the sacrifice. In great iron baskets raised on tripods standing in open ground at the four corners of the altar flames leaped up. Except for the light of these fires and the burning sacrifices only the moon illumined the white altar. Shadows lay among the cypress trees. All within the enclosure waited for the dawn.

Just as the first pale light appeared, the Son of Heaven

THE MING OR BRIGHT DYNASTY 169

took his solitary way to the altar, ascended its steps to the circular marble in the great white space at the top, its holy of holies. There he knelt and spoke to Heaven for his people.

In another enclosure stands the Temple of Earth. As the Temple of Heaven was circular to represent the dome of the heavens, the Temple of Earth was square to represent the Chinese idea of the earth. To this temple the Emperor went in the summer solstice to turn a furrow of earth with the plow. The Emperor, clothed in yellow ceremonial robes, offered sacrificial calves and yellow silk before the yellow jade tablet to the Earth. Thus he bespoke a good harvest for his people. These were ancient ceremonies which the Mings revived. From the days of the Mings until the passing of the Manchus in 1911, a period of some five hundred years, these ceremonies were performed every year.

There was yet another architectural form which the Mings perfected—the imperial tombs. Its distinctive features are a great burial mound and a ceremonial avenue of approach flanked by two rows of sculptured figures. The first Ming Emperor, Hung Wu, was buried outside the city walls of Nanking. There his tomb still stands. Guarded on either side by large stone figures of camels, horses, elephants, statesmen, soldiers, priests, a long approach leads to the hill, grass grown now, in which the tomb is located. The large sculptured figures are but a development of the crude stiff figures used by the Hans in front of their royal graves. During various civil wars the memorial halls, built by the Mings, have been destroyed; only the burial mound and the long avenue remain which give one an idea of the grandeur and dignity of the tomb of the first Ming Emperor.

The graves of the other Mings are some thirty miles northwest of Peking near the place where the southern pass (Nan Kou) breaks through the Great Wall. In general, the plan of these tombs is much like that of the first Ming Emperor, only all is on a grander scale. The thirteen graves of the later Mings cover an immense area, for each tomb has its long avenue of approach with huge carved figures on either side. The avenues lead from pavilion to pavilion and at last to ceremonial halls with yellow tiled roofs, marble steps and balustrades.

The Mings in their building of Peking gathered up the best traditions in Chinese architecture. With their delight in fineness of line and delicacy of color they made the palaces and temples buildings of rare beauty. They preserved the enchanting features of Chinese architecture; tiled roofs with curving ends on which are perched dragons and phoenixes, red lacquered columns, marble balustrades carved in dragons, and inclined approaches carved in bas-relief.

The Chinese during the Ming Dynasty may be said to have perfected rather than to have created. Hung Wu, as we have seen in his anti-Mongol policy, sponsored the old customs and practices. Neo-Confucianism, begun by the Sungs, was now an all-absorbing philosophy of the scholars and this, as we remember, looks back to Confucian thought and ideals. This spirit of the age tended to check aggressiveness and imagination and fix all kinds of endeavor in a traditional and conventional form. To make more perfect and refined the things of the past became the desire of men in every walk of life. In architecture and sculpture we have seen that this was true.

The painting of the Mings also shows this conventionalizing tendency. Painters studied the old masters instead of Nature itself and a whole set of little conventions was followed by all the artists. There is an example to illustrate this in a story told of a school of painting. A line of poetry, "The bamboos envelop the inn beyond the bridge," was given to a class as a suggestion for a painting. One of the

THE MING OR BRIGHT DYNASTY 171

students painted a heavy grove of bamboos with a tiny banner, the kind displayed on all wine-houses, above the bamboos. This hereafter became the convention for everyone who wished to paint an inn. Many of the paintings of the period are very charming and very excellent in technique but they tend to be overladen with details and meticulous in line. They lack the originality and mystic quality of the T'ang and Sung periods.

Besides architecture and painting the people of the Ming Dynasty developed the lesser arts of bronze casting, lacquer work and ceramics. These had all been begun in earlier times but the Mings brought them to a fine point of excellence.

The beginnings of the ceramic art go back, as we have seen, to the prehistoric period. Pieces of this earliest Chinese pottery found in the Neolithic and Shang villages furnish examples of the first efforts which the Chinese made in the art. Glazing was added by the Hans but further progress was slow for several centuries.

In the north, the early pottery was made of a very ordinary clay, but later in Kiang-si, Chekiang and Fukien Provinces excellent clays for porcelains were found and there potterymaking developed rapidly.

The noted factory of Ching Teh Chen in Kiang-si, established about 580 A. D., was famous during the days of the T'angs and Sungs, neglected by the Mongols, and now under the Mings came back to its own. At the height of its glory a great village devoted entirely to the pottery industry contained three thousand kilns. One part of the village was given over exclusively to the making of the imperial ware. Famous artists painted beautiful designs on the vases and dishes. The materials both for the pâte or porcelain and for the glaze were brought in boats from a place in the hills some sixty miles away. The Mings introduced many new features, bringing the porcelains to a higher and higher perfection and beauty. In the fifteenth century they began to use a blue coloring under the glaze which gave the beautiful blue and white ware—the ginger jars which we often see today.

In the later Ming Dynasty they painted in three and five colors over the glaze and in various designs, scenery in a rock garden or figures of people. The colors used were red, green, violet or purple, yellow, black or brown. Another favorite glaze was red, discovered in the time of the Mings and kept secret. They allowed outsiders to believe that powdered rubies were used to give the bright color, *pao-shih-hung*. It is now known that the ruby would have decomposed in the heat of the kiln.

The crackle glaze had been originated some time during the Sung Dynasty but was developed to its height under the Ming. One method of producing the crackle was the addition of soapstone to the glaze. This caused the glaze to contract during firing more than the body of clay beneath, thus producing irregular cracks on the glaze. Various decoctions were smeared into the minute cracks before the glaze was completely dry, thus producing patterns in different colors.

The range of articles was great: Figures particularly of *Kuan Yin*, Goddess of Mercy, libation cups, vases, bowls, cups, plates. The native writers say that at the time of the Mings there was almost nothing that was not made of procelain. In design also there was great variety. The blue and white ran mostly to the hawthorne and willow patterns. The dragon was much used, especially on the imperial pieces. Designs of the five-color variety were generally scenery with figures of people, for instance, beautiful willowy women standing near a rock or tree. The luxury of the court demanded great excellence of work and a large number of

THE MING OR BRIGHT DYNASTY 173

articles. Official records show that the court required in 1554 26,350 bowls, 30,500 saucers to match, 6000 ewers with 6500 wine cups and 680 garden bowls to cost 50 taels each. The loss of court patronage after the Ming and Ching Dynasties was undoubtedly the reason for the decline of the art.

The porcelains of the Mings made China famous in central Europe and England as silk in the days of the Hans had made her famous in Rome. There are reports of porcelains being imported into Europe as early as 1440, but if so it must have been only in small amounts. It was too fragile for the caravans. Even in the seventeenth century it was still treated as a curiosity in Europe. But in the eighteenth century when tea was introduced into Europe and warm drinks became the fashion the Europeans looked to China for their cups. The handleless cup of the Orient did not suit them so China made special cups with handles for export to the West. Some of this was known as "Cambron Ware" from the name of the English East India Company's station Cambron in the Persian Gulf. By 1840 England shipped goods from Canton and this porcelain was called "China Ware" simply because it was made in China.

By the middle of the dynasty the Mings had reached the zenith of their power and glory. During the last one hundred and fifty years there were nine monarchs all of whom were under the power of favorite concubines and eunuchs. Hung Wu had endeavored to do away with this evil by decreeing that no eunuch, under any circumstance, be permitted to meddle in state affairs, the punishment for the offense being instant decapitation. But the reform was short-lived for even in the next reign, the Emperor in gratitude to the eunuchs for their help in his struggle for the throne appointed them to high official positions. From this time on they gained in power, until finally they secured the office which had charge of state ceremonies. This office carried great influence as the holder of it was often called upon to frame decrees issued in the name of the Emperor. As time went on many state papers passed through the hands of a strong eunuch without reference to the Emperor. Also bribery, the custom of presenting to the eunuchs "yellow and white grain," gold and silver respectively, increased as the eunuchs grew more powerful.

At this juncture, when the government had been reduced to a low level, China was confronted with the question of her foreign policy. With the coming of the Mings the flourishing foreign trade of Mongol days had disappeared. The old northwest gateway was closed, partly because of the Mings' pro-Chinese policy and partly because of the Turks who were disrupting the caravan trade along the mid-Asian routes, those old trade routes of the Hans and the T'angs. But the disruption of trade in the time of the Mings began in the fifteenth century when Portugal and Spain and then other European countries began the quest for sea routes to China and the Indies to take the place of the former routes by land. At the very time when Europe was eager with a spirit of adventure, when scholars were busy developing maritime science and geographical knowledge and when inventors were producing the compass and astrolabe, China was more and more shutting herself away from the world, reviving and perfecting her past traditions. Consequently when the Westerners appeared at her southeastern gateway on the Pacific Ocean she was surprised and in no mood to receive anything foreign. Tolerance such as she had shown in the days of the Hans, the T'angs and the Mongols was a thing of the past and her history from this point on is practically a continuous struggle against foreign powers.

The Mings seem never to have adopted a definite policy toward the foreigners who came seeking trade privileges and

THE MING OR BRIGHT DYNASTY 175

places to open trading ports. At times they fought them off, at times they made a compromise with them, and at other times they received them more openly. Except in rare instances none came to Peking but all were kept at bay on the fringes of the empire.

China's first difficulty was with Japan. The Japanese had never forgiven the invasions made upon them under Kublai Khan and were also galled by the attitude of superiority which the Chinese assumed. The immediate cause of difficulty was the refusal of the Chinese to grant trading privileges to the Japanese. In consequence, the Japanese sent out piratical expeditions and harried the coasts of China, capturing the cities of Ningpo, Shanghai, Soochow, and carrying off much spoil. The Chinese finally sent out a large force against the Japanese *daimyo,* or lord, Fashiba by name, who in turn resolved to invade China. He began by asking the aid of Korea but when its king refused he invaded that country, advancing upon the capital, Soeul, forcing the King to flee. The King thereupon called for aid from the Chinese Emperor, who lost no time in sending an army to his assistance. There were no decisive results to the fighting and when Fashiba died in 1598 hostilities stopped and terms of peace were arranged. The Japanese were allowed to establish a settlement at Fusan (southeastern end of Korea) which gave them a foothold on the mainland of Asia.

Rafael Perestrello, a relative of Columbus, is the first European known to have landed on the China mainland by way of the sea. In 1516 he reached China in a Malay junk with thirty Portuguese. He was followed six years later by another of his countrymen, Fernando Peres de Andrade, who entered the Canton River with a fleet carrying pepper. He asked the privilege of opening commercial intercourse and was graciously received, even allowed to go to Peking to reside at the court. But this friendliness did not last long.

Another Portuguese fleet under Andrade's brother, Simon, appeared and unfortunately committed acts of lawlessness and piracy along the coast about Foochow and as far north as Ningpo. This naturally called down the hatred of the Chinese. The first Andrade was thrust into prison and later brought to Canton and beheaded to avenge the wrongs done by his brother and his fleet. A massacre of Portuguese at Ningpo followed, and all who were able to escape fled south in 1550 to Macao which is on the mainland opposite Hongkong. Here the Chinese Government finally allowed them to settle in return for an annual rental.

With the Spanish in the Philippine Islands, China also had difficulties. During the Ming Dynasty the Philippines became a Spanish colony. Magellan's fleet, coming from Spain by way of the Straits which now bear his name, appeared in the Philippines in 1520. In Manila, the capital of the Philippines, there seems to have been a very considerable Chinese population and the Spaniards, fearing this population might become too numerous, treated the Chinese cruelly, at one time inflicting a great massacre upon them. The Chinese Government took no steps to protect her people against these cruelties, evidently taking the position that if they wished to live in foreign countries they must do so at their own risk. In 1575 Spain sent an embassy to Canton, but there seems to have been no result from the mission.

The Chinese also discouraged the Dutch when they wished to open up trade with China. There was an attempt to settle in the Pescadore Islands (between Formosa and the mainland of China) but it got no farther than erecting two forts on the large island of Formosa. Even from this place of vantage they were driven out by a Chinese pirate, Koxinga, who got control of the island.

During the Ming period the English also made their first attempts to reach China. The lure of old Cathay started the

THE MING OR BRIGHT DYNASTY 177

English explorers in search of the Northwest Passage. In 1553 Sebastian Cabot and Sir Hugh Willoughby sailed from England, carrying letters from Edward VI addressed "to Kings, princes, and other potentates inhabiting the Northeast parts of the world in the direction of the powerful Empire of Cathay." Richard Chancellor in 1554 went by way of the White Sea—his goal, China. Finding himself in Russia instead, he obtained first licenses to trade with that country. Frobisher, Hudson, Baffin and many another were engaged in the search for the Northwest Passage to the Orient.

Apparently the first English ship to reach China was the *Unicorn* which, on a trip from Java to Japan, was wrecked near Macao. In 1600 the Merchant Adventurers sent out five ships and three years later the London East India Company, sometimes called the Old Company, was formed and given the monopoly of English trade in the Orient. It is reported that the *Hind* succeeded in reaching Macao, but trade was at a standstill because of the imminent fall of the Ming Dynasty.

The Jesuits wanted to enter China, but at first the Chinese refused them admittance to the mainland. St. Francis Xavier was only allowed to settle on an island near Macao, where he died. But Matteo Ricci, the most influential of Jesuits with the Chinese, somehow gained a foothold on the mainland. He learned the language, adopted the garb of a Buddhist priest and then that of a Chinese scholar and made his way overland to Nanking. In 1601 he reached Peking and presented the Emperor with some clocks—probably the first the court had seen. His knowledge of Chinese enabled him to publish a translation of Euclid and some astronomical works. In consequence the court granted to him and other Jesuits certain favors and honors, among them appointment to the Board of Astronomy. Probably the policy of the

Jesuits in adopting the customs of the Chinese and learning their language gave them greater privileges than the traders had received.

Besides questions of foreign policy and domestic administration, the later Mings were faced by economic conditions of the gravest sort. The reforms so auspiciously begun by the founders of the line unfortunately did not last long. The building of Peking had been a great financial drain. It is recorded that two hundred thousand men were kept busy for twenty years. Many of these were peasants who were forced to leave their fields and give their services to the work. Upon the rest of the population taxes for the enterprise fell heavily. The "palace farms" became a great grievance. These confiscated lands, set aside to yield income for the royal house, some claim to have been the cause of the Ming downfall. The upkeep of these "Royal or Imperial Farms" became a pretext for the imperial relations and court favorites to tax the people. The people complained and the government issued edicts for the suppression of the abuse. But to what avail? The treasury was empty; the Emperor was unable to give the courtiers money, so he was forced to let them keep the lands. Again and again we read of the rich occupying the fields of poor neighbors and shifting on them the burdens of taxation.

In face of all these troubles, the government tried various relief measures. Some were the time-honored ones: opening of the granaries, the sale of grain at reduced prices. They also resorted to new ones; they dug a canal from Peking to Peiho deep enough for grain junks; they confiscated Taoist and Buddhist lands; they launched a scheme for operating gold mines in central China in which a half million men were engaged. Many lives were sacrificed and the government failed to gain from this scheme the gold for which they had hoped.

THE MING OR BRIGHT DYNASTY

One futile effort followed another and the suffering among the people grew apace. At first the conditions were worse in the north. In Honan and Shensi the people lived on poor grass—the food supply of all the people. But later we hear of poor harvests in the south also. The supervisor of taxes of Chekiang says: "The people of Chekiang are suffering terribly and they are too busy to save themselves from starvation. . . . On New Year's Day there was no smoke from the villages, few were found walking about. . . . Dead corpses were lying on the roads. In face of all this there is no relief."[1] In 1595 it is reported that the people were wandering from north to south in search of food; women and children were sold for trifling sums; babies were thrown away; the aged were deserted. Robberies and the eating of human flesh became common practices.

In 1600 from Shensi in the north comes this stark story of distress: The people ate grasses and when the grasses were gone they ate bark. "Among all the trees, they considered the bark of the Yu the best. When the bark was exhausted they ate rock from the mountains which was known as 'Green leaves.'"[2] Of this it was said that it smelled like fish and had rather a delicate taste. One ate a little and felt satisfied, but in a few days the stomach swelled and burst, causing death. Some, not wishing to die, became thieves.

Some historians have wondered that the Ming Dynasty went down so easily before their successors, the Manchus. Others point to the utter misery of the people and only wonder that they did not sooner succumb. Half the population had died and those remaining lived miserable lives. The treasury was bankrupt. Honor and loyalty were lacking among the Emperor's generals and the depraved eunuchs were in power.

Rebellions broke out in various parts of the empire, the

most formidable in Shensi where misgovernment prevailed under a weak viceroy and where famine was unusually severe. The rebellion consisted of marauding bands of brigands who as they were not suppressed became more daring. Matters grew worse and the rebellion spread into five other provinces in the west. The empire found itself between two fires with this rebellion on its western side and a Tartar tribe, the Manchus, growing strong on the northeast and ravaging that part of the empire.

In the west the rebels finally found a strong leader in Li Tzu-ch'eng, a native of Shensi. Against him the imperial armies sent into this quarter made no headway. Li, after capturing several cities, proclaimed himself as emperor of the Great Shu Dynasty and made Sian, that beautiful capital of the T'angs, his headquarters. But this he thought of only as a stepping-stone to Peking. As he marched toward the capital, the forts between Sian and Peking the generals in charge gave up without the least attempt to keep. So Li appeared at the gates of the capital almost without warning. The armies were in the northeast fighting the Manchus and the garrison at Peking was abandoned by the few hundred eunuchs who were in charge of it. Li entered the city and immediately set to burning and pillaging.

The Emperor seeing the fire from his retreat on the top of Coal Hill knew the worst. He vacillated, unable to decide whether or not he could go out to meet the rebels. Finally he left the decision to three sticks of the fortune teller. He plays with his sticks; the long one falling upon the ground means he will go bravely forth to meet his adversary, the medium one he will await him in the Forbidden City. The short stick—all is lost. The Emperor of a great empire placing his destiny in the power of three sticks! The short one falls to the ground; the Emperor in futile rage curses the temple in which he stands and goes back to

THE MING OR BRIGHT DYNASTY

his splendid palace and hangs himself with his own girdle.

While this was going on in Peking, the Emperor's general, Wu San-kuei, was guarding the fort at Shanhai-Kuan, the gateway to the capital situated where the Great Wall runs down to the sea. He was holding back the Manchus when suddenly he heard the news from Peking—the Emperor was dead, the rebel Li Tzu-ch'eng held the city and worse yet had captured Wu's own father and given his best beloved concubine to another general. So throwing patriotism to the winds he allied himself with the Manchus in order to avenge himself on Li, the captor of his concubine. But again "the camel's head is within the tent," for the Manchus after aiding General Wu to push out Rebel Li, seat themselves on the Dragon Throne, thus beginning in 1644 the next dynasty, known as the Manchu or Ta Ch'ing.

CHAPTER XIV

The Chinese Again a Conquered People

To an outsider the mere thought on the part of the Manchus that they could win in a war against their big neighbor, China, would have looked foolish. Despite their growing powers, they could not match the Chinese in extent of territory, numbers of population, or wealth of resources. Furthermore, their only fighting equipment, bows and arrows, would be as weak as child's fists beating against the strength of the Great Wall, made even stronger by cannon which the Chinese had borrowed from the Portuguese and with the aid of the Jesuits had placed upon it at the fortress, Ning Yüan. What chance for victory had the Manchus barred by that Great Wall and those fearful cannon?

But we must not forget that the Manchus were blood brothers to the Kins who had conquered China in the days of the Sungs. They were still a virile people and while the Chinese had been growing effete and soft with too much luxury, the Manchus had been growing stronger and stronger in their native land of Manchuria, northeast of China beyond the Great Wall. An aggressive prince, Nurhachu, and his successors had been welding the Manchu tribes together and pushing out the borders of their territory to include Korea, China's ally, and even part of Mongolia, which the Chinese claimed as theirs. In our preceding chapter we have seen how the Chinese, in contrast with all this vigorous growth in stature and toughening in fiber of their Manchu rival and in the face of the danger which it created for them, had been made weak by dissensions and jealousies among themselves. In the end they virtually gave their empire to the enemy. After the fall of Shanhai-Kuan, that fortress on the Great Wall, the Manchus under the Prince Regent advanced upon Peking where they met with little if any resistance. The merchant guilds, worn out with strife and misrule, welcomed them. Apparently there was no group left which retained any loyalty for the Ming rulers.

The Prince Regent took possession of the throne in 1644 in the name of his nephew, the Manchu Emperor, and China was again under a foreign ruling house. In the interim, before the arrival of the Emperor, the Prince made a conciliatory gesture by ordering the remains of the late Ming Emperor and Empress to be buried in a fitting manner and by declaring three days of mourning. This act was especially designed to conciliate the scholar class. The region near the capital, on the east and northeast of Peking, promptly swore allegiance to the new dynasty.

After this conquest the men of China were made to bear a visible sign of subjection—a badge of servitude to their Manchu captors. All the men of the Empire were obliged to shave the front of the head and braid the remainder of their hair in a long queue which hung down the back. This forced custom prevailed in all China until the Revolution of 1911, after which the Republican Government ordered all Chinese to cut their queues. Long before that time the Chinese had become very proud of a well kept queue and if it were not long and imposing enough naturally, would braid a long, black silk tassel into the end of it. And when the order came to cut it they were very loath to do so; partly because the men of 1911 had never known any other custom and felt very strange without it and partly because the more ignorant of the population feared the Manchus might again come into power and wreak vengeance upon them for having abandoned the custom.

Although the Manchus forced the Chinese men to adopt the queue and the Manchu dress—a long outer garment buttoned on the shoulder and under the arm—they allowed the Chinese women to retain their own costume, short outer garment, hair brushed smoothly back and done low on the neck with no headdress except the jade and pearl ornaments which the wealthy women tucked into the knot at the back of the head. They also allowed them to continue the custom of binding their feet. The Manchu women who now were a part of every town looked quite different. On their natural-sized feet they wore silk embroidered shoes with a heel in the middle of the thick white sole. Their long robes fell to the ankles. They dressed their hair in a high elaborate headdress.

This taking of Peking by the Manchus did not mean immediately a completely conquered China. The rebel, Li Tzu-ch'eng, had fled to Shensi and his enemy, Wu San-kuei, was sent to put down his rebellion. Several Ming claimants to the throne raised their standards in various sections of the south, the most legitimate making Nanking its capital. The greatest difficulty came from a pirate chief who carried the fight onto the sea—a kind of fighting the Manchus knew little about. They offered him high official appointments if he would come to Peking and surrender, but he refused. So they continued their pursuit of him, finally accomplishing his capture and execution. After this the cities of Chekiang Province quickly surrendered.

But the proud people of the south, the fiery-tempered southerner, gave way slowly before the conqueror. The pirate chief left a son who became one of the Manchus' most formidable enemies. His mother was a Japanese; he himself is known as Koxinga. It is said that at the age

AGAIN A CONQUERED PEOPLE

of thirteen he had been successful in the imperial literary examinations. Gathering together a fleet, he harried the coast of Fukien, and advanced as far north as the mouth of the Yangtse with the hope of capturing Nanking—two hundred miles from its mouth. Unsuccessful, he was forced to retire to the island of Formosa out of which he drove the Dutch already established there and made himself king. This island of Formosa he held until his death at the age of thirty-eight. His death left the Manchus in control of Southeast China.

Resistance to the Manchus provoked rebellions in the southwest also, but by the time a quarter century had rolled around, the Chinese had settled down to the new order, willing again to endure a foreign dynasty if only it gave them peace and order.

Like the Mongols, the Manchus, once they had conquered the Chinese, took a conciliatory attitude toward them, especially in government matters. The Grand Council which stood next the Emperor in authority did not exceed five in membership, but the Manchus allowed even this council to be part Chinese. As the members of the Grand Council were entitled to a personal audience with the Emperor whenever they wished, such representation gave real recognition to the Chinese. The Chinese were also given equal representation with the Manchus in all official appointments. Through their two hundred and fifty years' reign, all Boards were organized with two presidents, one Chinese and one Manchu, and four vice-presidents, two of each race. The mandarinate was based upon the old system of examinations for official appointment. As soon as a province submitted to Manchu rule, it was rewarded by the restoring of the examination system. Such show of respect to the Chinese people and their customs lessened the hatred of the subjected Chinese toward their conquerors.

In one instance the Manchus retained their own custom—the military organization. The army was divided into sections called Banners, seventy-five hundred men in each. The name came from the fact that each section carried a different colored standard, hence the Red Banner, the Blue Banner and so on. When they entered China the Manchu army consisted of eight Banners. After Mongolia and China were conquered the army of each of these regions was organized with eight Banners. However, the Manchu Banners were not all left in Manchuria but a large part of them were used in the subjugated parts of the empire.

There were, however, two rulings which kept the Manchus and Chinese forever distinct. One was the Manchu ruling that there was to be no intermarriage. The other was the placing of Manchu Banners, or garrisons, in the provincial capitals. They and their families dwelt at the western side of the city, a little Manchu city within the big Chinese one with a wall separating them from the Chinese subjects. In the daytime conqueror and conquered passed freely back and forth, but at night throughout the next two and a half centuries the gates of the Manchu city wall were closed against the Chinese city, even as the gates of the Chinese city were closed against the countryside.

When the first Manchu Emperor died he was succeeded by his second son, K'ang Hsi, who became a great and wise ruler—a fortunate thing for the Chinese for so much of their happiness depended on the character of their ruler. Coming to the throne as he did at the age of eight, K'ang Hsi had a long reign (1662-1722). As he was contemporaneous with Louis XIV of France, it is interesting to compare the two. Mr. Steiger says:

"The greatness of K'ang Hsi does not rest upon the size of his empire and the length of his reign, but upon his sound statesmanship and good judgment. In character and ability, as well as in his success in securing the welfare of his people, K'ang Hsi was a far greater ruler than his French contemporary. Louis XIV plunged France into a series of disastrous foreign wars, which, undertaken merely to satisfy a thirst for glory, left his country exhausted and burdened with a mountainous debt. K'ang Hsi suppressed the last uprisings of the Ming supporters and, although he undertook several campaigns against the turbulent peoples of central Asia, China at the end of his reign was prosperous and well governed."[1]

K'ang Hsi proved himself in military affairs master of a constantly restive people whose threat lay in their numbers and the vast extent of their territory. But his real worth lay in his ability to give peace and prosperity to the country. K'ang Hsi thus stated his aim: "One vow have I resolutely made and that is to bestow the blessings of peace throughout this vast territory over which you have placed me." From the beginning of the dynasty he displayed a liberal policy and a solicitude for the welfare of the people. Wanderers were rounded up and settled on new lands. Agricultural experts helped start these new farmers, giving them seed and implements. Edicts were passed providing for drainage and irrigation, for the planting of mulberry trees, for the cessation of the killing of oxen, for the prohibition of seizure of lands by the rich. This was indeed a constructive program all too rare in the long history of China.

In consequence, during K'ang Hsi's reign China was a hive of workers. The industries were fostered as well as agriculture. Tax exemptions were applied to textile and dye industries. This indirectly helped agriculture as the dyes were vegetable dyes. The Ming disorders had reduced the population to about one-half so that with the peace and order of the Chings there was plenty of opportunity for the people to take up land and become prosperous. By the forty-sixth year of the dynasty, however, the increase in population forced the government to cut down its expenses to relieve the people.

K'ang Hsi at heart was a scholar. From childhood he loved the literary works of the Chinese and the philosophy of life set down by Confucius. In terse literary form he compiled sixteen moral maxims called *The Sacred Edict*. Later, his son enlarged these and they were printed in book form. In every town and village throughout the empire for two hundred years and more on the first and the fifteenth of every month they have been read and explained to the people.

> "Our Imperial Ancestor, the Benevolent Emperor, ruled the empire for sixty-one years. Those he held in the highest esteem were his ancestors; consequently he exhorted everybody to duteousness and subordination. Hence, in the sixteen sections of the Sacred Edict, duteousness and subordination are first in order.
>
> "What is duteousness? Duty to parents is a self-evident principle of nature and the root of virtuous conduct in man."[2]

> "You who are children and do not know how to do your duty by your parents, only think of their passionate affection for you and see whether you ought to be filial or not.
>
> "When you were (a babe) in arms, were you hungry? You could not feed yourself. Your parents looked upon your face, listened to your voice. Did you laugh? They were pleased: Did you cry? They were sad: Did you toddle? Step by step they followed you."[3]

> "Just think: You were born a little naked being and did not bring a stitch of silk or cotton with you. Up till now you have had food and clothing through your parents' kindness: Can you repay them? If you do not

realize the kindness of your parents, just think of the affection with which you treat your own children and then you will know. Well said the Ancients, 'Bring up children and you will then understand the kindness of your parents.' Now seeing that you are aware of the kindness of your parents, why do you not do your duty by them?"[4]

"If you are dutiful to your parents and are respectful to your elder brothers: then as subjects you will be well conducted; as soldiers you will be patriotic."[5]

It was because of K'ang Hsi that a great dictionary containing over forty-four thousand characters was compiled. For years he encouraged a group of literati to work day after day perfecting this dictionary. Under his patronage a vast encyclopedia and a concordance of literature were written.

Not only did the classical literature flourish but also that other literature written in the spoken language of the people—the novel. The earlier novels of Mongol times were worked over into a more polished form and new ones were written. One of these new ones, *The Dream of the Red Chamber,* is said to have attained the highest point of development reached by the Chinese novel. Its setting is that of a large patriarchal family of the high class. It is interesting as a love story and as a panorama of Chinese social life.

But matters of expansion, exploration and a foreign policy do not seem to have stirred the intellectual curiosity of K'ang Hsi. In the early days of his reign China's commercial contact with foreign countries had shrunk to almost nothing, just a couple of trading posts far away to the south, Macao and Canton. He knew nothing of, nor was he interested in, the great spirit of discovery and colonization abroad in the world, or the fact that Spain, Portugal,

Holland, France, England were all racing with one another in the colonization of the Americas, and in scouring the world for new trade routes. What might have been the result to China of future greatness if K'ang Hsi had been interested in a like policy, if he had encouraged the Chinese to build ships and hunt for trade, if they too had sailed past Arabia and around Africa, if they had traded with Japan, if they had sent their ships far afield to the Hawaiian Islands and across the Pacific to America?

Prof. C. Chapman, *History of California,*[6] raises the question as to why China and Japan did not colonize California during the two hundred years which it took the thirteen colonies to reach out to the Pacific Coast. During this period in which the European countries were setting the world ablaze with the fire of adventure and discovery, China was as powerful as any country in the world, perhaps better prepared for exploration than the West. Why did this spirit of withdrawal take possession of the Orient just when the Western world was reaching out? Probably no other country in the world surpassed China in extent of territory, amount of population, value of resources. Why then, indeed, did China not have within her that scientific spirit which was moving the West?

There was one contact with the West which interested K'ang Hsi, an intellectual one—the work of the Jesuits in astronomy. When he first came to the throne he freed from prison one of the Jesuits, Joannes Adam Schaal, whom the regents during the minority of the Emperor had condemned to die by the slicing process. The regents were jealous of this Jesuit because the Emperor had put confidence in his astronomical work. K'ang Hsi made Schaal head of the Astronomical Department and in that position Schaal directed the correcting of the calendar. A Dutch Jesuit, Verbeist, made several of the astronomical instruments which still stand on the city wall of Peking and wrote an astronomical work known as *The Perpetual Astronomy of K'ang Hsi*.

Then this one bond of understanding between China and the West snapped. Jesuits, Franciscans and Dominicans began quarreling among themselves over the Chinese word to use for God and also the place of ancestor worship in the Chinese Christian's life. Up to this time the Jesuits had allowed this worship to their converts. The three orders, unable to come to an agreement, appealed to the Pope who decided against the Jesuits in the matter of ancestor worship, forbidding the custom to those Chinese who accepted Catholicism. He also decided in favor of the word for God which the Franciscans and Dominicans had suggested.

K'ang Hsi was indignant that an appeal which concerned his people should be made outside his own dominions, especially as the verdict went counter to China's time-honored religious beliefs. It made him suspicious and fearful of these outside people who arrogated such power to themselves. He issued a decree forbidding missionaries to reside in China without his special consent. Many were expelled. A few were allowed to remain in Peking, but any found living secretly in the interior he ordered to be punished. Later in his reign he forbade by edict admission of missionaries into China.

Another foreign problem confronted the scholar, K'ang Hsi. Russia in her advance across Asia had erected a fort in the Amur River Valley and was sending out colonists to settle in this region. In this the Russians were resisted by the Chinese who seem to have been victorious in the fighting which followed. A treaty signed in 1689 at Nerchinsk made the boundary the watershed north of the Amur River. This treaty is notable as it was the first treaty that China signed with a European power and also was the basis of Sino-Russian relations until 1858, for a century and a half. In addition to the boundary question it provided for trade and arranged that subjects of either country who committed crimes in the country of the other should be arrested and sent to their own country for punishment. Here was the germ of extraterritoriality. This was a far-seeing policy on the part of Emperor K'ang Hsi. As a result of this treaty a large caravan trade sprang up between the two countries, and Peter the Great in the year 1719 sent an embassy to Peking headed by M. Ismaloff. His embassy was received graciously, and a permanent Russian envoy was allowed to stay at the Manchu court. The ceremony of the *kow-tow*, the stumbling-block in foreign intercourse, was performed on both sides. A high Chinese official *kow-towed* before the letter of Peter the Great and Ismaloff did the same before K'ang Hsi.

But notwithstanding the increase of trade resulting from the mutual agreement between the two great countries, Russia and China, the great K'ang Hsi felt some apprehension, some strange foreboding of trouble in foreign intercourse. Very late in his rule he wrote that he feared that sometime there would be a clash with the powers beyond the seas. Two years before his death all foreign boats were forbidden to come to any Chinese port save Canton. In this Canton situation was the germ of much future misunderstanding between the West and the East.

In response to the insistent attempts of foreign countries to trade with China, the Mings had granted the privilege of a trading post at Canton, but not a trading post wherein the foreigner and the Chinese could mingle freely. China regarded these foreign traders with both disdain and suspicion and she was at no pains to conceal it. Just enough foothold on the soil of China was given them so that they might fill the holds of their ships with the precious things of the

East—ivory, tea, silk, spices, bought with silver, Spanish dollars.

The trading post was but a collection of warehouses and offices called a factory, the name being derived from the customary term factor for trader. In the beginning, the Chinese allowed not one of the Western "barbarians" to reside there. They must live on their boats or at the Portuguese settlement of Macao. It was at best a precarious trade existence for the Chinese officials demanded large export and import duties, a major portion of which went as "squeeze" to the officials. The Chinese did everything they could to hinder imports which they believed would take silver from China and thus impoverish their country. China was not alone in adhering to this doctrine. It was the old Mercantile Theory of the European countries.

In 1720, toward the close of K'ang Hsi's reign, the famous *Co-hong* system, which was to last over a hundred years, came into existence. The *Co-hong* was a league or combination of the thirteen leading Chinese merchants of Canton to whom the Emperor gave a monopoly of all the foreign trade. It was to stand between the Chinese Government and the foreign merchants, the "go-between." On the one hand, it was responsible for any misdeed committed by the foreigners and, on the other, for any indebtedness of the Chinese to the foreigners. With the *Co-hong* also lay the task of collecting duties. The amount of the duties charged on any cargo was whatever the *Co-hong* thought wise to extort. It was always a large tax for the government at Peking must get no insignificant sum, the local official (the Viceroy of the two southern provinces) must get his squeeze, the *Co-hong* merchants must have a profitable return on their business, but withal, the amount must be nicely gauged so that it would not be bigger than the foreign merchants would or could pay. It was too profitable a business to throttle by too greedy taxation, and none knew it better than the *Co-hong*.

The *Co-hong* merchants were often as badly off as the foreigners in this matter of trade. They had to pay large sums to the local officials before they could join the *Co-hong* and once a member always a member. No matter how unfortunate anyone had been in a business deal, he was not allowed to resign from the *Co-hong*. However, in the end most of them became enormously wealthy. Although China scorned trade, her men are universally good business men.

Later the traders were allowed to live at the factory, but they could not set foot beyond the narrow strip of land outside the city walls where the warehouses were located. No pleasure boats were allowed them on the Pearl River, which the warehouses faced, nor were any of their women privileged to dwell in the factory. In such fashion did K'ang Hsi seek to avert the danger that he saw lurking in international trade.

Some sixteen years after the death of K'ang Hsi China entered into one of her most illustrious periods under the rule of K'ang Hsi's grandson, Ch'ien Lung (1736-1799). T'ang, Ming, Ch'ien Lung are still magic words in China. A ballad runs: "O, the cash of Ch'ien Lung, may he live millions of years."

Ch'ien Lung was a benevolent ruler and strong enough to keep his vast empire in order. His reign was for China a time of prosperity and peace, of development of literature and art, of expansion of its territory. He showed a thirst for conquest and pushed out his borders in every direction, regaining the lost territories—Northeast Korea, Manchuria and Mongolia. He reconquered Tibet and Chinese Turkestan, the scene of the ancient trade routes of the days of Han. He forced tribute from Annam and Burmah even as the Mongols had forced tribute from them.

He devoted much time to the perfection of literature and art and the magnificence of the ceremonials of the court. The Emperor was trained a scholar and interested himself both as an author and as a collector. He worked diligently for the perfection of the Manchu language and translated many works from Chinese into Manchu. On tablets, memorials, names over doorways and buildings are seen the Manchu as well as the Chinese characters. He himself wrote poetry in both Chinese and Manchu, it being said he wrote over thirty thousand poems. The best known are *The Eulogy on Mukden,* the ancient capital of the Manchus, and another entitled *Tea.* Aside from his own writings, Ch'ien Lung was interested in collecting and compiling all the written works of the country from the time of antiquity to his own day. These were reprinted at the expense of the government and libraries of these reprints were presented to the cities of Hangchow, Yangchow and Chinkiang which were the chief literary centers of the day.

Probably the patronage of literature by these two illustrious Emperors, K'ang Hsi and Ch'ien Lung, grandfather and grandson, is one of the factors responsible for the so-called literary renaissance of the seventeenth and eighteenth centuries. The scholars, in a revolt against the Sung interpretations of the classics which had stamped philosophy since the eleventh and twelfth centuries, went back to the Han texts and examined critically all the canonical books.

Hu Shih says, "By the middle of the seventeenth century Chinese scholarship had developed a genuinely scientific method of study and investigation. With the aid of this methodology, the scholarship of the last three hundred years became quite scientific and a number of historical sciences, notably philology, higher criticism and archaeology, reached a high stage of development. Yet with all this achievement in the humanistic studies China remains in the backward state where we find her today."⁷

In Europe during the fifteenth century the Revival of Learning "did not affect agriculture, industry, commerce, law, medicine, government, religion, invention and exploration. It did not directly touch the life of ordinary men and women but only the literary and scholarly few."⁸ The revival of learning in China during the seventeenth and eighteenth centuries seems to have followed the same lines. It made progress in some subjects such as archaeology but did not improve the standard of life in China by inventions or scientific discoveries. It did not filter down to the people. Education was still the privilege of the few. And apparently it did not create a spirit of critical-mindedness which challenged tradition. That was left to a later day.

The population which had begun to increase in K'ang Hsi's reign continued to increase, due at least in part to the Chinese belief that sons were necessary to worship the ancestors: sixty million in 1736, one hundred million in 1753, and three hundred million in 1792. In half a century the people had increased fivefold. In 1740 an edict was promulgated exhorting the people to use odd pieces of land— and the mountain tops. Then they terraced the sides of the mountains, using every possible bit of land. The government reclaimed wastelands and helped the farmers to intensive agriculture. In places two crops of rice were raised on the farms. The most successful farmers were rewarded with honors and decorations. By such means the Emperor sought to relieve the distress of the people.

In the conduct of foreign affairs Ch'ien Lung was no more progressive than his predecessors. Like his grandfather, he believed that China, the Middle Kingdom, was the center of the universe, the one great powerful country of the world and that all other nations were inferior and only

AGAIN A CONQUERED PEOPLE 197

might have intercourse with China if they played the rôle of tributary nations and *kowtowed* to himself, the great ruler of the universe. Throughout his reign the *Co-hong* system with its lack of official recognition of other countries continued to be the only means by which the growing trade could be carried on.

And now the United States entered the race for the China trade. About 1784 a new flag appeared floating from the mast of a ship sailing into Canton, the flag of the American republic. The profits of the first boat, *The Empress of China,* were so great that all the Eastern cities, Salem, Nantucket, Boston, New York and Philadelphia, entered the trade. The New England women waited for the return of the boats and the coveted dinner and tea sets, ivory fans, satins and crêpes they brought.

From the time of Columbus when Europe sought spices in the East it had been very difficult to find foreign articles for Chinese consumption. The Americans were singularly successful in this matter. The first boats, for lack of cargo, took out large quantities of Spanish "pillar" (dollars which were for many years the only foreign coin accepted by the Chinese). Even today the silver dollar in China is called "mex" or Mexican dollar. The root ginseng they shipped in large quantities hearing that the Chinese supply was running low and that it was very much desired because of its medicinal qualities. Luckily for the American traders, some pioneers found it growing in the Hudson Valley and along the Ohio River in Kentucky. The Chinese desire for fur was another discovery made quite by chance by the Americans. Some Chinese came on board one of the sailing ships when it was at anchor at Canton and saw some worn skins on the bunks, and eagerly bought them. So the next ships carried furs from the western coast of North America. And the third lucky find on the part of America was sandalwood in the Hawaiian Islands which the Chinese wanted for the offerings in the temples. By the early part of the eighteenth century the American trade had reached such proportions that it stood second only to that of the English.

England had been taking to China cotton cloth and in 1773 began the taking on of cargoes of opium at Calcutta and selling it in China. The Chinese had since the days of the T'angs used opium, but by the end of Ch'ien Lung's reign it had become a universal habit and the trade in opium had grown to enormous proportions.

As trade with China increased the English became anxious to do away with the inconveniences of the *Co-hong* system. Therefore, in 1792, four years before Ch'ien Lung abdicated in favor of his son, the British Government sent Lord Macartney to visit Peking to ask for the recognition of a British ambassador who would care for British interests in China. The Emperor, Ch'ien Lung, received him with ceremony and apparent respect, but on the flag of his vessel was printed in Chinese characters "a tribute bearer from the country of England." The Chinese officials who were conducting him demanded that he *kow-tow* before the Emperor, but Macartney refused unless a Chinese official of equal rank with himself would *kow-tow* before the picture of George III. The ceremony was waived and Macartney succeeded in getting two interviews with Ch'ien Lung—not in the capital, Peking, but at the less important palace, Jehol. Although Ch'ien Lung treated Macartney with much courtesy, Macartney battered in vain against the wall of exclusion Ch'ien Lung erected. The "Imperial Mandate" to King George issued by His Majesty (Ch'ien Lung) a few days after his reception of the British Embassy at Jehol reads thus:

"You, O King, live beyond the confines of many seas, nevertheless, impelled by your humble desire to partake of the benefits of our civilization, you have dispatched a mission respectfully bearing your memorial. . . . I have perused your memorial: the earnest terms in which it is couched reveal a respectful humility on your part, which is highly praiseworthy. In consideration of the fact that your ambassador and his deputy have come a long way with your memorial and tribute, I have shown them high favor and have allowed them to be introduced into my presence. To manifest my indulgence I have entertained them at a banquet and made them numerous gifts. . . .

"As to your entreaty to send one of your nationals to be accredited to my Celestial Court and to be in control of your country's trade with China, this request is contrary to all usage of my dynasty and cannot possibly be entertained. It is true that Europeans, in the service of the dynasty, have been permitted to live in Peking, but they are compelled to adopt Chinese dress, they are strictly confined to their own precincts and are never permitted to return home. You are presumably familiar with our dynastic regulations. Your proposed Envoy to my Court could not be placed in a position similar to that of European officials in Peking who are forbidden to leave China, nor could he on the other hand, be allowed liberty of movement and the privilege of corresponding with his own country; so that you would gain nothing by his residence in our midst. . . .

"Swaying the wide world, I have but one aim in view, namely, to maintain a perfect governance and to fulfill the duties of the State; strange and costly objects do not interest me. If I have commanded that the tribute offerings sent by you, O King, are to be accepted, this was solely in consideration for the spirit which prompted you to dispatch them from afar. Our dynasty's majestic virtue has penetrated into every country under Heaven, and Kings of all nations have offered their costly tribute by land and sea. As your Ambassador can see for himself, we possess all things.

I set no value on things strange or ingenious, and have no use for your country's manufactures. This, then, is my answer to your request to appoint a representative at my Court, a request contrary to our dynastic usage, which would only result in inconvenience to yourself."[9]

With this attitude on the part of the Emperor we are not surprised to know that foreign trade went on after the same old manner—at Canton alone and only as long as the traders were obedient to the local officials and the merchants of the *Co-hong*.

The Chinese consider Ch'ien Lung's reign one of the greatest in Chinese history and great praise must go to this Emperor, Ch'ien Lung for the prosperity the people enjoyed. He never spared himself in their behalf. He seems not to have been weakened by the luxuries of the court. He never let the luxury of life keep him, in the beautiful yellow-roofed palace, from spending long hours at work or from traveling to distant parts of the empire to study his people, hard though the travel was. He made every effort to avert the disasters caused by the floods of the Yellow River, was generous in remitting taxes in times of disaster (an old Chinese custom), punished severely unfaithful officials. Often at the age of eighty, he arose in the middle of the night to hold audiences in matters of state. The mistake of his reign was his short-sighted policy in foreign matters, his lack of interest in what was going on in the rest of the world.

CHAPTER XV

Foreign Trade Advances

Ssu-ma Ch'ien's prophecy was again to be fulfilled—after the flow, the ebb. The evils which had undermined the T'angs and the Mings had just as surely been at work undermining the Manchus. No ruling house, whether native or foreign, seemed able long to withstand the degenerating influence characteristic of China's court life. Again and again when a new dynasty came into power was the palace purged of its indulgences, hundreds of concubines sent home, the eunuchs shorn of their power, only to have these evils creep back. For a long time, behind the vermilion walls of the Forbidden City luxury, indulgence and intrigue had been at work among the Manchus.

For the next forty years after Ch'ien Lung we read of emperor after emperor, weak or dissolute, unable to cope with the problems which confronted the empire. Ch'ien Lung, when an old man, abdicated in favor of his son and thought he had bequeathed to him a powerful empire. He felt that his campaigns had made the frontiers safe and he prided himself that he had won the affection and respect of the Literati, the powerful official class of the Chinese. But the real fact was that the Manchu Dynasty had passed its crest of strength and had started to decline. Under the surface were seething all kinds of restlessness and disorders.

The population of the country had increased enormously. By 1850 it had, according to the best estimates, reached three hundred and sixty-two million. Great wisdom was needed in the administration of the finances, the development of agriculture, constructive policies to lessen the evils of flood and drought. Yet one emperor at least dismissed such problems with the comment that "famine, crime, and robbery seem a providential check to overpopulation." Quite different this from the beneficent attitude of K'ang Hsi and Ch'ien Lung.

The populace again grew discontented. Secret societies, an ancient institution in China, became anti-dynastic. At one time, in an effort to suppress the societies, thousands upon thousands of people were executed. Such cruelty only increased the discontent which had been the cause of the secret societies' anti-dynastic trend. Many from the highest ranks of society joined the societies. They became so bold that one band found the way in broad daylight into the very palace and all but succeeded in killing the Emperor.

Another indication of chaos in the country was the power of the pirates. China had never quite been able to exterminate them and now on the Pearl River and along the southern coasts pirates boldly preyed upon the ships and the near-by countryside. They would dart out from their strongholds and attack native junks, tribute-bearing ships from other countries and the coastal provinces, and occasionally the trading boats of the West. No shipping was safe from their attack and they became so feared that at one time the governor at Canton did not consider himself safe in that city and sought refuge in the Portuguese settlement at Macao, where he could be defended by the foreign firearms and ships.

During all this chaotic time the foreign trade continued to grow. The representatives of the Western nations, for the sake of the trade it brought them, still accepted the position of semi-prisoner, although their self-respect was undermined by the knowledge that the Chinese considered them inferior; their self-control was strained to the breaking point by the strict regulations that controlled so narrowly the life of the traders. Often in desperation at the semi-imprisonment which lasted from October (when the ships arrived) until the following March (when the winds were favorable for their departure), the sailors defied the regulations and went into the city. Many were the annoying affairs between Chinese and foreigners in Canton, delicate affairs which the *Co-hong* must settle satisfactorily lest the Emperor get wind of the trouble and suppress the trade. It speaks well for the traders and the merchants of the *Co-hong* that there were comparatively few clashes. In fact, as time went on, very real friendships grew up between various sea captains and *Co-hong* merchants.

Ever the central figures in all this complicated life was Houqua—the senior merchant of the *Co-hong*. In *Gold of Ophir* he is described thus:

> "His wealth and power grew day by day, and as the weight of his business increased, his face became more cadaverous, and his eyes more and more melancholy, albeit more wise, his manner more serious and resigned. But his reputation never altered. We see him moving in and out of every affair at Canton between Chinese officials and foreigners, shrewd, impersonal, serene."[1]

For him there seems to have been a real affection on the part of many. An American firm named one of its clipper ships after him and many are the tales of kindness told about him. Often Houqua stood between some hapless Britisher or American, who had got into trouble, and the local officials.

Houqua, although made immensely wealthy, often wished to resign, for his duties were many and arduous, standing as he did as a kind of buffer between his friends, the merchants, and the local officials, even the Emperor when difficulties took on serious proportions. If the merchants became vocal enough to make their very obnoxious persons known to the "Son of Heaven," the Emperor in a moment of anger might demand the head of luckless Houqua. Notwithstanding this, Houqua ran many a risk to accommodate his friends, the white man, winking at their visits into the city and little trips down the Pearl River, even at two or three adventurous wives who came to share their husbands' exile and donned men's clothes in order to see Canton.

He even went so far as to entertain some of his merchant friends at his own home. The homes of the *Co-hong* merchants were large and beautiful, rivaling in splendor the imperial palace. "Great gardens elaborately and curiously designed, with grottoes and lakes spanned by carved stone bridges and pathways that were inlaid with stones representing birds, fish, and flowers, afforded never-waning pleasure to the invited foreign guests. The seat of Houqua was on a scale of great magnificence: It is a village or rather palace divided into suits or apartments which are highly and tastefully decorated."[2]

Great sights indeed for the Puritan straight from the rigorous simplicity of New England! In 1825 the *Co-hong* and the factories came to the heyday of their glory. H. F. MacNair in his *Modern Chinese History; Selected Readings,* gives a most interesting map of the narrow space along the Pearl River—the scene of all the activities of the trade. Half the nations of the globe had their factories and their representatives there.

In a few sentences he gives a picture of the homes of the English merchants:

"The 'Factory' entertained with unbounded hospitality and in a princely style. Their dining room was of vast dimensions, opening on the terrace overlooking the river. On the left was a library amply stocked . . . on the right a billiard room. At one extremity of the room was a life size portrait of George IV in royal robes, with crown and sceptre, the same that had been taken by the embassy of Lord Amherst to Pekin, offered to and refused by the Emperor Keen-Ling (Ch'ien Lung) and brought to Canton overland. Opposite to it hung a smaller full-length portrait of Lord Amherst."[3]

Mr. MacNair has salvaged too from some accounts of an obscure young American of those days a vivid picture of the Chinese warehouses situated in that same narrow strip of land:

"Those of importance cover an immense area, and being divided into sections with open spaces intervening, they are light and well aired, being also wonderfully clean and well ordered. The great gate of entrance is closed at night, and they are then left in the charge of one or more keepers whose quarters are close to it. Under exceptional circumstances, however, such as a press of business, merchants remain in them night and day. . . . It was in the establishments of the *Hong* merchants where teas were weighed, marked and rattaned for shipment to foreign vessels at Whampoa, where the boats lay at anchor, and silk and silk piece goods examined and weighed before being shipped off. On the other hand, they received all import cargo from Whangpoa which, if woolens or cottons, were stored on joists or beams of wood raised a foot or more from the ground, and resting immediately on paddy husk, to preserve them from white ants, which abound and are very voracious, but to which 'paddy chaff' is obnoxious.

"The *Hongs* of the 'security merchants' (that is, members of the *Co-hong*) were on the city side of the Pearl River, and bordering it for the convenience of landing and shipping off cargo. Several, however, had vast warehouses or go-downs across the river on Ho-Nan, in which were stored immense quantities of raw cotton from India, woolen and cotton goods and other merchandise from England and the United States, as well as from the Straits of Malacca, say rice, pepper and betel nut, rattans, tine, etc. These articles arrived in the southwest monsoon in quick succession at Whangpoa, and were immediately landed in presence of an officer from the *Hoppo's* office, who attended with a large staff of pursers to examine and take note of the duties to be collected."[4]

Neither the American nor the Englishman in these descriptions say anything of the vast shipments of opium, which had now become contraband cargo. In 1800 the Chinese decided that opium was harmful to their people and prohibited the importation of foreign opium and the cultivation of the poppy in China. The English East India Company forbade it to be a part of the cargo declared on the manifests of their ships. But neither the royal decree on the part of the Emperor, nor the banning of opium as a legitimate cargo by the East India Company, ended the trade. Chinese and foreigners alike engaged in smuggling. Li Ung Bing, a Chinese historian, says:

"In 1800, the Imperial Government made renewed efforts to suppress the use of opium. Stringent decrees were issued in rapid succession. China, indeed, can boast of many good laws, but not always of good men to enforce them. So it was in this case. As long as the demand for opium existed, the supply came; and if it could not be brought into the country openly it was done clandestinely. By means of systematic bribery, opium smuggling, therefore, went on at Canton without hindrance. Large receiving ships were stationed at Lingting and vicinity, while numerous smaller craft under the English and other foreign flags plied back and forth on the Canton River in their attempts to land opium. To the officials and their subordinates, to the foreign capitalists, to the local bad characters and to the pirates along the coast, opium smuggling meant a short-cut to wealth. It is estimated that three thousand, two hundred and ten chests of opium valued at $3,657,000 (Spanish) were consumed in China in 1816, and eighteen thousand, seven hundred and sixty chests valued at $12,900,031 (Spanish) in 1830."[5]

Professor MacNair found this old account written by one of the smugglers of that day:

"We anchored on the inside of the island of Namoa on the third day close by two English brigs, the 'Omega' and 'Governor Findlay.' Inshore of us were riding at anchor two men-of-war junks, with much bunting displayed; one bore the flag of a *'Foo Tseang'* or commodore. Knowing the 'formalities' to be gone through with the mandarins, we expected a visit from one, and until it was made no Chinese boat would come alongside, nor would a junk, not even a gunboat. We had no sooner furled sails and made everything ship-shape when his excellency approached in his 'gig,' a sort of scow as broad as she was long. Besides the oarsmen, there were official and personal attendants, in grass cloth with conical rattan hats and flowing red silk cord surrounding them to the brim. He himself sat majestically in an arm-chair smoking quietly. A large embroidered silk umbrella was held over his head, while servants with fans protected him from the attacks of flies and mosquitoes. He was received at the gangway by Captain Forster. His manner and bearing were easy and dignified. When cheroots and a glass of wine had been offered, the 'Commodore' enquired the cause of our anchoring at Namoa. The Shroff gave him to understand that the vessel, being on her way from Singapore to Canton, had been compelled, through contrary winds and currents, to run for Namoa to replenish her wood and water. Having listened attentively, the great man said that any supplies might be obtained, but when they were on board, not a moment must be lost in sailing for Whampoa, as the Great Emperor did not permit vessels from afar to visit any other port. He then gravely pulled from his boot a long red document and handed it to his secretary that we might be informed of its purport.

"It was as follows:

"'An Imperial Edict. As the port of Canton is the only one at which outside barbarians are allowed to trade, on no account can they be permitted to wander about to other places in the 'Middle Kingdom.' The 'Son of Heaven,' however, whose compassion is as boundless as the ocean, cannot deny to those who are in distress from want of food, through adverse seas and currents, the necessary means of continuing their voyage. When supplied they must not longer loiter, but depart at once.

"'Respect this.

"'*Taou-kwang* 17th Year,

"'6th Moon, 4th Sun.'

"This 'Imperial Edict' having been replaced in its envelope and slipped inside of his boot (for service on the chance of another foreign vessel in distress), His Excellency arose from his seat, which was a signal for all his attendants to return to the boat except his secretary. The two were then invited to the cabin to refresh, which being done we proceeded to business. The Mandarin opened by the direct questions, 'How many chests have you on board? Are they all for Namoa? Do you go further up the coast?', intimating at the same time that there the officers were uncommonly strict and were obliged to carry out the will of the 'Emperor of the Universe' etc.; but our answers were equally as clear and prompt that the vessel was not going north of Namoa, that her cargo consisted of about two hundred chests. Then came the question of '*Cumsha*' and that was settled on the good old Chinese principle of 'all same custom.' Everything being thus comfortably arranged, wine drunk, and the cheroots smoked, his Excellency said, '*Kaou-tsze*' (I announce my departure). We escorted him to the side, over which he clambered with the aid of his secretary; we saw him safely deposited under his brilliant silken canopy, and in a short time rejoin his junk.

"Chinese buyers came on board freely the moment they saw the 'official' visit had been made. A day or two after, several merchant junks stood out from the mainland for the anchorage. As they approached we distinguished a private signal at their mastheads, a copy of which had been furnished to us before leaving Capshuymun. We hoisted ours, the junks anchored close to us, and in a surprisingly short time received from the 'Rose' in their own boats the opium which had been sold at Canton and there paid for, deliverable at this anchorage. It was a good illustration of the entire confidence existing between the foreign seller in his Factory at Canton and the Chinese buyers and of a transaction for a breach of any of the conditions of which there existed no legal redress on one side or the other. This parcel, whose value was $150,000 had been already packed in bags, marked and numbered at Capshuymun. The Chinamen who held the order of the Canton house for its delivery, on coming on board unfolded it from a cotton handkerchief, smoked a pipe or two and drank a cup of tea with the Shroff while it was going over the side, then took leave of us with the usual 'Good wind and good water,' or 'May your voyage be prosperous.' The junks had anchored, mainsail to the mast, and as the last bag was received on board the anchors were at the bow and they standing to the northward."[6]

The failure of the Chinese Government and the East India Company to regulate the opium trade was the cause of growing irritation between the two countries. The English became convinced that nothing permanent would be accomplished until the Chinese became willing to recognize the legal equality of nations. An excellent opportunity presented itself for the English to renew their efforts, when in 1834 the charter of the English East India Company expired. England wanted to abolish this monopoly and put the trade directly under a superintendent appointed by the British Government who would communicate directly with the Chinese Government at Peking.

The English first sent Lord Napier to take up this matter of equality. He proceeded to Canton attempting to get into direct touch with the Viceroy. As a commissioner of the British Government he refused to do business through the *Hong* merchants, as the traders had always done. But the Viceroy was unwilling to grant any privilege other than those enjoyed by the traders. Lord Napier insisted on equality; the Viceroy refused and suspended the English trade.

This question of the equality between foreign nations was the stumbling block. Before 1834 China had governed the foreign trade as she saw fit, and the traders had accepted the restrictions and the inferior position as long as they were making money. But now the governments behind these traders, England and later all other nations, made the claim for equality of treatment between nations. And this China refused to give. Lord Napier died of a fever, without accomplishing anything, and later representatives were no more successful.

At this juncture the opium question loomed again upon the horizon. The feeling against the trade became more acute because it was tied up with a financial problem. For many years great quantities of silver had been going out of the country, for, as contraband cargo, opium was not exchanged for other cargo, but paid for in silver, either Spanish or Mexican dollars. In consequence, China was faced with a specie famine. There was also the moral question—the undermining of the health and character of the young men who indulged in the habit. One account tells us that the hatred of opium and detestation of the foreigner became nearly synonymous, because the opium that enervated the Chinese enriched the foreigner.

The court had held various opinions regarding the suppression of the trade. In fact the royal family was divided and nothing definite was done toward suppressing the vice until the Emperor's beloved son died from the effects of opium. Then the Emperor took a stand on the question. He sent Lin Tse-hsi early in 1839 to Canton as Imperial Commissioner to carry out his wishes; and now in the city of Canton, where two years before the Viceroy of Canton had been building a flotilla to carry the merchants' drug from the receiving ship to his provincial capital, Commissioner Lin, a few days after his arrival, demanded that the foreigners should give up all the opium stored on the boats in the harbor. At first they refused, whereupon Lin closed the gates of the factories so no one might leave. The innocent as well as the guilty were thus imprisoned, as the Chinese laws made the family or a group responsible. So Lin held all the foreign traders prisoners until the opium should be delivered. He also withdrew the Chinese servants and cut off all supplies of fresh food. For forty-eight days, three hundred men were thus imprisoned, until at the end of that time, twenty thousand, two hundred and ninety-one chests of opium, valued at nine million dollars had been turned over to the Commissioner. He had it taken out and mixed with salt water and thrown into the sea. He furthermore demanded that the traders sign for themselves and their respective governments that there should be no more opium imported. The foreign merchants explained that they had no authority to sign for their governments. So Lin accepted their individual signatures and let them embark on their boats.

By the summer of 1839 relations between the Chinese and English were so strained that war seemed inevitable, though there was no formal declaration on either side. The grievance of China was the opium smuggling and that of the British the failure to secure recognition of the principle of the equality of nations.

Actual war began in November, 1839, when the English opened fire on the fleet of Admiral Kwan. The British with their superior firearms and ships easily took Canton, Amoy, Ningpo, Chapel and Shanghai on the coast, and Chinkiang up the Yangtse River. The Chinese became alarmed and in 1842 signed the Treaty of Nanking with Great Britain.

This treaty virtually abolished the *Co-hong* system by permitting foreign representatives to communicate directly with Chinese officials. It provided for a regular and published tariff instead of the previous uncertain bargaining and extortion. Five ports (Canton, Amoy, Foochow, Ningpo, Shanghai) were designated as the places where foreign merchants might in a restricted area build residences and warehouses. These settlements were the first of the so-called "treaty ports." The island of Hongkong was ceded to England and indemnity was laid upon China sufficient to pay England's expenditures in the war and for the opium destroyed by Commissioner Lin.

The next year another treaty was signed between China and England stating that other nations trading with China should have the same privileges as those granted to England and that if additional privileges should be granted other nations, the English should also have those same privileges. This is known as the "most favored nation" clause.

As America stood second in the Chinese trade, the American Government after the signing of the Nanking Treaty sent Mr. Caleb Cushing as Commissioner and Envoy Extraordinary and Minister Plenipotentiary to negotiate a treaty with China. The treaty was especially interesting as extraterritoriality was one of the things agreed upon between China and the United States. This meant that Americans living in the treaty ports were to be tried for criminal offenses in consular courts established by their own country, while a Chinese in a criminal offense against a foreigner was to be tried in a Chinese court. This was not a new idea for China. In the Nerchinsk Treaty of 1689 Russia and China had agreed to return each other's nationals for trial. The laws of the Chinese and Manchus were so different that they had always found it expedient to live each under his own law. The Chinese at the time were quite willing to make a like arrangement with America, for its laws, too, were so different from theirs. The West believed in individual responsibility rather than group responsibility. Trial by jury was an equally baffling idea to the Chinese; on the other hand, the Chinese punishment, strangulation, offended the white man. Extraterritoriality whereby nations controlled their own nationals seemed an advantageous arrangement. By the "most favored nation" clause all the Treaty Powers obtained the same privileges. In the French Treaty, the same year, toleration was granted to Christianity.

By these treaties, the Western Powers had partially gained what they had so long been striving for. Trade was extended beyond Canton and there were to be regular customs charges. In the five treaty ports Chinese and foreign representatives might meet for business purposes, a step toward equality of nations.

CHAPTER XVI

THE TAI PING REBELLION

DURING the period that China was engaged with her foreign trade problem her internal affairs were going from bad to worse. The Manchu Dynasty was growing more effete; the officials more corrupt. The increasing population, floods, famines, the indemnity to be paid the English were more than the government could manage. After 1850 the Emperor financed the country by voluntary contributions from the rich, who in payment received official honors. As riches thus became a basis of choice, the illiterate often bought official position—and this in a nation where since time immemorial official appointment had been based on the civil service examinations. Much corruption was the result of this system of official tenure. Those who bought offices recouped themselves by "squeezing." Taxes of necessity were heavy, justice was corrupted, a favorable decision was sold to the highest bidder. More and more often the populace broke out in sporadic rebellions which finally culminated in the 'fifties in the Great Tai Ping Rebellion.

One phase of this rebellion which is of particular interest to Westerners concerns the question of Christian missions which became entangled in the upheaval.

The Roman Catholics had been alone in the missionary field until the nineteenth century when the Protestant English and American missionary societies became interested in taking Christianity to China. The first Protestant missionary was an Englishman—Robert Morrison, who arrived in

Canton in 1807. The Chinese would allow no one to go anywhere except Canton, so the Mission Societies decided that the work must be one largely of preparation. Morrison's time was spent first on the study of Chinese and then in literary production; the preparation of a dictionary, translation of the Bible, and the writing of short pamphlets or "tracts." As life for the foreigner was so precarious in Canton, most of this printing was done in the Chinese colonies of the Malay Peninsula.

After the 'forties and the treaties granting something of toleration to Christianity there followed a rapid expansion in the Protestant missionary campaign in China. In addition to the evangelical activities, medical and educational features were added. A hospital at Canton and a school at Hongkong were among the first ventures. Protestant activities grew rapidly and resulted in many converts to the new religion. The tracts spreading new ideas were eagerly read by the restive young men of the educated class. Christian doctrines became entangled with revolutionary tendencies of the time, which unfortunately created a confusion of religious and revolutionary ideas in the minds of some of the Tai Ping leaders.

Hung Hsiu-ch'uan, the leader of the movement, was born near Canton. He was the son of a farmer but desirous of obtaining the degree at the literary official examinations. Three times he failed and this seems to have preyed upon his mind. In a dream he saw the Almighty enter his room, place a sword in his hand and command him to begin a crusade for extermination of devils. He later studied some Christian tracts and became convinced that in them he found the meaning of his dream. He organized his family and neighbors into the Shang Ti Hwei, a Society for the Worship of the Almighty.

The movement gained momentum and spread from

province to province. Idols were destroyed and temples razed to the ground. Then the leaders demanded that the people pay tribute of grain or cash to the society. The Imperial Government, fearing the growing strength of the movement, sent two commissioners to put it down. This unwise attempt to suppress a purely religious organization turned it into a dangerous anti-dynastic movement which took up the cry "Exterminate the Manchus." Evidently, it was not Hung himself but two other men who joined the movement who gave the organization its political bent. They saw in the fanatic Hung and his religious propaganda the material for the making of a powerful rebellion. Hung's talk of a heavenly kingdom made an excellent slogan for the common people who would not be moved by a more abstract political aspiration. A man named Feng, Hung's first convert, and later a man from the province of Hunan, Chu Kui-tao really organized the society into a military power, but they always kept Hung as its nominal head, making him serve as cat's-paw for the movement. His visions supplied the superstitious elements which brought the masses under their standard. Religious enthusiast, Hung was called the Heavenly King, but the other two, called the Eastern and Western Kings, less visionary men, exerted the temporal power. In 1850 the rebels seized several towns and set up a kingdom styled the *Tai Ping Tien Kuoh* (the Peaceful Heavenly Kingdom). In Chinese annals the movement is known as the Long-haired Rebellion because the members of the society no longer shaved the front of their heads as prescribed by the Manchus.

The rebellious army headed by the Heavenly King came up from the south, the Yangtse their objective, moving over practically the same route which the revolutionist army of 1927 took. When they started out, the Tai Pings had but one division but as they advanced northward toward Hunan many joined them, attracted either by religious zeal or, more often, purely by the love of murder and plunder, for the Tai Pings devastated the cities and towns they captured, and the one division grew into many divisions. Like crusaders they marched forward, women as well as men swelling the ranks, wearing red cloth turbans which tied up their long hair.

It was in Hunan that the astute Chu Kui-tao joined them. As it was he who is recognized as the great executive, possibly he it was who gave the Tai Pings their complete military system of squadrons, companies, battalions, divisions. Against the onslaught of this organized rabble the Manchu Dynasty was powerless. The garrisons of Manchus, stationed in each city, had through the centuries lost their virility; of late years there had been little for them to do and they had grown lax in matters military. As they were supplied with rice, work was not necessary so they had become weak and lazy. Now when put to the test these garrisons proved themselves valueless. They gave way ingloriously before the Tai Pings, thousands strong, marching forward, the ends of their red turbans streaming to the wind, a mighty band devastating the countryside and the cities, destroying the temples and the works of art, the bronzes and the paintings, and the books.

A barren waste lay behind this advancing horde. Even today in the Yangtse Valley there can still be found deserted villages—one or two families living among the ruins the Tai Pings made seventy odd years ago. In cities like Hangchow, once full of beautiful buildings with colored tiled roofs there are now only the gray tiled roofs; the beautiful palaces which Marco Polo tells about are gone. The spade of the workman tells the melancholy tale. Each spade of earth thrown up holds more broken tile than dirt.

The movement was a great perversion of the Christian doctrine, for these marauders called their heavenly king the younger brother of Christ; they called themselves "thy little children," meaning the children of the Heavenly Father who came to earth to speak to them. They said they based their punishments on the old Mosaic law. To such a cruel practice as soaking the clothes of their victims in oil and then burning them they gave the name, Heavenly Lamp.

Their Christian catchwords and their destruction of idols confused the missionaries at first, causing them to believe that there was a great conversion among the Chinese. They wrote their churches in America rejoicing over the movement, only to find later how great was their mistake and to mourn over the cruelties and destruction committed in the name of Christianity.

But to go back a little. By the time the Tai Pings had reached Hunan the Manchus in Peking were thoroughly alarmed. Manchu garrison after garrison had fallen before the red turbaned throng. Changsha, the capital city of the province, was threatened. Whom had the Manchus to depend upon? Sadly enough, no one of their own blood. The Emperor now found how wise it had been on the part of the founders of the Manchu Empire to associate the best Chinese with them in the government of the country. Tseng Kuo-fan, a scholastic official, a man of great integrity and great ability as a statesman, had long been a personal friend of the Emperor. Just now he was at home in his native province of Hunan, the province so sorely threatened, observing the three years' period of mourning for his mother—which the superior man, according to the teachings of Confucius, must observe at whatever cost.

In his hour of need the Emperor called upon Tseng Kuo-fan to come to the aid of his country and Tseng Kuo-fan, scholar, statesman, follower of Confucius, responded to the urgent appeal of his sovereign, obeying the high duty which Confucius also laid down that, if the State needs the superior

THE TAI PING REBELLION

man, he sacrifices his mourning and gives his services gratuitously to the State.

Although untrained in military matters Tseng Kuo-fan set to work to organize a volunteer army in Hunan which later came to be know as the Hunan Braves. With admirable foresight he also had built a fleet of wooden junks.

While he was thus engaged the Tai Pings swept on down the Yangtse, gaining in numbers. With their ranks swelled to six hundred thousand men and five hundred thousand women, they came under the shadow of the high walls of Nanking. In ten days they succeeded in making a breach in the wall, until then thought to be impregnable, and took the city by storm. Not one brick of the houses of the Manchu garrison was left standing upon another; the city became a shambles; every Manchu man, woman and child was killed. The bodies thrown into the Yangtse were so many in number that tradition has it one could walk across the river. For many miles below the city the river ran red with blood. So terrible was the destruction that even today there are great unoccupied spaces within Nanking's city wall and the people still carry the dread of being trapped within the city; horrible in their minds is the scene of the Tai Ping slaughter which their fathers and mothers have described to them.

Here in Nanking the Tai Pings set up their capital. The religious enthusiast Hung, the Heavenly King, gave himself over to a life of luxury and vice, spending most of his time with the women of his large harem. Dissensions also ran rife among the political leaders of the movement. During the next three years the Tai Pings continued their military exploits. At one time they advanced north to within two hundred miles of Peking, where they were checked by the Mongols whom the Emperor called to his aid.

And all this time Tseng Kuo-fan had been busily making preparations so that he might go out to meet the Tai Pings.

In April, 1854, he at last emerged from Hunan with a force of twelve thousand men and a fleet of war junks to come against the Tai Pings on the Yangtse. The next four years gave defeats as well as victories to Tseng Kuo-fan and his Braves. However, Tseng steadily made progress down the Yangtse, taking Wuchang and Chinkiang. At last only Anking and Nanking were left to the Tai Pings. The end of the rebellion seemed in sight but, unfortunately, just at this time the Imperial Government again became embroiled in difficulties with the foreigners which gave the Tai Pings time to recoup their fortunes.

The cause of foreign complications was the old issue of trade relations. We remember that, by the treaties of the 'forties, trade was to be regulated by a fixed tariff to be collected at the seaports.

In the turmoil and panic during the Tai Ping troubles, the Chinese officials utterly failed to regulate the collection of the tariff. At Shanghai the Chinese customs officials fled and in the emergency the British, French and American consuls took upon themselves the task of collecting the duties and turning the proceeds over to the Imperial officials. They managed the collection so successfully and turned in so much more money than the Chinese that the Chinese Government asked the foreigners to assist in the creation of a customs service. Thus began the Chinese Maritime Customs Service, still in existence. The service included both Chinese and foreign officials, all appointed by the Chinese Government. A foreigner was put in charge of the customs returns in each treaty port and at the top of the service was the Inspector General, appointed from the nation having the most trade with China. This office has always been held by a Britisher. Sir Robert Hart held the post from 1861 to 1909 and it is due to him that a wonderfully honest administration has been developed which has, more than any one thing, kept China from becoming totally bankrupt. The proceeds from it have guaranteed many of the loans China has been forced to make of late years. This high honor on the part of the West in discharging an obligation to the Chinese, the faith of the Chinese in the Westerner, is a bright spot in the dark picture of distrust and misunderstanding between China and the West painted during these years.

Another sore spot in the trade difficulties was at Canton where the foreign traders, or factors, were constantly harassed by the strict regulations thrown around them in the factory—that narrow strip of land along the river which had been allotted to them. By the treaties, Canton was one of the treaty ports or cities where foreigners might come and go but the Cantonese refused to admit them within their walled city. Further fuel was added to the sullen flame when the Emperor rewarded with the order of the Chinese nobility the High Commissioner of Canton, who had been so flagrantly disregarding the treaties. It seemed to the foreigners that the Emperor thus encouraged his representatives to break faith with them.

Matters came to a head in 1856 over the affair of the *Lorcha Arrow,* a boat flying the British flag. As the *Lorcha Arrow* sailed up Pearl River to Canton the Chinese boarded her in search of opium, hauled down the British flag, and carried off fourteen sailors under the excuse that the officials suspected them of piracy. The English consul, Harry Parkes, demanded the return of the sailors and an apology for hauling down the flag. The Chinese official refused, then finally agreed to return the sailors but not to make the apology. This was unsatisfactory to the British Consul.

At this juncture the British Admiral took possession of the defenses at Canton and demanded that the treaty obligations—the opening of Canton to foreign residence—so long evaded, be fulfilled. As China still hedged, the English, assisted by the French, who had been unable to get any satisfaction for the murder of a missionary, entered upon another war with China—a war the Manchus could ill afford with the Tai Pings destroying them from within. Canton was bombarded and captured. With Canton in their hands the Allies again sought to get into direct communication with the Central Government but when the four powers, England, France, Russia and the United States, asked for the appointment of a representative of the Imperial Government who would have authority to negotiate with them, the throne refused and again told them to apply to the Canton Viceroy.

It was then that the representatives of the Powers set out for the north. At Taku, the fort at the mouth of the river on which the city of Tientsin is located, the foreign representatives were met by Chinese officials, but as these were not clothed with full powers the English and French refused to treat with them. Again the Allies were thwarted in their attempt to deal directly with Peking. The Allies, resolved to push this matter to a conclusion, now resorted to force. It was only after they had captured Taku and had proceeded up the river to Tientsin that fully accredited officials of the Peking Government were sent to treat with them. The English Treaty of Tientsin (1858) and similar ones with France, Russia and the United States resulted. The most important provisions were: the addition of three Yangtse cities to the treaty ports; the privilege of allowing foreign diplomats to reside in Peking; the toleration of Christianity; and China's new indemnity of four million taels. The treaties were to be ratified the following year. But the government still harassed by the Tai Pings was hesitating about the treaty ratification, hoping to play some card that might save it from signing the treaties. During

THE TAI PING REBELLION

the year they had agreed upon tariff rules which gave to the Treaty Powers the right to regulate the rate of duties levied on foreign goods coming into the treaty ports.

The year rolled around and the British and French set out for Peking, the place insisted upon by all but America as the only sufficiently dignified spot for the ratification of international agreements. The commission refused to go to Peking by the old overland route used by the tribute-bearing nations because of the implication in such a route. The allied fleet of thirteen gunboats reached Taku and started to pass up the river, when stopped by heavy firing from recently erected fortifications. In the fight which followed they lost six of their boats and many of their number were killed and wounded. They retired to Shanghai, again thwarted in their efforts to deal directly with Peking.

Not daunted, however, the next year (1860) Lord Elgin and Baron Gros, British and French Ambassadors, set out again for Peking, supported by eighteen thousand men. The Taku forts were taken and also the city of Tientsin.

Then the Allies sent Mr. Parkes with a party under a flag of truce to Tungchow (a village twelve miles from Peking) to discuss terms of an armistice. The flag of truce was disregarded by the Chinese and these envoys were arrested, tortured, and carried to Peking where they were imprisoned for two months. Many of them died during this time. The allied troops in retaliation forced their way to Peking and burned the lovely Yuan Ming Yuan palace just outside the city and captured Peking.

What disaster! China who in her proud aloofness had meant to keep the inferior nations of the globe at bay, and to gain the advantages of foreign trade without granting official recognition was now confronted with the spectacle of her beautiful capital, the city of the Mings, held by those inferior nations. The Emperor and his great court fled to

Jehol, the summer palace—the Yellow, the Forbidden City was abandoned!

The Emperor's brother, Prince Kung, negotiated new treaties. The ratifications of the Tientsin Treaties were exchanged as formerly provided for, at the same time the new treaties known as the Peking Treaties were signed (1860). These provided for an increase of the indemnity and the Emperor expressed his regrets for the misunderstanding at Taku. The captured cities were to be returned to China and Tientsin was added to the list of open ports. The British obtained Kwoloon Point, opposite Hongkong, on the mainland, and the French secured, in Chinese text, the right for Catholic missionaries to own land in the interior, that is outside the treaty ports. The Tsungli Yamen, a department for dealing with foreign affairs was established. Opium was to be admitted at all treaty ports upon payment of an import duty.

At last the hard fought question of international trade was temporarily settled. But just under the surface of peace existing between China and the Western countries lay germinating the seeds of distrust and rancor which had been sown. The West resented the dissimulation of China; the Chinese resented the often truculent show of force of the Westerners. So foreign intercourse which should have brought strength and increased revenues to the Manchus left them an exiled court, prestige lost with the populace, their resources drained by indemnities, to go back to their internal struggle with the Tai Pings.

Thus did Peking struggle ineffectively with her right hand against the foreigners and quite as ineffectively with her left hand against the Tai Pings who, while the foreign difficulties were acute had forced their way out of Nanking and were by the time of signing of the treaties in 1860 working southeast toward the rich city of Shanghai.

THE TAI PING REBELLION 225

Emperor Hsien Feng who had called for the services of Tseng Kuo-fan later wisely added to his power by making him viceroy of the Liang Kiang provinces and Imperial High Commissioner. These offices gave to Tseng the power he needed for now he had authority to commandeer supplies and men. Even though the Emperor died while the court was in flight at Jehol, still the regency, appointed for his six-year-old son, retained Tseng in his appointment.

Tseng Kuo-fan was an example of what the Chinese civilization at its best could produce. He was modest, patient, with no desire for self-aggrandizement or material gain. He did not stoop to the temptation of "squeezing" from the public funds as so many officials did.

He made no spectacular play to the gallery, swooping down upon Nanking with much display. Instead he said frankly that he could not take Nanking in the beginning; that he must move upon it only after he held the other forts on the Yangtse, that he must take Anking, a city near Nanking, and there establish a base. Furthermore, he did not try to do all this himself, in demonstration of his own power. He gathered around him able men. Li Hung-chang he placed in command in Kiangsu and Tso Tsung-tang in Chekiang. But even so the struggle against the Tai Pings was long and bloody. The rebels put up six months of stubborn fighting before they at last surrendered the city of Anking to the Imperialist troops.

And even with this important city in his hands, Tseng Kuo-fan worked for three more years before he finally put down the rebellion. They were years dotted with defeats as well as victories. At one time Shanghai would have been captured by the rebels had the English and French not taken up arms in defense of the land they had made their home. After that the Mayor of Shanghai enlisted foreigners in the service of the Emperor. General Ward, an American adventurer, became a commander in the Chinese Army and rendered valuable service. When he was killed the Chinese erected a shrine to his memory. His commandership was given to an Englishman named Gordon, nicknamed Chinese Gordon. Ward's and Gordon's Army was a motley crew but they released the main body of Tseng Kuo-fan's troops for the great encounter with the Tai Pings at Nanking. However, the sturdily independent Tseng Kuo-fan would have preferred to fight the thing out alone even if it took him longer. With quiet dignity he said: "China's rebels are China's own children and China's force should certainly be sufficient to quell her small disturbances. . . . Why should we lightly borrow soldiers and leave a legacy of ridicule to future generations?"[1]

Finally Tseng Kuo-fan led his troops against Nanking, but even after the wall was breached and the Imperial troops streamed into the city street fighting went on with the last of the Tai Pings. Although their Heavenly King, Hung, had poisoned himself, the remnant of the once vast Tai Ping army was loyal to their cause. But the organization and system of Tseng Kuo-fan's army at last won over the corrupted and vice-ridden Hung and his followers. Tseng Kuo-fan was made a marquis for his valuable services, and his brother and Li Hun-chang, earls.

For fifteen years the Tai Ping Rebellion had laid China waste. Life and property had been ruthlessly destroyed. Six hundred towns and cities lay in ruins, trade and art and literature all had suffered. Thousands upon thousands of the patient people had met horrible deaths.

CHAPTER XVII

The Empress Dowager

THROUGHOUT the history of China whenever great disaster had overtaken the country it had been the custom to question the character of the "Son of Heaven." Time and time again an effete dynasty had been overthrown. And now the Manchu Dynasty was proving itself to be corrupt and ineffective. The Tai Ping Rebellion had shown how weak the ruling house had become; the continued conflicts with the West had made evident the inability of the government to handle international trade problems without strife and loss. It is hard to estimate how much prestige had been lost in the eyes of the Chinese when they saw the Manchu court fleeing from Peking before the despised barbarians, the French and English troops.

To the casual observer it would seem that the moment had come for the Chinese to wrest their country from under the weak hand of the Manchu invader. The opportunity would seem to have presented itself, when, in 1861 in the midst of the court's ignominious sojourn in Jehol, the Emperor, Hsien Feng, died leaving as heir to the throne a boy of only six years of age. But the Chinese made no move and the Manchu Dynasty lasted another forty years.

A strange thing happened—a woman, by quick and decisive action in the moment of dissension and intrigue following the death of the Emperor, took the affairs of China into her own strong hands. This woman was Tsu Hsi, concubine to the late Emperor and mother of his son.

For many years thereafter she ruled China, coming to be known over the whole world as the Empress Dowager. A masterful woman was Tsu Hsi; to accomplish her ambitions she sometimes used real statesmanship, sometimes cruelty and intrigue, sometimes simply the charm of her personality.

At the time of the Emperor's death the court was in the midst of its retreat at Jehol and for two years past Su Shun, an imperial clansman, had held almost absolute power. When the Emperor died, Su Shun naturally wished to continue his hold upon affairs so he planned to preserve the child but to do away with the Empress, lawful wife of the late Emperor, and with Tsu Hsi, the mother of the boy, heir to the throne. By ancient custom and court etiquette the new boy Emperor and the dead Emperor's wives, after they had offered libations and prayers at the start of the journey, were required to hurry ahead of the cortege so as to be ready to perform the proper ceremonies when the Emperor's catafalque reached the capital. Su Shun, taking advantage of this procedure, planned to have the Empress and concubine Tsu Hsi murdered on the way.

But Tsu Hsi, hearing through court whisperings of Su Shun's plan, secretly informed Prince Kung, brother of the late Emperor, who had come to Jehol to offer sympathy to the Empresses. With the help of the Prince who had been won to their side, the Empresses were able to avoid the place of the proposed murder and to arrive in Peking before the conspirator. Then backed by Prince Kung and the Imperial Army Tsu Hsi and the Empress went out to meet the cortege on its approach to the capital.

After dutifully performing the ceremonies of reverence, Tsu Hsi suavely thanked Su Shun and his fellow conspirators for bringing the Emperor's body to Peking and for the services which they had rendered as regents. Of this office she now relieved them. When they protested

THE EMPRESS DOWAGER 229

that they were legally appointed regents, Tsu Hsi had them arrested. As the streets of the capital were lined with troops loyal to Prince Kung and to Tsu Hsi, the conspirators saw that they were outwitted and they made no further protest. Tsu Hsi had won her first great battle and had shown herself as a manager of men and as a past master in guile and craftiness.

By Imperial Edict the lawful Empress and Concubine Tsu Hsi were now made joint regents. To the Empress of the late Emperor went first place, but as she was a woman of retiring and gentle disposition, Tsu Hsi, the masterful and ambitious, held the real power in her own hands. Prince Kung, for his part in putting down Su Shun, was made Prince Councilor and Head of the Grand Council.

At the beginning of her regency Tsu Hsi showed her good judgment by avoiding the appearance of power. She seemed to realize the delicacy of her position—that women as rulers had never been popular with the Chinese. She had studied Chinese history and she did not forget in the flush of her first victory that even the Empress Lu of the Hans in the second century was considered a usurper by the Chinese people. How much more would they be inclined to think of Tsu Hsi, the Emperor's favorite concubine, albeit the mother of his son, as a usurper.

Sensing this she was in the beginning benign, sparing the lives of many who had been in the intrigue against her. Thus she gained for herself many friends among her erstwhile enemies and built up for herself a reputation among the people for almost "quixotic gentleness."

However, whenever she was really thwarted, she did not hesitate to show her power as she had on that day when she gained for herself the regency. With the late Emperor's brother, Prince Kung, to whom she owed much for his help in putting down the conspiracy against her, she early came into conflict. Proud and domineering as she, he resented any show of superior power on her part. On the other hand, Tsu Hsi exaggerated his independence, accepting as true all the tales of him her favorite eunuch brought to her ears.

Very early Tsu Hsi had come under the influence of eunuchs and gave them great power. An affair over one of them brought her into her first difficulty with Prince Kung. Tsu Hsi sent one of her trusted eunuchs on a journey to the south, forgetting or ignoring the rule that no eunuch might leave the capital on pain of death. His mission was discovered and an order for his arrest obtained from the First Empress and he was killed before Tsu Hsi could save him. She blamed Prince Kung for a share in this matter; this was probably the beginning of the difficulties between them. The rupture widened, until finally when the Prince half rose from his knees during a court audience she cried out that he was attacking her. By royal decree she took from him his high positions in the palace only later to restore them to him, striking the former decree from the records in order that the "white jade" of his reputation should remain unmarred.

As time went on, Yehonala, as Tsu Hsi was called in her girlhood, became bolder in the manifestation of her power. And in spite of repeated protests from the bitter officials, she openly flaunted before the kingdom her reliance upon the eunuchs. "Even before the appearance of Yehonala their evil influence had again become paramount in the Forbidden City; with her accession to power all the corruption, intrigues, and barbarous proceedings that had characterized the last Mings were gradually re-established and became paramount features of her Court."

In spite of memorials begging that the abuses of the eunuchs and their interferences in state matters be done away with, in spite of the Empress Dowager's written documents deploring such practices, J. O. P. Bland tells us that

> "The Chief Eunuch's influence over the young Empress became greater every day. It was common knowledge, and the gossip of the tea-houses, that his lightest whim was law in the Forbidden City; that Yehonala and he, dressed in fancy costumes from historical plays, would make frequent excursions on the Palace Lake; that he frequently wore the Dragon robes sacred to the use of the sovereign, and that the Empress had publicly presented him with the jade '*ju-yi*,' symbol of royal power. Under these circumstances it was only natural, if not inevitable, that unfounded rumors should be rife in exaggeration of the real facts, and so we find it reported that An Te-hai was no eunuch, and again, that Yehonala had been delivered of a son of which he was the father; many fantastic and moving tales were current of the licentious festivities of the court, of students masquerading as eunuchs and then being put out of the way in the subterranean galleries of the palace. Rumors and tales of orgies; inventions no doubt, for the most part, yet inevitable in the face of the notorious and undeniable corruption that had characterized the court and the seraglio under the dissolute Hsien-Feng, and justified, if not confirmed, as time went on, by an irresistible consensus of opinion in the capital, and by fully substantiated events in the Empress Dowager's career."[1]

Of the eunuch, Li Lien-ying:

> "It is recorded on trustworthy authority that at an early stage in his career he had so ingratiated himself with Her Majesty that he was permitted unusual liberties, remaining seated in her presence, aye, even on the Throne itself. In the privacy of her apartments he was allowed to discuss whatever subjects he chose, without being spoken to, and as years passed and his

familiarity with the Old Buddha increased, he became her regular and authoritative adviser on all important state business."[2]

And all these years the young Emperor was growing up with the licentious eunuchs for his companions instead of the able officials and Literati of the empire who would have taught him scholarship, statesmanship, and the high responsibility of his position. He is a pathetic figure as we see him at seventeen, in 1873, taking upon himself the duties of the "Son of Heaven." All the cards are stacked against him and his patrician wife, A-lu-te, the virtuous. His character and health had already been undermined. From the start he knew that his only course was to be completely submissive to his ambitious mother and let her continue to rule.

From the very first the fate of these royal children—for they were little more—was sealed. The Empress Dowager encouraged the young Emperor's dissipations. It became a matter of common knowledge and notorious in the capital that the Emperor and his colleagues consorted with evil characters in the worst localities of the city and often returned from a night of orgies too late for the audience with the Ministers of State, held by custom at dawn.

It is not surprising that the Emperor contracted smallpox, wandering in the lowest dens in the city. In a few days the Emperor died, only two years after he had ascended the throne.

Then the Empress Dowager, leaving the Emperor's wife, A-lu-te, mourning at the side of her husband's couch, hastily called a meeting of the court. Ignoring the possibility that A-lu-te's unborn child might be a son, she set aside also the next in line, the long hated Prince Kung's son, a youth nearly old enough to assume his kingly duties. Without

THE EMPRESS DOWAGER

any authority but her own bold statement, she decreed that another baby, the son of her younger sister who had married a prince royal, be declared Emperor. Late in the evening though it was and with a dust storm raging over Peking, she sent the yellow imperial chair to bring the child to the palace. The little boy, known as Kuang Hsü, as if he foresaw the misery the future held in store for him, arrived weeping miserably. That very night before he slept he was taken to the room where the late Emperor lay in state and made to *kowtow* before him. Thus did he in 1875 begin his royal duties, duties which for many years must be carried on by his regent, the Empress Dowager. As in the days when she first made herself regent, the Empress Dowager had acted quickly in this crisis, forgetting no detail that would insure the success of her schemes and that would put her once more upon the throne.

Soon after, A-lu-te died and with her perished the Emperor's unborn child. Gossip ran rife through the empire and many claimed that the Old Buddha had killed A-lu-te. Memorials from all over the empire poured in protesting at this violation of ancestral custom in the choice of an emperor. Nevertheless, the Empress Dowager continued to reign—soon it was as sole regent, for the other Empress died, whether naturally or violently, no one can really say, although again gossip had it that the Old Buddha poisoned her.

Now Tsu Hsi and her favorite eunuch could manage matters as they wished. They practically made common cause and a common purse in collecting tribute. It is said that the favorite eunuch held in his supple hands the lives and deaths of thousands, making and unmaking the highest official of the empire, levying rich tribute on the eighteen provinces. At one time the vast quantities levied by the court from the southern provinces passed first through his hands and the share he took, dragon robes, tribute silk, etc., was stacked high in his apartments; of the bullion he took a fifth, after the Emperess Dowager had taken half. Such was the extravagance and degeneracy of the court. We find little in the records to show that the Empress Dowager interested herself in promoting the culture or material well-being of her people.

No more able to cope with the situation were the provincial governments. They lacked both the will and the power to handle the larger problems; over-population, banditry, piracy, the recurring floods and famines, and the great problems of communication in a country as vast as China, education, and the general well-being of the people. The maintenance of peace and order rested upon the immemorial unit of local government, the village. The town fathers were powerful in their small communities so that throughout the empire the daily life of the people went on much as it always had. The Literati also were an element of strength. By them the traditions of hundreds of years of scholarship were treasured as well as the moral teachings of the sage Confucius.

At this juncture some of the more thoughtful of the statesmen began to talk of reform and to advocate the adoption of certain innovations from the West. The foreign missionaries and business people, accepting the privilege of residence granted according to the treaties, now had little centers of Western civilization in many of the important cities of the country. Consuls from foreign countries were stationed in the ports and diplomatic representatives now resided in Peking. Among the Chinese junks along the coast were seen steamboats of Americans, British and other nationals. Then an American put the first steamer on the lower Yangtse following which city after city up the Yangtse was opened to foreign trade. Thus the attention of China had of late years been constantly called to certain aspects of Western civilization.

Earlier than this, in 1867, Anson Burlingame, United States Minister to China, became very much interested in the Chinese people and the possibilities of the country. After he had retired from office he induced the Chinese Government to send a commission abroad to promote a knowledge about China and amicable relations between China and the West. Burlingame and two Chinese composed the commission which went first to the United States and then to Europe. Unfortunately, Burlingame on their return trip to China died in Russia, but his enthusiasm led the West to become interested in the Chinese as a people. Understanding between China and the West seemed about to be born. A few years later a group of young students was sent to the United States to pursue studies in Western sciences.

Tseng Kuo-fan, the savior of his country from the destructive Tai Pings, now showed his power as a constructive reformer. Though desirous for China to adopt Western methods in the army and navy and to add a specific training to the old examinations, he wanted to keep what was of value in the ancient system, particularly the morality of Confucius. He believed that the teachings of the Confucian classics should remain everlastingly unchanged. His ideals of character were those of the classics, filial piety, brotherly submission, benevolence, right and the eight virtues, industry, frugality, stability, clear perception, faithfulness, modesty, integrity, reciprocity (doing to others nothing which you dislike done to you). There was hope in China if men of this caliber could be friendly to the idea of reform. But alas, there were not many and the country just at this moment suffered a bitter loss in Tseng Kuo-fan's death. In his memorial he left these suggestions for reform:

1. The removal of the capital to some central point.
2. The abolition of the corrupt practices of officialdom and the establishment of right methods of government.
3. The erection of a modern army and navy both to be placed under the Central Government.
4. Reorganization of the Treasury to be placed under the Central Government.
5. Reform in the method of recruiting the Civil Service, the dismissal of useless officials, the specific training of those who are capable.

Li Hung-chang, whom Tseng Kuo-fan had been instrumental in raising to high office during the latter part of the Tai Ping Rebellion, though not of the intrinsic moral fiber of Tseng, helped to bring about a better understanding between foreigners and his country. It is significant, too, that he realized that one of the greatest contributions that the West could make to China was mechanical in character—the railway. He saw that China's poor transportation facilities, then as today, were the cause of the deaths by starvation of such large numbers, isolated in the famine districts. One wonders that he did not see, too, that the railroad would bring about the political unity so much needed in the country; that quicker transportation would pull the provinces together, would bring about exchange of products, would intermingle the thought of north and south and by degrees build up a common language understood by all.

The means of transportation still in use were those which had been used since ancient times. In the south, where the countryside for centuries had been interlaced with canals, primitive sailing vessels were used. When there was no wind men hauled these boats along by means of towing ropes. On the rivers when the trackers pulled against the swift currents they were not able to make more than ten miles a day. Nowhere on these waterways were there any fleet steamers except where the foreigners had introduced them in the Yangtse and the Pearl Rivers. And they were few in number compared to the junks. Salt—a monopoly of the government—has never been carried by any but the old flat-bottomed junks.

On land, coolies still carried the heaviest loads hung from poles on their shoulders. When the officials traveled on urgent business, they must go by junk or sedan chair. In the north where there were few rivers and canals, men, donkeys, mules and camels were the only means of transportation. Two-wheeled, springless carts, drawn by mules, lumbered over the uneven roads, which were impassable in time of thaw and rain. Then the cart-wheels settled up to the hubs in the mire or were completely engulfed. Some of these roads used for centuries had been worn down fifty or even a hundred feet below the surrounding land. As in the days of the T'angs and Mongols, letters and even edicts from the throne must be sent by couriers on foot or horseback. And the horses were not the fleet-footed horses that the Mongols in their day had kept stationed along the main highways. The court had long before let this system of relays lapse and there were now more mules than horses in use in China.

In 1876 Li Hung-chang interested a group of foreign merchants in constructing China's first railroad. It led from Shanghai to Woosung, at the mouth of the Yangtse, a distance of twelve miles. But the illiterate and superstitious masses opposed the educated reformers. They would have nothing of reform. They saw in a railroad only an evil power disturbing the graves of their ancestors. Believers in *Feng Shui,* they thought the luck of the land would be destroyed. Taught for years to distrust the foreigner, they considered the railway an outgrowth of foreign influence. Maybe deeper yet lay the economic opposition of the carrying coolies and the boatmen, who saw the railway taking their jobs and only means of subsistence. It was the beginning of China's fight against the industrial revolution—men against machines.

As soon as the railway line was in operation the people deliberately walked in front of the engines, believing that in death they would be transformed into powerful hostile spirits which would combat the railroad. Excitement ran so high that the government was obliged to buy the road from its foreign owners and dump the engines in the river. No further attempt at railroad building was made until five years later when a short line was laid between the Kai'ping mines and a canal. In 1886 this line was lengthened and soon after an Imperial Chinese Railway Administration was formed. By 1894 a line was complete between Tientsin and Shanhaikuan.

This first reform movement suffered another great loss in 1885 in the death of Tso Tsung-tang, who, through Tseng Kuo-fan's efforts, had risen to a position of importance during the Tai Ping Rebellion. He, too, urged upon the now effete Manchus the need of changing the ancient and outworn industrial pattern. Like Tseng Kuo-fan, in a dying memorial, he petitioned the throne to construct railways, improve the navy, strengthen the coast defenses, introduce scientific mining and manufactures, regulate finance and encourage foreign studies. Thus did this man of seventy-three plead for his country. With prophetic vision he saw disaster ahead for an unprogressive China. Had his advice been followed the outcome of the war with Japan, just ten years later, might have been different. But the voices of these old men were the voices of prophets crying in the wilderness. The Empress Dowager and the people heard them not.

CHAPTER XVIII

CHINA'S VAST EMPIRE IS SHRINKING

FOR fifteen years the Empress Dowager enjoyed the second regency. But in the year 1887 the child, Kuang Hsü, brought to the palace that ill-omened night of the raging dust storm and of the death of the young Emperor from smallpox, had become a youth of seventeen, deemed old enough to take over the government of the great Chinese Empire. But for two years more, in response to the many memorials from those who had enjoyed her patronage, the old Empress Dowager continued to rule. Finally there seemed no further excuse to prolong her regency and at the marriage of the "Son of Heaven" to her niece, a woman loyal to herself, the Empress Dowager relinquished her second regency and retired to the Summer Palace just outside Peking. However, you cannot imagine so masterful a person abandoning her power so easily. Nor did she. She kept a close watch on the lad, forcing him to make frequent visits to her. She insisted upon approving official appointments and other important matters of state. In order to reach the Summer Palace in time for the morning court audience, the Emperor had to arise very early, as it took several hours to make the journey in the two-wheeled, springless cart—the fastest means at his disposal. Often the chief eunuch kept him waiting, kneeling reverently at the gate before he announced the Emperor's arrival to the Empress.

Very early in his reign Kuang Hsü showed an interest in

international affairs and two years after coming to his majority, he received the foreigners of Peking in audience. The impression they carried away was of a young man of dignity and intelligence, but of no great physical strength, displaying none of the military attributes of his Manchu forefathers who had conquered China. Very marked were his melancholy and sadness. Unfortunately, early in his reign two of his most able ministers died: one of them the son of the illustrious leader, Tseng Kuo-fan. These men had been interested in the creation of a navy and with Li Hung-chang were appointed to a commission known as the Board of Admiralty and had attempted to carry out Tso Tsung-tang's recommendations given in his dying memorial. Two fleets were organized, the northern and the southern, and ironclads were ordered by Li Hung-chang from Germany and other boats from England. Foreign experts were engaged to construct fortifications at Port Arthur and Wei-hai-wei and other experts to train both naval and military forces. Prince Shun was particularly interested in the navy and his death proved to be a great loss to the young Emperor and to the program of naval reform.

With these two strong men gone, the Empress Dowager's influence again became the paramount one. Funds that had been bespoken for the navy she had diverted to the beautifying of the Summer Palace where she lived. The Board of Admiralty was abolished. This impoverishment of the navy proved a poor preparation for China in her struggle, already begun, with the "earth-hungry Powers," grouped on her frontiers. Already China's outlying districts had been lopped off—here a little, there a little. The tributary states of Burmah and Annam had been lost respectively to Great Britain and to France.

In the Empress Dowager's first regency, China had lost

to Japan her first near-by islands—the Liu Chiu Islands, a string stretching from the southwestern tip of Japan to Formosa. Both the Liu Chiu Islands and Formosa China claimed as part of her empire, although she really had never governed them. In 1868 Japan had protested the massacre of some fifty Liu Chiu sailors on the Island of Formosa on the ground that Liu Chiu sailors were her nationals. China claimed they were hers. Then Japan landed her troops on Formosa. War seemed inevitable when the British Minister in China, Sir Thomas Wade, intervened and the matter was amicably settled, China paying for Japan's expedition. Two years later, Japan annexed the Liu Chiu Islands.

Ever since, there had been a growing rift between China and Japan which had constantly widened as their dissension grew over China's tributary state, Korea. Although China claimed suzerainty, she rarely troubled herself about the country, except to receive the tribute, unless some other country attempted aggression there. Japan, it seems, had had various commercial difficulties with Korea and as China was loath to assume responsibility, Japan concluded a treaty directly with Korea, assuring its independence. China then tried to get back the ground she had lost and had several times been on the verge of war with Japan. Finally Li Hung-chang and Count Ito, representing China and Japan respectively, had come to an understanding by which the troops of both nations were to withdraw from Korea. Furthermore, they agreed that neither nation should send troops to Korea unless due notice of such an intention be given to the other government. This had brought about an uneasy peace lasting until 1894, the fifth year of Kuang Hsü's reign, when Japan claimed that China broke the compact. The Korean Government, unable to quell a religious rebellion, had appealed to her suzerain, China, who had sent troops to aid her without giving notice to Japan. Japan claimed China had thus broken her promise.

Japan in her new nationalism was alarmed, also, at Russia's activities in northeastern Asia. Russia, in her march across Siberia to the Pacific, had obtained the seaport of Vladivostok, but it was ice-bound for several months of the year. To get an ice-free port she was looking southward either to Manchuria or Korea. Japan was keeping a close eye on Russia's activities for she, too, was looking with envious eyes on both Korea and Manchuria. By 1894 Russia and Japan were eying each other across Korea. Japan made the first move to take Korea from the Chinese. Why not test her new modern army and navy in a conflict with China? She was trying to make herself into a strong modern nation which might command the respect of the Western powers and free her from the restrictions put upon her. If she won, she would acquire respectful treatment from the West.

War between China and Japan was declared August 1, 1894, and was fought in Korea and Manchuria. After the first encounters, Japan won everywhere, not alone in Korea but on Chinese territory, in Manchuria, gaining control of the Liaotung Peninsula and winning the naval battle of Wei-hei-wei off the coast of China proper. Too late China realized the strength of the "dwarf men," as she called the Japanese, who, while the Empress Dowager had been using the naval funds on the Summer Palace, had been perfecting their country in modern warfare. China, realizing the day was lost, sued for peace, which was signed in the Treaty of Shimonoseki. The terms provided for:

1. The independence of Korea.
2. The cession to Japan of the Liaotung Peninsula, Formosa, and the Pescadores Islands (between Formosa and the mainland).

CHINA'S VAST EMPIRE SHRINKING

3. The payment by China of two hundred million taels indemnity to Japan.
4. The opening of more treaty ports: Shasi on the middle Yangtse, Chungking above the rapids on the upper Yangtse; Soochow and Hangchow, rich cities near Shanghai.

But Japan was not so easily to gain territory on Asia's mainland. The three Powers, France, Russia and Germany, objected to the cession of the Liaotung Peninsula to Japan, arguing that it was a violation of China's integrity. Japan was thus forced to retrocede it, receiving from China an additional indemnity of thirty million taels as recompense.

Overnight almost, the West changed its opinions about the Far East. Until this defeat of China by Japan there had very generally prevailed an opinion that China was a sleeping giant who was about ready to wake up and show his tremendous strength. It was known that under the guidance of Li Hung-chang a navy department had been created and steps had been taken toward building a fleet and a telegraph system. How great might be the hidden strength of China once she embarked on a course of developing modern armaments and communications had been a matter of much conjecture. This war with Japan pricked the bubble of China's military prestige and showed the world the weakness and corruption of the Manchu Dynasty.

What the whole world also now realized for the first time was the growing power of the Japanese Empire. What might this new power mean in the future affairs of the Pacific regions? Sir Robert Hart voiced the fears of the West. "Japan wants to lead the East in war, in commerce, and in manufactures, and the next century will be a hard one for the West."

The knowledge of China's weakness and of Japan's strength changed the attitude of other Powers regarding their future course in China. Now was the moment for the "earth-hungry" to press their demands. Germany and Russia, Powers who had successfully protested Japan's acquisition of the Liaotung Peninsula at the end of the Sino-Japanese War, were the first to be heard from. Russia's acquisition in years past of the territory (now a part of Siberia) north of the Amur River and along the seacoast east of Manchuria, with the Pacific seaport, Vladivostok, had led her to make plans for a transcontinental railroad known as the Trans-Siberian Railroad to connect Russia with Vladivostok. The eastern part of the railway Russia hoped to build through China's possessions, Manchuria and Mongolia.

By providing China with a loan with which to pay her indemnity to Japan, Russia now acquired the privilege of leasing Port Arthur as a naval base and the Liaotung Peninsula (the territory denied Japan in 1895) for a period of twenty-five years. With this lease went the right of Russia to build a railroad connecting Port Arthur with the Trans-Siberian line, later built and known as the Chinese Eastern Railroad. This agreement was signed March 28, 1898.

But even earlier, on March sixth of the same year, a similar document regarding other territory was signed by China and Germany. It granted concessions in settlement for the death of two German missionaries who had been murdered in Shantung Province. As soon as this incident was reported a German squadron steamed into Kiaochow Bay and Germany demanded reparation from the Chinese Government. In due time a Sino-German agreement gave Germany a lease of Kiaochow Bay as a coaling station and naval base for ninety-nine years, while a separate agreement provided for Chinese and German cooperation in building railroads and working mines in Shantung Province.

CHINA'S VAST EMPIRE SHRINKING

France also obtained her bit of China, the lease of a coaling station to the south of Kwangtung Province. And England! She had much at stake in Asia. To protect India was her one thought and she must not let any Power become strong enough in Asia to threaten that. Of Russia she was always wary. So she demanded and obtained the privilege of having for a naval base, Wei-hai-wei, across the bay from Russia's base, Port Arthur. Thus China found herself shorn of the places along her coast which were suitable for naval bases.

But this was not all. The foreign powers began to develop Spheres of Influence in the interior of China. These were the parts of the country mapped out by various nations in which they were to have peculiar rights and privileges. Under this policy Russia considered Manchuria the territory or sphere in which she had special rights. To her only in this region should China give the rights of building railroads, of opening mines. In like manner, Germany claimed Shantung as her sphere; France, Yunnan Province; England, the Yangtse Valley. So great was the rivalry for special spheres that it looked almost as if China were to be carved up among the European nations. Books were written on the subject, one bearing the title, *The Breaking Up of the Chinese Empire*. Only the jealousies of the nations among themselves prevented China from losing more of her sovereignty than she did.

Besides losing temporary and partial sovereignty in the leased territories and the Spheres of Influence, China lost in another way, namely the control over railroads in the interior of the country. Ever since the war with Japan, China's foreign indebtedness had been increasing. In order to pay the indemnities she had been forced to borrow from European nations and because of the political weakness of China the nations lending money to her demanded as a guarantee a provision that the interest should be allocated from the revenue of the Maritime Customs. Likewise when China wished to enter upon any new enterprise, such as railroad building, she found herself in the same difficult position, lacking both money and credit. Foreign nations in lending her money for projects demanded guarantees for the protection of their interests. So in railroad building China was forced to grant concessions which gave to the lender the right to finance and build railroads in Chinese territory with whole or part management in the running of the road when completed. Thus the Belgians built the Peking-Hankow line; the Germans, the Shantung lines and the northern part of the Tientsin-Pukow line which united Peking and Nanking; the English the southern part of the Peking-Pukow line and its extension to Shanghai. Peking and Tientsin were connected with the Russian railroads in Manchuria.

Although China lost many sovereign rights and much prestige in the granting of the railroad concessions yet she probably gained more than enough to offset the disadvantages. By connecting the Yangtse Valley with Peking and the north there developed a greater trade in all domestic products and opportunities for remote regions to get their goods to the coast. A variety of goods both native and foreign began to penetrate the communities along the railroads and raise, bit by bit, their standards of living. People came to see other districts and hear the strange dialects of other villages and towns. Despite the political difficulties the railways were a boon to China.

During this period of "land grabbing" and concession hunting the United States stood aside. Our position differed from that of the European nations in that we were still occupied in the development of our own large territory. Accordingly, we had always taken the stand that we wished none of China's territory ourselves and furthermore desired that her integrity be preserved. But by 1898-99, after the Spanish-American War, our interests in the Pacific had very much widened and somewhat changed in character by the acquisition of the Hawaiian Islands as a territory and the Philippines, at least as a temporary possession. With these new interests our trade and commerce in the Orient developed tremendously and we came to view with concern these European Spheres of Influence in China. In the spheres we feared restriction of our trade as the nationals of the country controlling the sphere were in a favorable position. Special privileges made it impossible for the merchants of other nations to compete with them. At this juncture, our Secretary of State, John Hay, sent identical notes to the Western Powers and Japan saying that he understood that in the Spheres of Influence there was entailed no loss of sovereignty on the part of China and that, therefore, by the treaties China was open on an equal basis to the trade of all nations. In other words, he objected to special privileges being given by China to any one nation in any part of the Chinese Empire. Whatever rights of trade China gave to one nation she gave, by the "most favored nation" clause, to all the treaty powers. This declaration of the equality of trade opportunity in China to all nations is known as the "Open Door Policy." It did much not only toward doing away with special privileges in the foreign trade but also in keeping for China her sovereign rights.

However, as China faced the twentieth century, her vast empire had indeed shrunk: Annam, Burmah, Korea gone, Formosa and the islands close to China's coast gone, naval bases occupied by other nations, special Spheres of Influence taking some of her sovereignty. Like tigers who close in upon their leader when once they find him weak, so had the other nations now closed in upon China. Once China had been strong and then she had conquered the weak and demanded tribute of Korea, Mongolia, Tibet, Burmah and Annam. Now she was weak and the earth-hungry nations had not spared her.

PART FOUR
REFORM AND REVOLUTION

CHAPTER XIX

Reform and Reaction

BITTER as was the loss of territory through foreign aggression during the closing years of the nineteenth century, it yet had its salutary effects. It acted as a sting, rudely awakening China to her military weakness and her bankrupt condition. The new intelligentsia of the country—a small per cent of China's four hundred million—boiled with alarms and theories; some others looked deeper as had Tseng Kuo-fan and Li Hung-chang in an earlier period to find the causes of their country's recent defeat. They realized that there was value in the heretofore despised Western civilization. Once they had wished to get only its military strength; now they began to look deeper. Might it be possible that some of China's old institutions of government were outworn and that Japan's course of following the West might not be altogether bad? Students, returning from Europe and the United States and Japan, were bringing with them ideas of Western philosophy, science, history, literature, law and custom. Then, too, many Western ideas had unconsciously filtered into China through the foreign trade centers and missionary communities which by now were scattered well over China.

Among the wisest of the Chinese statesmen who advocated reform was Chang Chih-tung. Like Tseng Kuo-fan, who saved the country from the Tai Pings, he was one of the few officials who did not use his office to become rich. It is said that all the wealth that flowed through his *Yamen* was spent on public works and public charity. The defeat of China at the hands of Japan made him fear for the safety of his country. Out of the question, "How can China be saved?" which he put to himself over and over, came this solution, which he put in a book entitled *China's Only Hope*.

A true patriot, he looked within for the causes of China's defeat and used the clean knife of criticism on his country. He says:

> "Of all countries China has alone for these fifty years proved herself almost irreclaimably stupid and not awake. Many of the officials and people are proud and indolent. They contentedly rest in the belief that the old order of things will suffice for these dangerous times, and in the end become the easy prey of outsiders. Among our officials there is not one man of discernment: we have no real scholars and no skillful artisans. We are not represented abroad and at home have no schools. So our incompetences are not supplied. With nothing to stimulate the mind, harden the nature, or supply the deficiencies, there seems nothing left for China but to perish miserably in the slough of despondency and despair."[1]

Chang Chih-tung was not a radical reformer like many of the young students, and would not throw away that part of old China that he thought was good. In education he did not advocate the destruction, wholesale, of China's ancient teachings. Loyalty to Confucianism he preached. Students, he said, must be well grounded in a knowledge of their own language and Confucian literature. He wanted schools established throughout the country, money for which he would obtain by using Buddhist and Taoist temples and confiscating the property of these religions which he believed were degraded and dying out. After a grounding in China's best teachings, let the nation acquire Western learning from translations into Chinese of the best of the West. The "Eight Leg Essay," that stereotyped form of writing brought in during the Ming Dynasty, he would abolish from the official examinations and introduce Western science in its place. Also, he advocated sending students not to Europe and America, but to Japan, where the language difficulty was less.

Although he believed they could learn much from Western methods of government, he would have none of republics and parliaments. He exhorted the Chinese to be loyal to the Throne. He favored a modern navy and army and deplored the fact that Tso Tsung-tang's suggestions and the beginning made by the Board of Admiralty had not longer been followed.

He, too, like Li Hung-chang, saw that the building of railroads was essential. He says:

"Is there any one power that will open the door of learning for the scholar, the farmer, the workman, the merchant, and the soldier? To this question we reply emphatically—there is, and it is the railway. The potentialities of the scholar lie in extensive observation; of the farmer in finding a ready sale for farm products; of the workman in the increase of machinery; of the merchant, in cheap and rapid transit; and of the soldier in the quick dispatch of the munitions of war. . . . The railway is the source of wealth and power of Western countries. The laws of China make no provision for the building of thoroughfares. . . . Let us build railways. . . . The whole country will become really ours and China will be one great united family with no fear of famine or war."[2]

This book was written in faultless Chinese and it is estimated a million copies were sold in the country, so enthusiastic was its reception. As some one has said, if there had been twenty officials in China like Chang Chih-tung, the country might have worked out its salvation. But as there were not, Viceroy Chang was unable to graft a vigorous new life on the sturdy branches of China's old civilization. He was doomed to see China fall upon yet more evil days.

Others, deeply dissatisfied with China's Government, voiced their complaints and desires for reform in a much more vehement manner. The most outspoken were some young Cantonese whose leader was Kang Yu-wei. He was a student and philosopher who believed, like the philosophers of the Chinese Renaissance period in the seventeenth and eighteenth centuries, that many of the ancient texts of the Han Dynasty were spurious, among them the *Book of History*.

Kang Yu-wei again opened the way for historical criticism of ancient literature. Besides his interest in literature he was at heart a political and social reformer. To find sanction for his ideas of reform he printed a book entitled *Confucius as a Reformer*. He wished to destroy for the people the "model Emperor" lore of Yao and Shun and put in its place a picture of Confucius as a reformer. The aim was the same as that of Confucius—to give an authority for the social reforms he was convinced China must have.

Associated with him was another Cantonese scholar, Liang Chi-chao, who was hardly less important than Kang Yu-wei in the reform group. He was an exceptionally brilliant writer, editor of a newspaper which was the organ of the reformers.

They saw one hope in the dynasty. They hoped the young Emperor, Kuang Hsü, might be persuaded to back the reformers. At this period the relationships between the Empress Dowager and the Emperor were becoming strained; he was beginning to break away from her tutelage. Outwardly,

REFORM AND REACTION 255

they were still friendly, but actually they were in severe conflict with each other as the conservatives looked upon the Empress as their leader and the younger reformers were beginning to look to the Emperor as their leader. The Empress's party was nicknamed the "Old Mother's Set" and the Emperor's "Small Lad's Set."

The Emperor had already been reading and studying foreign books, a Bible, maps, globes, charts, and now suddenly to the horror of the conservatives of the court the Emperor received the radical reformer, Kang Yu-wei in frequent audiences and made him Secretary of the Bureau of Foreign Affairs. In three months the reformer, Kang Yu-wei, managed to place around the Emperor men of his ideas. Day in and day out they filled the Emperor's mind with the need for drastic reforms and suddenly the Emperor startled the empire by issuing in rapid succession a series of edicts. In the next one hundred days he issued twenty-seven such reform proclamations. It has ever since been known as "the one hundred days." Some of the most important of the edicts were:

> "Changes in the examination system so as to include questions on history, political economy and scientific knowledge.
> "The establishment of public schools throughout the Empire and the conversion of temples and monasteries into school buildings.
> "The extension of railroads.
> "The abolition of many superfluous offices both in the capital and throughout the Empire.
> "The complete reorganization of the military system."

Had he worked slowly he might have succeeded in instituting the reforms regarding education, reorganization of the navy and army and even the changes in the examination system. But when he went so far as to issue edicts regarding reforms in government machinery, which included cutting down the number of officials, the Manchu and Chinese officials throughout the land raised a cry of alarm and disapproval.

The reformers showed the greatest lack of foresight in dealing with the reactionary party centered around the Empress Dowager. Kang Yu-wei became so bold that he suggested to the Emperor that they capture and imprison the Old Buddha. To this the Emperor assented. He called in Yuan Shih-kai and taking as much precaution as he could in the palace where the Empress Dowager's eunuchs and other henchmen spied constantly upon him, the Emperor outlined the plot to Yuan and the part he was to play in its accomplishment. Yuan was to go to Tientsin to kill Jung Lu, one of the men who had so loyally supported the Empress long ago when that group of conspirators had plotted to take her life on the road to Peking. After killing Jung Lu, Yuan Shih-kai was to rush back to Peking and seize the Empress herself. Yuan consented. All seemed propitious for the carrying out of the plot. He departed, seemingly to carry out the Emperor's order and the Emperor proceeded to the gate of the Western Park to greet the Old Buddha when she arrived from her palace for the purpose of sacrificing at the altar to the Goddess of Silkworms. But the Emperor's feeling of security was ill-founded. Yuan Shih-kai gave the plot away and he and Jung Lu made plans to support the Empress. Before night the men surrounding the Emperor had been replaced by the henchmen of the Empress. The next morning, as the Emperor was leaving one of the halls in the palace, he was seized by the eunuchs and taken to an island in the middle of a little lake in the palace grounds. The tables were turned—the Emperor was the prisoner!

The Old Buddha, hard and ambitious, again held the supreme power in her own hands. She forced the Emperor to sign his own edict of dethronement. Making ill health the cause of his inability to rule, he implored the Empress Dowager again to take over the arduous task of regent and appoint an heir to the late Emperor Tung Chih. The Emperor remained for ten years, until his death, virtually imprisoned on his island, a puppet Emperor performing the filial ceremonies incumbent upon the "Son of Heaven," attired in his blue robes, kneeling in the Temple of Heaven alone in prayer for his people, but in state affairs sitting on a throne below the Empress, listening and assenting to her word of law.

For the third time the Empress Dowager, through her quickness of action, stood at the head of the government. She showed no mercy to the reformers; she judged them guilty of treason and had six decapitated. The two leaders, Kang Yu-wei and Liang Chi-chao, were fortunate enough to escape to Tientsin from whence they fled by boat to Hongkong—British soil—beyond the power of the Empress. They were considered as outlaws and forced to live in concealment or out of China until the Revolution of 1911 in which they took a prominent part.

The Empress now entered on a strong reactionary program. The reform edicts were quickly rescinded; reactionaries, most of them Manchus, were put in office. For two years a program anti-reform and anti-foreign in all its aspects was reinstated.

The Empress Dowager saw all too clearly that the dynasty was threatened: from within the country by the spirit of criticism and reform, and from without, by the foreigners who were asking so many privileges. She saw one last hope of reestablishing the dynasty; she would turn the criticism from the dynasty to the outside nations who had made so many aggressions on Chinese territory.

Envisioning war against the foreigners, the Empress Dowager appealed to the people to help her. She issued edicts calling upon the Northern Provinces (Chili, Manchuria, Shantung) to strengthen or create, if they had none, the old local militia or train bands. They should drill and be ready to support the dynasty. As they organized, there were enrolled into these bands desperadoes and ne'er-do-wells and members of societies—the Big Sword Society, Plum Blossom Fists, and Righteous Harmony Fists, the latter giving the name, Boxers, by which the foreigners know the movement. The superstition that they were immune to death gave a fighting enthusiasm to these members of the secret societies.

The movement began in Shantung and spread into Chili. There the soldiers displayed huge banners on which were written, "The Gods assist us to destroy all foreigners! we invite you to join the Patriotic Militia." Their venom was aimed against Christian missionaries and their Christian converts. The missionaries had been criticized for aiding their Chinese converts politically. The non-Christian Chinese felt that the missionaries used undue influence to help their converts when they got into difficulty with the law. Capitalizing this feeling abroad in the land, they launched a campaign against the missionaries. Railroads, steamboat and telegraph lines also came under the displeasure of the Society. These were the visible expressions of the West. A bad famine in the north convinced the populace that these Western innovations had disturbed the *Feng Shui,* the luck of the land, by displeasing the gods.

As reports came to the court of Peking of the spread of the movement and of the massacre of foreigners in outlying districts, the Empress Dowager worked herself into a kind

REFORM AND REACTION

of frenzy against all foreigners. To her ministers like Jung Lu, who knew that the killing of a few foreigners in the country of China would not rid China of them but merely bring hardship to the country, she refused to listen. She was carried away with the advice of Prince Tuan and her favorite eunuch, both of whom deceived her with promises that the Boxers would be successful in killing every foreigner in China. By June, 1900, so obsessed had she become with the idea of the extermination of foreigners, that she offered rewards for the heads of those foreigners residing in Peking and ordered the Governor of Shansi to kill every foreigner in his province. Obeying her command, the Governor saw to it that all the foreigners of Shansi, mostly missionaries, many of them women and children, were massacred.

Great bravery was shown by some of China's officials in attempting to stop this tragedy. Five paid for their opposition with their lives. Three the Empress Dowager had put to death for opposing the declaration of war and two because in telegraphing the Empress's order to the provinces *to slay* all foreigners, they telegraphed the order *to protect* all foreigners. Officials on the Yangtse, Chang Chih-tung and Liu K'u I among them, refused to carry out the edicts of slaughter which they received.

The Legations at Peking were at first unwilling to believe that any such fantastic thing as the killing of all foreigners in China would be undertaken. So the foreigners stayed on in Peking. They were a not inconsiderable group now. Every country of any size had her minister and a corps of lesser officials housed in Legations. Both Catholic and Protestant missions had large centers in Peking. There were, however, no business people there, as the capital never had been opened to international business.

These few hundred foreigners scattered about over the

huge city of Peking now became definitely alarmed as the reports kept coming in of the massacre of missionaries in outlying districts. They wired Tientsin for help and four hundred and fifty men from the foreign warships were sent quickly to Peking for the purpose of getting the foreigners away. They reached Peking but neither they nor those that had been sent to protect were able to leave Peking. Both the railway and telegraph lines were cut. The group of foreigners were now out of touch with the rest of the world.

The troops had no more than arrived when the Boxers in their red sashes spread over Peking terrorizing the native Christians. One night the foreigners, most of whom had taken refuge in the Legation quarter, were horrified to see the great Catholic Cathedral in flames. When at last some of the foreign troops managed to reach the place a terrible spectacle greeted their eyes. Hundreds of native Christians who had taken refuge in the church had been burned to death, driven back at the point of the spears of the red-sashed Boxers when they tried to escape. The remnant of native Christians, hunted and terrified, now appealed to the foreigners as Christian brethren to save them and some two thousand of these Christians were added to the already crowded Legation quarters.

And then came a day when an ultimatum was received from the Chinese Department of Foreign Affairs saying that as China could no longer protect the Legations, the Legations would have to protect themselves. In a last effort to prevail upon the Empress Dowager to stop this mad program of the Boxers, Baron Von Kettler, the German Minister, started bravely forth in his official chair to call upon the Department of Foreign Affairs. Putnam Weale says, "There were only two Chinese outriders with him as Von Kettler had refused to take any of his guard. I remember Von Kettler was smoking and leaning his arms on the front

REFORM AND REACTION

bar of his sedan, for all the world as if he were going on a picnic. The little cortege soon turned a corner and was swallowed up."[3]

Fifteen minutes later the two outriders, yelling and lashing their ponies into a wild gallop, charged back through the hastily created barricades of the Legations. Von Kettler was dead! Shot!

Then for two months, almost under the shadow of the pink wall of the Forbidden City, the Legations were besieged by the Boxers and the Imperial troops. Day after day as best they could the besieged strengthened their barricades. Men, women and even children worked filling hastily made bags with dirt. In their desperate need even rich silks and satins found in native shops within the Legation Center were made into bags. Peking carts, commandeered from near-by Chinese streets were overturned and built into the barricades. Food became a problem and mules and horses were killed for meat. Day by day, the strongly built barricades of the Chinese were pushed nearer and nearer. Fires, too, increased the danger of the beleaguered. Filled with priceless treasures, beautifully illumined books, rare old manuscripts, even the wonderful Hanlin Academy which touched on one side the British Legation was set on fire in the Boxers' efforts to rid the country of the hated barbarian. And day by day the besieged community grew smaller as officers and men guarding the barricades were killed.

And all this time behind the vermilion walls of the Forbidden City the struggle of the groups surrounding the Empress Dowager went on, the wise at her court attempting to stop such a disastrous policy. Twice they succeeded in making themselves heard and then the siege was lifted for a few days. Once in a mood of relenting the Empress Dowager sent melons to her friend, the white man. But each time the counsel of Prince Tuan and the eunuchs was in the end accepted and the siege was renewed.

If the Manchu troops had been undivided in their determination, there was not a time when they could not have taken the thinly manned barricades of the foreigners. Only the indecision at the court saved the Legations. But the time came when those within the Legation center could not hold out much longer: both food and ammunition were low. The messages the besieged had tried to send to Tientsin by faithful Chinese had brought no answers. Had the men been captured? Then at last one of these Chinese messengers, then another, returned bearing messages—the one on a strip of paper braided into his queue, the other on a little wad of paper in his ear—telling that troops were on the way. If the Legations could hold out a few days more they would be saved. The food and ammunition were then divided up, and spread over those days that must elapse before help could come. And during these days the attack became fiercer.

Putnam Weale, a participator in this grim struggle, tells of that last night of the siege.

"It was the night of the 13th. Not a word had been heard of the relief columns, not a message, not a courier had come in. But could anything have dared to move to us? Even the *Tsung-li Yamen,* affrighted anew at this storm of fire which it can no longer control, had not dared or attempted to communicate with us. We were abandoned to our own resources. At best we would have to work out our own salvation. Was it to be the last night of this insane Boxerism, or merely the beginning of a still more terrible series of attacks with massed assaults pushed right home on us? In any case, there was but one course—not to cede an inch until the last man had been hit. . . . By two o'clock every rifle that could be brought in line was replying to the enemy's fire. If this continued, in a couple of hours our ammunition would be exhausted, and we would have only our bayonets to rely on. . . . Suddenly above the clamour of rifle-fire a distant boom to the far east broke on my ears, as I was shouting madly at my men. I held my breath and tried to think, but before I could decide, boom! came an answering big gun miles away. I dug my teeth into my lips to keep myself calm, but icy shivers ran down my back. They came faster and faster, those shivers. . . . You will never know that feeling. Then, boom! before I had calmed myself a third shock; and then ten seconds afterwards, three booms, one, two, three, properly spaced. I understood, although the sounds only shivered in the air. It was a battery of six guns coming into action somewhere very far off. It must be true! I rose to my feet and shook myself. Then, in answer to the heavy guns, came such an immense rolling of machine-gun fire, that it sounded faintly, but distinctly, above the storm around us. Great forces must be engaged in the open. . . . I had been so ardently listening to these sounds that the enemy's fire had imperceptibly faded away in front of me unnoticed, until it had become almost completely stilled . . . again the booming dully shook the air. Again the machine-guns beat their replying rataplan. Now every rifle near by suddenly was stilled, and a Chinese stretcher-party behind me murmured, '*Ta ping lai tao liao*'—'the armies arrived.'[4]

But it was not until the next afternoon that the foreign troops at last reached the Legation quarters.

"As we stood about, twisting our fingers and cheering and trying to find something sensible to say or to do, there was a rush of people towards the lines connecting with the American Legation and the Tartar Wall. This caused another tremendous outburst of cheering and counter-cheering, and led by C——, the American Minister, columns of American infantry in khaki suits and slouch hats came pressing in. In they came—more and more men, until the open squares were choking with them. These men were more dog-tired than the Indian troops, and their uniforms were stained and clotted with the dust and sweat flung on them by the rapid advance. Soon there was such confusion and excitement that all order was lost, until the Americans began filing out again, and the native troops were pushed to the northern line of defences. In the turmoil and delight everything had been temporarily forgotten, but the growing roar of rifles had at length called attention to the fact that there might be more fierce fighting. Every minute added to the din, and soon the ceaseless patter of sound showed machine-guns were firing like fury. Somebody called out to me that there was a fine sight to be seen from the Tartar Wall. . . . Every street and lane from the Ch'ien Men Gate was now choked with troops of the relieving column, all British and American, as far as I could see, and already the pioneers attached to each battalion were leveling our rude defences to the ground in order to facilitate the passage of the guns and transport wagons. . . . Strange cries smote one's ears—all the cursing of armed men, whose discipline had been loosened by days of strain and the impossibility of manoeuvring. . . . The firing, in all truth, had increased enormously, and now rang out with a most tremendous roar. It always came from over there to the northwest, round about the Palace entrances. Evidently Chinese troops were holding all the Palace gates in great force, and for some reason wished to keep the relief columns at bay at all costs until nightfall . . . I soon understood. A mass of Indian infantry, with some machine-guns, had established themselves for hundreds of yards along this commanding height, among the old Chinese barricades, and were now firing as fast as they could down into the distant Palace enclosures."[5]

So as joy came to the foreign Legations, consternation settled down upon the court of the Manchus and upon the Empress Dowager. Fearing to face the tragedy her mad-

REFORM AND REACTION

ness had brought upon the dynasty, she made hasty plans for the escape of herself and the Emperor. They fled the city in the carts of the commonest of their people, the proud and haughty Old Buddha disguised in the coarse blue cotton of the humblest old woman of the land. She and her attendants, among them her favorite eunuch, fled to the west— to Tai Yuan-fu and thence to Sian-fu, China's ancient capital. The ministers were left with the unhappy duty of making peace as best they could with the nations she had outraged.

It is ever to the discredit of the West that the international troops looted the palaces and killed many Chinese, innocent as well as guilty. The troops after their long forced march from Tientsin crowding into the city were out of hand, the people who had been besieged for two months were bitter against the treatment they had received from China. The spirit of revenge took possession of many; before discipline was established, looting and carnage by foreigners and Chinese raged over the hapless city of Peking.

Dearly the outraged nations felt China should pay for the attack on their diplomatic representatives. The death sentence was passed upon eleven princes and ministers who had led in the Boxer movement, among them, Prince Tuan and Yu Hsien (the Governor who had had all the foreigners of his province massacred). Missions of apology for the murder of their diplomats were sent to Germany and Japan. The *Tsung li Yamen* (Department of Foreign Affairs) was reorganized, and the importation of arms forbidden. The amount of indemnity which China should pay the Western powers varied in their opinions. Some believed China should pay heavily for her international misdemeanor. The United States felt that if she paid as heavily as some desired she would be permanently bankrupt and would forfeit her national integrity.

In the end the bills for reparation were pared down, but even so, China was saddled with an indemnity of four hundred and fifty million taels (about three hundred million dollars), the interest upon which was guaranteed by the revenue from the Maritime Customs. The United States returned part of the indemnity due her in the form of funds to be used for the education in Western sciences of Chinese young men. A school was established in Peking called Tsing Hua College, familiarly known as the Indemnity School, where the boys sent up from the provinces were prepared for college and each year one hundred graduates were sent to America to study.

To safeguard the Legations in Peking from ever again facing destruction at the hands of the Chinese, a protocol was added to the treaty in which the Chinese agreed that walls could be erected around the Legation quarter and gave to each Treaty Power the right to maintain in Peking a Legation guard. To keep an approach open to the sea, the nations also insisted that they be allowed to guard the railroad to Tientsin whenever they deemed it necessary.

How far proud China had fallen since the days of Ch'ien Lung! And yet may not the seeds of this decline be found in the very course which he had adopted in the heyday of Manchu power? To Lord Macartney, he said, "We possess all things. I set no value on things strange or ingenious and have no use for your country's manufactures."[6] This view became the cornerstone of China's policy with the outside nations. Had she followed the liberal path of free intercourse practised by the Hans and the T'angs, might she not have entered easily into the latest phase of world culture—the modern industrial civilization and saved herself the revolution that was to come in only a few years after the Boxer debacle?

CHAPTER XX

THE EMPRESS DOWAGER AGAIN AND THE LAST MANCHU EMPEROR

EIGHTEEN months after the flight of the court from Peking, the Empress Dowager returned to her capital—a return in striking contrast to the flight. Now she and the Emperor, the young Empress and the concubines were accompanied by retainers, eunuchs, ladies in waiting and servants. Trains and carts were piled high with tribute which she had demanded from the provinces while she was in exile at the ancient capital of Sian. She herself, clothed in the richest satins and jewels, showed herself at the cities along the way to let the populace view their great Empress. And for part of the journey she rode on the hated foreigners' railroad train and enjoyed it immensely! Greeted by the highest officials of the country, she was led into the Forbidden City and to the old life of intrigue and extravagance. But not quite the old life. Convinced, maybe against her will, that neither the foreigner nor reform could be done away with, she adopted a more conciliatory attitude, in time even sponsoring in her edicts the reform cause.

But China was to have only a breathing space from war. She was soon disturbed by another conflict, the Russo-Japanese War of 1904-05, fought in Chinese territory. Before and during the Boxer Uprising Russia had been advancing her interests in Manchuria by building the Chinese Eastern Railway through Manchuria to Port Arthur and placing military guards along the road. The Powers called

China's and Russia's attention to these military guards, whereupon Russia promised to evacuate them in eighteen months after July, 1902. When that date rolled around, as there was no sign of evacuation, Japan, who had been eying with concern the movements of Russia, again objected, but she received no satisfaction. Tension between the two countries increased to the breaking point, and Japan and Russia went to war in 1904. In spite of the protest of the Manchu Government the war was actually fought on the soil of Manchuria.

Russian lost her Far Eastern fleet and her Grand Fleet. On land she fared no better; her army badly led and badly organized was pushed back by Japan. Through the good offices of President Roosevelt representatives of the two nations were brought together at Portsmouth, New Hampshire, and a treaty of peace was signed on September 5, 1905. Under its terms Japan, besides receiving a heavy indemnity, acquired the Russian lease of Port Arthur and her interests in the Liaotung Peninsula and the southern half of the island of Saghalien. Korea was left nominally independent, but Japan in 1910 quietly annexed it to her empire. China stood weakly by and viewed the shuffling of her outlying possessions.

This war had a tremendous effect upon China, continuing the process of her awakening begun by the earlier victory of Japan in the China-Japan War. Now she saw a European power defeated by an Asiatic one! What had made Japan so powerful that she could defeat a European power? Was it not that she adopted Western science in her education, modernized her army and navy, and put her finances and government in order? Might there not be something after all in these modern ideas? If Western methods could do all this for a little country like Japan, what might not such methods accomplish in China with her large population, her huge resources?

Even the Empress Dowager could no longer stand out against these arguments. She bowed before the Reform Movement and in 1905 and 1906 issued decrees ordaining that the educational system be modernized, the army and navy reorganized, and the Manchu garrisons disbanded, the laws and government renovated, and the growing of opium suppressed. A strangely familiar sound these edicts had! How much bitterness their publication must have brought to the soul of the hapless Emperor, lonely and discredited, living out his monotonous life on that small island. The Old Buddha sponsoring the program which had cost him his throne six years before!

These reforms were more than mere strokes of the vermilion pen. They were actually accomplished facts in those provinces where the officials and gentry were interested in the ideas of reform. The ancient examination system was abolished. In Peking and in some of the provincial capitals the examination halls were torn down. In most cases normal school buildings took their places. Under the Board of Education, schools multiplied: the Imperial University at Peking was started, and all over the empire colleges, normal schools, secondary and primary schools sprang up. The Minister of Education, aided by Chang Chih-tung, drew up a plan providing for a regular graduated system: colleges, middle schools and primary. A good many of the higher schools were opened but very few primary because of lack of funds and possibly even more because of lack of teachers.

As one wandered through the streets of the richer cities in those days one would find primary schools in old Buddhist temples. Coming along the streets you could hear a tremendous shouting and as you advanced nearer and peeked into the dimly lighted temple, you saw sitting below the dusty god a man with horn-rimmed spectacles, bent over a table. Before him at smaller tables sat the urchins of the neighborhood swaying back and forth on their stools singing the classics at the tops of their voices. These schools reached only a few of the hundreds of thousands of China's illiterate, but at least they were an attempt to carry out the edicts for education. At first there was no provision for the education of girls. But rich women became interested and began to open schools in their own houses. There was one edict for the benefit of girls, the abolishing of foot binding.

The edict for the modernization of the Army and Navy provided for two armies, the Northern and the Southern, altogether to be composed of thirty-six divisions of ten thousand men each, the whole to be completed by 1922. By 1908 the Army was in part organized, the Northern Army being about twice the size of the Southern. There was no uniformity in the troops as it had been left to each province to raise its own division. The Navy fared even worse than the Army. By 1908 there were only two cruisers of three thousand tons, one of four thousand, and a few smaller boats. And this was about twenty-five years after Tso Tsung-tung's memorial advocating a modern navy.

To carry out the edict regarding the reform of laws and government an Imperial Commission was sent to foreign countries to study forms of government. The next step was the promulgation of a program of preparation. There was to be a gradual progress toward constitutional government to be attained by 1915. In the meantime, National and Provincial Assemblies were to be called which were to be "nurseries" for the real Parliament of 1915. The "nurseries" held advisory power only. The National Assembly was to consist of two hundred members, half appointed by the throne and half by the viceroys and governors of the provinces. The National Assembly was to meet in 1910 and the provincial assemblies a year earlier.

Some of the provinces were up to schedule. In Chekiang, for example, a new building on a foreign model was completed and the assembly began its meetings with little power, however, but that of debate. But advisory power alone was not enough to satisfy the awakened part of China. Many Chinese both at home and abroad (where the most radical ones were forced to live) felt that the Manchu Dynasty did not wish to carry out a true reform but were only conceding enough to keep themselves on the throne.

Perhaps the brightest spot in all the picture was the condition of foreign trade. In spite of the disorders in the country and its bankruptcy, in spite of the Boxer attack on foreigners, China's international trade had steadily increased. The trade after it had become more regularized by the treaties of the 'forties and 'sixties is often spoken of as the new trade.[1]

Besides the increase in volume, the character of imports and exports had changed considerably. Some articles which had long held first place in China's foreign trade were losing out in the new trade. Tea, which in the 'sixties had comprised three-fifths of the value of all exports, by 1905 constituted only one-tenth. India had improved her tea and taken the trade from China, who followed the methods of centuries. For centuries China had led the world in the export of silk, her most unique product. It still was a leading item of export, but Japan was beginning to surpass because the Japanese were using scientific methods in dealing with disease among the silkworms and were willing to accommodate themselves to the demands of customers as to length of thread spun.

Other exports first appearing in the new trade were

bristles, cotton, principally to Japan, firecrackers—eight times as many in 1905 as in the 'sixties and all going to the United States—hemp, jute, matting, straw braid and furs. The fur trade shows a reversal of former days for now skins mostly from Mongolia and Manchuria were going to the United States whereas in the days of the *Co-hong* trade the western coast of America was sending large quantities to Canton.

Even greater differences perhaps are to be seen in the articles that China was importing. Opium was still on the list though in lesser amounts. It had been regularized in the 'sixties and thenceforth went in as legitimate cargo. Cotton cloth, sheetings and shirtings, constituted in the 'sixties twenty-one per cent and now forty per cent of all imports. Metals, copper for coinage, lead for packing tea, tin for making tin foil for idol money in religious ceremonies, iron and steel—mostly old iron discards of Western markets—comprised ten per cent of all imports.

Cigarettes, unknown in the 'sixties, were by 1905 valued at four million taels, one-half coming from the United States. Kerosene oil was another new import. Beginning in the 'sixties it had reached some importance by the 'seventies. At this time it came entirely from America but later Russia, Sumatran and Borneo oils were introduced so that by 1905 American oil comprised only fifty-two per cent of the whole quantity imported. The trade in oil was large for it was a great boon in a land which had nothing but peanut oil or tallow candle. America's share in 1905 reached one hundred and fifty-seven million gallons.

Rice, strangely enough, also appeared on the import list. As China was able to sell her finest grades to Japan for a high price she exported these and then imported poorer grades for the mass of her people who could not afford to buy the better grades. Lumber—always deficient in amount

THE LAST MANCHU EMPEROR

and that little used recklessly long ago—was now being bought in large quantities from foreign countries.

This increase in foreign trade was of great benefit to China during the impoverished last years of the Manchus. The Maritime Customs Service, organized during the Tai Ping Rebellion, had all these years functioned admirably and had brought in a goodly income to the financially embarrassed dynasty. It had been ample to keep up interest on China's foreign obligations (to which specific allocations had been made in various treaty arrangements) and to hand over a surplus to the central government. This surplus, if wisely used, would have been sufficient to have brought the Manchus out of their difficulties but much of it was wasted in official squeeze and in buying the favor of this or that power or of some influential individual. Therefore in spite of the lucrative trade which might have been the strength of the dynasty the Manchus were rapidly losing in power and prestige.

The Empress Dowager did not live long enough to see the total collapse of the dynasty, since she died in 1908. On the ninth of November, the Emperor Kuang Hsü died and on the next day the Empress Dowager. In many circles the opinion was expressed that the old Empress so hated her nephew and so feared the possibility of his gaining the throne and overturning her policy that she had seen to it that he should die before she did. Well may history ask the question: Did poor hectored Kuang Hsü possess a latent ability that might have been of benefit to China had not the Empress overpowered him?

The Empress Dowager was buried as extravagantly and regally as she had lived. One hundred and twenty bearers carried her catafalque the ninety miles to the Eastern Tombs where her tomb stood waiting for her, built at an expediture of eight million taels. Within, "sacrificial vessels of carved jade, massive vases and incense burners of gold and silver" adorned the mortuary chamber, the richly jeweled couch to receive the coffin and the carved figures of serving maids and eunuchs who stand forever in attendance." Her funeral cost one and a quarter to one and a half million taels while the Emperor's cost only four hundred and sixty thousand. After the closing of the tomb the conveyance of the Empress' ancestral tablet was scarcely less impressive. When the tomb is closed, the spirit of the departed is supposed to descend into the tablet so it must be carried with great ceremony in a gorgeous chariot attended with a large escort back to the Forbidden City to the temple of the dynasty's ancestors. And there it took its place among the tablets of the Emperors and their consorts of the Manchu Dynasty, to be worshiped by the living "Son of Heaven."

Powerful to the last, the Empress Dowager had decreed that a child of three, Hsuan T'ung, now Pu Yi of Manchuria, should ascend the Dragon Throne. "The Little Emperor," as he has been styled by the West, became Emperor with his father, Prince Ch'un, as regent. But things went badly during the Regency. Never before had there been so many Manchus in power, never before had the throne acted so independently—the court extravagant and profligate, the eunuchs wielding much authority, the people neglected and heavily taxed. Though outwardly everything seemed the same, there was beneath the surface a discontent among many classes. The Chinese official was dissatisfied. Since 1908, the beginning of the Regency, the Manchus had departed from their policy of dividing the high offices between Manchus and Chinese. Manchus alone were holding the highest offices in the state and holding them for the very definite purpose of reaping the spoils. Squeeze was in higher percentage than ever before in every department of the government. The princes of the blood were vying with one another in the accumulation of wealth; officials and eunuchs were lining their pockets at the expense of the public.

The Chinese high officials had either been dismissed or had retired voluntarily—the customary mode used to express disapproval. Yuan Shih-kai, the man who had saved the life of the Empress Dowager from the hands of the reformers, was among those who was retired. The Regent, Prince Ch'un, because he considered Yuan Shih-kai had betrayed his brother, the former Emperor, into the hands of the Empress Dowager, virtually dismissed him. Yuan, realizing his ignominious situation, retired to his ancestral home, pleading a sore leg. The Regent with less reason eliminated one Chinese official after another from high state offices, thus foolishly creating wide displeasure among the Chinese at a time when the Manchu Dynasty sorely needed their support.

The railway schemes of the dynasty provoked the greatest antagonism in the provinces. The provinces objected to the Central Board of Control of Railways. They were bitterly opposed to the government's policy of accepting foreign loans, with the attendant privilege of foreign administration of the lines. The provinces wished to finance, build and manage the roads in their own territories, pointing to the Shanghai-Hangchow line which had been financed by local capital, as an example of what could be done. Chang Chih-tung, favoring a scheme by which the profits of the railroads should be divided between Peking and the provinces, unfortunately died in 1909. After that matters went from bad to worse. The provinces of Hunan and Hupeh demanded that the provincial governments should be allowed to approve of all loan agreements before they were made by the central government. In Szechuen the arguments about railroad building and control became so bitter that they grew into riots against the dynasty. Peking was unable to cope with these various disturbances throughout the empire.

Again as so many times in China's history the people's suffering and discontent became so great that they felt that the encumbent of the Dragon Throne was showing his inability to govern the country. High Heaven was displeased! It was time for a change. Only this time, instead of a military leader overpowering the Emperor and setting up a dynasty of his own, the voices of the reformers were heard and the people revolted not only against an emperor and a dynasty but against the old imperial system.

CHAPTER XXI

Reform Changes into Revolution

CAUSES for the revolt of the people of China in 1911 against the Manchu Dynasty were many. The dissatisfaction of imperial officials and the complaints of the provinces against the central government were only surface manifestations of a deeper discontent seething underneath. It was not only a revolt against a dynasty grown corrupt but a revolt against an autocratic system which had long pressed hard upon the masses of the people. The fact that at length the common people joined in open revolt was due to new forces which had been at work for some time breaking the old mold of China's civilization. The infiltration of new ideas was instigating revolt against ancient custom and against the ancient philosophy of life.

These revolutionary ideas in the thinking of China were being developed and disseminated by the modern educated youth of the land. Since the 'seventies, as we know, students had been going to Europe and America to study in the universities. Since the edicts of 1905 the Chinese had been establishing schools of the Western type in China. And the Mission Boards in England and America, realizing that China was entering upon a new era, seized their opportunity and redoubled their efforts to Christianize China, sending teachers and money for the establishment of schools. All these students were being taught to look to the future, rather than to the past—a doctrine contrary to the fundamental principle of Confucianism. They were coming to believe that the individual had liberties and rights—a death blow to the very spirit of the ancient system, which made the individual subservient to family and clan. The idea of individual liberty was crowding out that of exaltation of the family; democracy was undermining belief in the Emperor's high position as the "Son of Heaven." From the student class these ideas began filtering down through the masses—those ninety-five per cent illiterate of China. Unconscious though most of it was, there was developing a new viewpoint. Everywhere there was a reaching out for some new thing. Some desired a modern education; some, a constitutional form of government; some, leather shoes.

A new conception of matters international was growing too. Since the beginning of the twentieth century many Chinese had been going to Japan. The distance was shorter, the expense less, language difficulties fewer than in going to Europe, England or America. This neighbor of theirs was a kind of hero to these students, for Japan, accepting modern ideas in government and education, had been able in a short time to beat both China and Russia in warfare, and to throw off extraterritoriality and other restrictions of the West. It is not strange that these Chinese youths returned to China determined that their country should follow the example of Japan. Little did they realize that the situation in their country was a far more complicated one than that in the small and unified country of Japan. To Westernize China meant the economic and social change of four hundred million people, scattered over a vast country divided by mountains and without even the connecting tie of a common spoken language. To gain a conception of the magnitude of the task which the reformers were setting for themselves one needs only to glance at China as she was in that year of 1911.

As soon as the coast and the treaty ports, where were

REFORM CHANGES INTO REVOLUTION 279

berthed the great ships of Western countries, were left behind one seemed to have stepped back centuries into another civilization. The mass of the people were going about the selfsame tasks in the selfsame way as had their forefathers. China's rich men and scholars were living after the same pattern as had their forefathers for generations, even centuries.

In quiet corners all over China the houses of the rich and of the scholars stood, filled with porcelains and bronzes, works of art done by the masters of the T'ang and Ming Dynasties. We went one evening in that year to a dinner given at the house of a Peking literatus. The head of the family, a man in his fifties, honored us with his presence. During the meal we were served tea in delicate cups which our host told us, with the pride of a collector, were made in the time of K'ang Hsi. After dinner in the front rooms of the house he showed us collections of vases, bronze, amber and jade. And then from a drawer he brought out scrolls which he unwound, and a servant was called to hang them from a great beam of the ceiling. These were paintings of scenery with a bit of poetry in exquisitely done Chinese characters written in the upper corner. The paintings and poetry were both the work of our host.

The dwellings of such men as this host of ours were surrounded by high walls which shut out the life of China's millions. In some building facing an inner court the men often sat at their library tables—perfect pieces of the cabinet-maker's art—turning the pages of the old classics, meditating over the philosophy of Confucius and the Neo-Confucianists—those philosophies which emphasized the realization of nature within one's self, nature something to be adjusted to, not to be conquered.

If perchance they lifted their eyes, on the pearl-colored paper panes of their library windows they saw silhouetted the exquisite curved roof line of the building across the court, or the intricately carved love-pheasant which adorned the ridgepole. All around them was beauty.

If they became tired, they could stroll through court after court without ever stepping into the street until they reached their own gardens, places of studied beauty. There, in teahouses overlooking rockeries and miniature rivers and bridges, they sipped tea made from the choicest spring leaf tips, scented with jasmine or rosebuds. As they sipped their tea, these rich men discussed the things that interested them: a passage from Confucius or a bit of Tu Fu's poetry.

But their charming houses in 1911 were, as they had always been, unheated except for a charcoal brazier or a *kang*—a brick platform with a small fire underneath it. The people slept and sat on it for warmth. Wind blew through loosely fitted windows and doors, matting did not keep out the dampness of stone floors and in consequence even the rich of China shivered in their padded silks and fur garments and suffered from chilblains and disease.

With a few noticeable exceptions, the women of such households led meager lives. Very few of them could read; work was considered beneath the wealthy and high born. Rarely did custom allow them to go beyond the women's quarters. So they gambled and gossiped their days away in the courts set aside for the women—those farthest removed from the street. Amahs made them beautiful for their lords and relieved them of the care of their children. Theirs were lives of idleness and emptiness until middle or old age put them in positions of importance in the family. The head ladies of the patriarchal families, then, were busy managing the servants, attending to the ancestral ceremonies and teaching manners to the young children.

China in 1911 was a land with no middle class so that the contrast between the lives of the people of leisure and those others, the workers, was great indeed. The mass of the Chinese people lived lives little better than beasts of burden. Of them Hu Shih says:

> "Let all apologists for the spiritual civilization of the East reflect on this. What spirituality is there in a civilization which tolerates such a terrible form of human slavery as the 'ricksha coolie? Do we seriously believe that there can be any spiritual life left in those poor human beasts of burden who run and toil and sweat under that peculiar bondage of slavery which knows neither the minimum wage nor any limit of working hours? Do we really believe that the life of a 'ricksha coolie is more spiritual or more moral than that of the American workman who rides to and from his work in his own motor-car, who takes his whole family outing and picnicking on Sundays in distant parks and woods, who listens to the best music of the land on the radio almost for no cost, and whose children are educated in schools equipped with the most modern library and laboratory."[1]

Beyond the gates of the rich the people worked far into the night. In all the vast expanse of China there were practically no machines to do the work in the fields. Neither were there animals sufficient to do this work. Men not only took the place of the machines, they took the place of draft animals. The great quantities of rice and grain needed to feed four hundred million people were raised literally by hand. Early and late the peasants labored. They used homemade plows pulled by a water buffalo, a mule or a man. The rice fields were planted by the men, women and children standing knee deep in slimy mud. When the rice and millet were ready to harvest, the peasants went into the fields with rude sickles to harvest them. Then they beat the grain on the edge of crude boxes or broke it with flails to separate the grain heads from the stalk. This slow method of agriculture required eighty-five per cent of the people working from dawn until dark.

Neither the peasant nor the coolie had a chance at the richness of life. Those long hours of animal labor dulled their faculties past the point of enjoyment or the ability to learn. Even the children, compelled to work if the family was to be kept from starvation, had no energy or time to study, even if there had been schools for them, which there were not.

The peasants, as in the days two thousand years before Christ, lived in huts made of mud. Only a few had brick houses with tiled roofs. But even in these the floors were of hard-packed dirt. A rough table, a bench, two or three stools, and a bed in which the whole household slept, were the possessions of the average family. In the south, the bed was an unfinished wooden frame with a latticed string spring, or in many cases no spring at all—simply a series of boards. In the north it was a brick platform, the *kang,* heated by flues running from an open fire at one end. There was no other heat in these millions upon millions of peasant homes, except that under the cooking pot. This fire was often fed with grasses, as long ago the hillsides had been stripped of their trees. At night, home-made drip candles burned before the tablets of the ancestors, and a chimneyless lamp with a two-inch bowl filled with peanut oil gave out a smoky fitful light.

In the towns and cities, the conditions were much the same. In some respects they were worse, because of the overcrowding. In every town and city in southern China tiny, dirt-floored huts, with the fronts taken away during the day, faced each other across narrow streets, often so narrow that the sun never penetrated. In the north the streets were sometimes wider, the little cubicles of houses

REFORM CHANGES INTO REVOLUTION

were of brick, but the interiors were much the same as in the South.

In the shops men squatted upon the dirt floors or sat on stools, plying their trades. They hammered pots and pans out of sheets of copper and tin and welded them together over an open forge. They wove baskets slowly and painstakingly out of reeds and thin strips of bamboo. They wove silk and cloth on hand looms such as had been used for centuries. A man sat above the weaver and with his fingers pulled strings which lifted various strands of the warp, allowing the weaver to throw his shuttle over and under, thus creating a pattern.

In many shops the beautiful old handicrafts of China were carried on—lacquer, cloisine, pottery, took shape under the delicate hands of the workers. But as Abel Barnard says, "The arts had perished, only the handicrafts continued like branches on a fallen oak, which put forth green, without knowing the tree is dead."

By the majority of the population these living conditions were taken for granted as something inherent in life which could not be avoided. *Mei-yu-fah-dz*—it cannot be helped—was the accepted version of life. But among the students there was a growing feeling that such meager life was unbearable and something that might be remedied.

Aside from the students there was another group, a group that was perhaps even more powerful than the students. These were the exiled sons of China wandering in foreign lands with a price upon their heads—Kang Yu-wei, the man who had led the young Emperor Kuang Hsü to launch the reform movement of the Hundred Days, Liang Chi-chao, Sun Yat-sen and many others. They wandered from community to community of expatriated Chinese in Europe, America and elsewhere, influencing them to back the reformers in the mother country and raising money to send back to China for the day when the Revolution should break.

Of these leaders Sun Yat-sen became the most radical—an open revolutionist. Born in a little village of South China near Canton, a precocious child, full of questions, which the village schoolmaster, with no knowledge except the classics, was unable to answer, he early rose in revolt against old Chinese custom. The cries of his little sister when her feet were bound made him beg his mother to undo them. The distress of his family made to pay taxes on land they had already sold caused him to lose faith in the government at Peking. When he was about thirteen years old, he went to Honolulu to join an older brother who was in business there. He saw in the iron girder of the steamship the symbol of Western power and his soul was stirred by the orderliness of law.

After three years of study in Honolulu he went back to his native village, but when he tried to show the youths of the town the ineffectiveness of the idols by breaking off a finger of one, the village would have none of him, and he was exiled, a disgrace to his family. He went to the British city of Hongkong where he studied in a medical college, taking his degree in 1892. While at Hongkong his revolutionary ideas took shape in a Chinese declaration of independence, "Divine Right does not last forever."

> "No longer shall we reverence the throne
> The Son of Heaven is incompetent
> His officers are corrupt
> His rule is an abomination
> He shall give way to the rule of the people
> No longer shall we reverence the throne."[2]

He also organized the secret society, Dare-to-Dies, which attempted an attack upon the Canton *Yamen* that ended in failure and Sun was obliged in 1895 to leave the country, wandering to Hawaii and later to London. In London he was kidnaped by the Chinese Legation, but through the kindly offices of some English friends he was released.

For the next fifteen years he lived abroad, going from place to place, always working on his plan for revolution, before him always the vision of his people harassed and downtrodden by unjust laws and customs and by a cruel foreign dynasty. He saw the overthrow of the dynasty as the first step in obtaining justice and liberty for his countrymen. During his wanderings he absorbed ideas of constitutional government, republicanism, socialism, what not. He was patriotic, impulsive, magnetic, visionary. Visiting the Chinese communities scattered over the globe, in Japan, the Philippines, Siam, Singapore, South America, the Hawaiian Islands, the United States, he spoke untiringly of revolution and change until these communities made up of Chinese full of the initiative which had carried them to foreign lands for a bigger opportunity than they found in their own country, were a vital unit of rebellion. These foreign-living Chinese had acquired money, many of them fortunes, and from this source came much financial aid to the movement. Up to 1911 neither students nor revolutionary-inclined patriots had strength enough to stage a revolution, but suddenly all these various bits of unrest fused into revolution. A chance happening brought action.

On October 9, 1911, a bomb in a revolutionary house in Wuchang exploded, forcing a band of revolutionaries to stage a revolution in order to save their lives. Acting quickly, they captured the three cities, Hankow, Wuchang, Hanyang. Li Yuan-hung was their chief military commander. Revolution had begun. The Manchus were not ready to meet the situation any more than they had been ready in the 'fifties and 'sixties to meet the Tai Pings.

There was little warfare or destruction—some fighting at Nanking, the burning of Hankow. It was not war between contending sides; simply a series of unchecked local revolts. Each province in turn deserted the dynasty and alligned itself on the revolutionary side. What happened in Hangchow, the capital of Chekiang, where I was living at the time, is typical.

News of the happenings at Hankow and along the Yangtse threw the city into a panic for the populace feared such destruction as had always made the memory of the Tai Ping Rebellion a horror. With the first news of the fall of Hankow, the wealthy families closed their houses and sought safety in the foreign settlement at Shanghai. At news of each new victory for the Revolutionists the middle and poorer classes packed their worldly goods and fled to the country districts. The city was possessed by panic; the station platform was piled to the ceiling with household goods; the people themselves waited hours that lengthened into days to get a place on the overflowing cars. Through the crowded canals of the city the native boats crowded with frightened people moved slowly out into the country. The streets and alleys were filled with fleeing people, terror on their faces. Then the city streets became quiet, almost deserted. At the sound of our footfalls on the stone flaggings as we passed down the empty streets, a door would partly open and a scared woman's face peer out to ask the news. Only the poorest remained; fully three-fourths of the population had gone.

Late one afternoon a telegram told us that the government arsenal at Shanghai had been taken. What would be the course of events in Hangchow? There was nothing to do but await the move of the Revolutionists. The city gates were closed, the city as quiet as a city of the dead. At three in the morning a big blaze leaped up in the south of the city.

The Revolutionists were in charge and had fired the provincial governor's *yamen*. When dawn came, a steady firing of rifles began and the heavy booming of cannon. The Revolutionists were bombarding the Manchu city, that garrison placed there by the Manchus two hundred and fifty years before when they first came. On the streets a few men with white bands tied around their arms (the sign of the Revolutionists) moved about. At nightfall the firing ceased; the Manchu garrison had succumbed. Thus was revolution accomplished.

The next day we were allowed to visit the Manchu city. How those fierce Manchus, the mighty, had fallen! With their women and children the Manchu men, the so-called warriors of the garrison, the defenders of Manchu authority, stood about, quiet but sullen, no vestige of military glory about them. Their arms—bows and arrows of the seventeenth century—used when their forefathers first conquered the Mings, were piled before them by Revolutionary soldiers. This had been a bloodless revolution. There was no destruction except at the *yamen* of the Manchu General. There the walls were torn with shots and the furniture was broken to pieces, but there were no personal effects about. The General and his family had escaped before the advent of the Revolutionists! And the garrison had surrendered with scarcely an effort. Worn out and effete, it was typical of the dynasty.

Scarcely three weeks since the bomb had exploded at Wuchang and (except for Nanking) all south of the Yangtse was lost to the government at Peking.

Province by province, city by city, not waiting for any national program, the local governments went about the business of putting their houses in order. The Revolutionists put a city under military rule and armed pickets patrolled the streets. Gradually as the days and weeks passed and no slaughter nor violence occurred, the people who had fled filtered back into the cities and went about their old occupations. The new buildings which had been erected for the Provincial Assemblies became busy places as the new governments were put in order. Some outward signs there were of the new order. The queue, inflicted upon the Chinese by the Manchus, was by decree abolished. The upper class conformed, but the coolies, inhibited by fear and superstition, clung to this long-established custom. Suppose the Manchus should come back! But the Revolutionists were firm. Soldiers armed with large shears stood at the city gates and on important thoroughfares. A snap of the shears as a man with a queue passed, and the mark of bondage to the Manchus disappeared.

And the Manchu garrison, this little city within a city—what was to become of it? What was to become of these men, women and children who were not accustomed to work but only to idleness, living upon the rice and silver doles from the court of Peking? Some tried to get work in the Chinese city. But they were not used to work, and then they were Manchus, who, only so short a time before, were the oppressors of those from whom now they sought aid. There was no work for them, so they sold their personal effects to buy rice. Those who had money left for Manchuria, their ancient home. Many died of want. The Manchu garrisons disappeared. In many cities the land was taken to build modern cities for the Chinese, broad streets, two-story brick buildings after the manner of the West. These Revolutionists believed not in the old ways.

While the provinces were thus engaged, much was happening in Peking. Very early it became evident to the Manchu Dynasty that they were unable to cope with the situation. They must look to some Chinese as they had looked to Tseng Kuo-fan in the Tai Ping revolt. Where was there an able

REFORM CHANGES INTO REVOLUTION 289

one? Finally in desperation they called in Yuan Shih-kai, the man whom the Regent had exiled from the court three years earlier. He hesitated, but finally obeyed the call of the dynasty. It was already too late to try force against the Revolutionists. He resorted to negotiations, hoping that the moderates in the Kuomintang (People's Party) would take a stand for a monarchy even if they insisted that the Manchus must go. But he found them determined, not only to do away with the dynasty, but with monarchy; nothing but a republic would satisfy the Revolutionists.

While Yuan Shih-kai sought to piece the shreds of monarchy together, the leaders of the Kuomintang were meeting in Shanghai and laying plans for establishing a republic in the Yangtse Valley. With the vitality given to them by the sudden appearance of the returned exile, Sun Yat-sen, in the midst, they came out boldly and declared themselves a Republic on January 1, 1912, with Nanking as their capital and Sun Yat-sen their Provisional President. Yuan Shih-kai saw now he could do nothing but advise the Manchus to abdicate. This they did on February 11, 1912, with the promise that the "Little Emperor" should live at the palace in the Forbidden City and the Imperial family should be paid a yearly allowance. Yuan was now left in charge of affairs at Peking and the country was split in two once more. In the old capital of Peking sat Yuan Shih-kai, the head of the government. In the new and yet old capital of Nanking sat Sun Yat-sen as president. Again conservative north faced radical south. Could they come together?

Yuan wanted a constitutional monarchy, Sun and the radicals of the Kuomintang wanted a republic. The Kuomintang found that without Yuan they could not get the allegiance of the north. Clearly a compromise was the only way out. The compromise was made. Yuan agreed to accept the Nanking constitution; the Kuomintang agreed to accept Yuan Shih-kai as Provisional President. Yuan insisted upon Peking for the capital. Doctor Sun retired from the presidency and assumed the office of Director of Railways. The Republic was proclaimed and received the recognition of foreign countries. The dragon flag was put into the discard and the flag of the republic was unfurled— five stripes, a color for each of the five peoples who swore allegiance to it: red for the Chinese, yellow for the Manchus, blue for the Mongolians, white for the Mohammedans (of the Northwest Marches), black for the Tibetans.

It had been easy to create these outward forms of a republic, but far more difficult did it prove to create the spirit within. It has often been pointed out that China has always been democratic and therefore it should not be difficult for her to swing into a republican form of government. But it was a different democracy from ours of the West. The family, craftsman's guild, and the village were self-governing units, but they had never united and sent delegates to form a representative government. Theirs was the pure democracy of the Greek city-states or the New England town, where the units were small enough for all citizens to meet and consider any matter. The ideas of representation and obedience to a majority were unknown to Chinese thought. Obedience to father, or elder brother, or loyalty to friend were all habitual. Loyalty to country and obedience to laws made by a representative assembly were new ideas to China. Like the Greeks their ideal was a state governed by the ruler and his assistants, the educated men who were guided by the restraints of gentlemanly conduct. The masses had never been considered. The conception of a democracy based on the participation of all the people could not be grasped in a moment simply by declaring a republic. There had never been choice of officials by the method of election.

REFORM CHANGES INTO REVOLUTION 291

How the First Parliament was got together is hard to say. There could have been no voting for representatives as we understand it. But men from each province were there. When I visited Parliament in 1913 I saw delegations from the different provinces—even from Mongolia. They could not understand one another's speech so their meetings were much like an international conference with the necessary interpreters.

Yuan Shih-kai bore the title of president, but his ideal was a constitutional monarchy, he its strong executive, a virtual dictator. The Parliament, composed mostly of Kuomintang members, was naturally hostile to Yuan and his ideal. Conflict resulted. Parliament refused to approve of the loan Yuan wanted to get from a consortium of foreign bankers; Yuan made the loan on his own responsibility. President Yuan made government appointments; Parliament opposed them. As time went on Yuan was forced more and more to act on his own initiative. Parliament, besides obstructing his schemes for reorganization, was unable to agree on any plan. Sun Yat-sen, assuming the leadership of the radical wing of the Kuomingtang, induced them to start another revolution in 1913. Its failure forced Sun to take refuge in Japan.

Yuan now increased his power. He ordered the arrest of those radicals in Parliament who had not already fled south. The President now ruled as a benign dictator. "His power was firm, his military governors kept order in the provinces, the recrudence of opium was suppressed, education was fostered, government finances were improved, and trade prospered. One of the best indications of confidence in him was a domestic loan made by Chinese bankers."[3] The great majority of the nation was satisfied. The masses, as always, wanted only peace and order and a chance to work.

It was not a democratic government but, in the opinion of many, one far more suited to a country where ninety per cent of the people were illiterate.

Only the comparatively small group of Revolutionists was not. They made the dictator's path a hard one.

In addition, affairs in other parts of the world were increasing Dictator Yuan's difficulties. The Great War was now in progress, and Japan, one of the Allies, seized the German concessions in Shantung Province and the leased territory at Kiaochow Bay. Yuan Shih-kai protested over this seizure of China's territory without taking China into consideration. Resenting his stand, the Japanese militarists who were then in power went still farther in their aggressive plan and in May, 1915, presented the now famous twenty-one demands upon China, arranged in five groups. The first demanded that China recognize Japan's right in Shantung; the second, that she do the same in Manchuria and Inner Mongolia; the third, that she give the Japanese special rights in the Han Yeh Ping Company, an iron mining and smelting company owned jointly by Japan and China; the fourth, that China lease to Japan harbors in Fukien Province and that China herself should lease no bays or harbors along the coast without the consent of Japan. The fifth group demanded that China's Army and Navy should be trained by Japanese experts and that her finances should be reorganized by advisers from Japan. She was to allow Japan to open schools throughout China and Manchuria and in them to teach the Japanese language and to allow the Japanese to send missionaries to China. It was felt by many that an ulterior motive lurked behind such a request as China had the same religions as Japan, except the state religion of worship to the Emperor. And finally, China shall first consult with and obtain consent of Japan before she can enter into an agreement with another power for making loans, for railway contracts and harbor works in Fukien Province.

President Yuan Shih-kai realized that these demands, especially the fifth, if agreed to by China, made her virtually a vassal of Japan. Europe was too busy with the war to come to his aid. What was he to do? He surprised the world by publishing these supposedly secret demands. The United States, the only great power not distracted by the war, was shocked, but took no strong stand. President Yuan had played his last card. With the threat of war from Japan and no country in all the world to protest, he was forced to sign the first four groups. The fifth, which was the most humiliating, he managed to leave for future negotiations. That was the best he could do. But this poor best placed him in a yet more awkward position. The Militarists in Japan, because he refused to sign the whole document, became his personal enemies, and his own countrymen, because he had signed the first four groups, hated him, unable to see that hopelessly divided as they were, they could not stand against Japan's demands.

Then Dictator Yuan made his fatal mistake. He decided to increase his power and make himself Monarch Yuan. What was his motive? Was it simply love of personal power, or was it clan spirit actuating him, the aggrandizement of his clan, the perpetuation of his power for his family, or did he feel that a limited monarchy was better adapted to the country's needs? None will know. At any rate, the cry of the Revolutionists had been a republic and they were in no mind to give up their cherished ideal. Liang Chi-chao in his writings shows that he thought Yuan had betrayed the Revolutionists. Scarcely anywhere was there any sympathy with Monarch Yuan Shih-kai! Some of his ministers resigned; Yunnan Province revolted and none came to his support in putting it down. He gave up the plan and in the spring of 1916 died suddenly, whether from disappointment and chagrin or from sickness or in some more violent way no one knows.

Li Yuan-hung, the military hero of the Revolution and Vice-President under Yuan Shih-kai, now became President and Parliament returned. Li was a most exemplary man of the moderate reform type, but neither political leader nor statesman. He could manage neither Parliament nor the military governors of the provinces who since the Revolution had shared control of the provinces with the civil governors. As time went on some of the military governors became stronger than others and got control over several provinces. *Tuchuns* they came to be called, or, in English war lords. Early in Li's administration their power began to be felt. Parliament produced a draft constitution but as this was unacceptable to the northern war lords they compelled the President in the early summer of 1917 to dismiss Parliament. Li, of course, was criticized for his weakness in thus playing into their hands. President Li, in weariness apparently over the whole thing, resigned in favor of the Vice-President and retired to private life.

China's first two presidents had failed.

The spring and summer of 1917 was a time of great confusion. China declared herself on the side of the Allies in the Great War. This decision was largely due to the fact that the United States had come out on the side of the Allies and many of the young Chinese wished to follow her example. A more important reason was that China wished to sit at the peace table when the disposition of Shantung should be decided. In the midst of this rapid change of presidents, friends of the Manchu Dynasty, in the middle of the summer, staged a coup d'etat, and the Little Emperor was placed on the throne of his ancestors. He sat there just twelve days, then was dethroned.

REFORM CHANGES INTO REVOLUTION

After Li's retirement, the northern war lords kept up the fiction of a government at Peking, making and unmaking presidents at will, controlling the remnant of Parliament. They carried on by borrowing from Japan, giving as security customs revenue and salt taxes, even land and tobacco taxes. First one and then another war lord pulled the strings that worked the puppet President and Parliament. Whatever of government, law and order existed (and there was considerable) was the work of provincial and local officials.

In the south, Kuomintang members, whom President Yuan Shih-kai had expelled from the National Parliament, met at Canton, set up a government which they claimed to be the rightful government of China as the north, they felt, had repudiated the spirit of the Revolution. In 1921 they elected Sun Yat-sen their president. Again the north and south, so different in temperament and philosophy, were politically divided. Canton and Peking went each its own way. Though the outside world recognized Peking as China's capital, it served the country little except as a base from which to carry on diplomatic correspondence.

Though the reform in government was meeting with vicissitudes, there were many changes evident in the social life of the country. The lunar calendar, which had seen very little change since the time of the Chous, was legally abolished and the solar one of the Western world was adopted. Officially it was followed, but it was hard for the masses to give up the old accustomed holidays. The student class began to keep one day in seven—the Western Sunday—as a day for recreation. But the mass of the Chinese continued to go about their business every day of the year, except China's New Year, as they had always done.

Among the masses of the people the only sign for a long time of a new order was certain surface changes. Often trivial and even ludicrous were the innovations: bits of

Western costume, foreign hats and leather shoes, knitted socks and the Boston garter outside the trousers, strange knitted creations worn by the women as hats to satisfy their craving for Western accessories, scented soaps, perfumes. Foreign clocks and watches had a large sale. Other commodities they bought affected the home life of the people. Kerosene oil was shipped to China now in ever-increasing quantities. A Western firm had invented a tiny lamp they sold for five cents. These with surprising rapidity began to take the place of the smoking, chimneyless oil lamps and the dip candles. Students and workers could now work at night without injury to their eyes. In one city the makers of firecrackers were given so much oil each evening. According to their contracts they could cease working only when the oil gave out and the lamps went out.

There were other changes that cut to the very root of China's social system. Women and girls were abandoning their seclusion and walking on the street. Many in the more advanced cities were obeying the edict of 1903 against foot binding. They were demanding the chance to be educated on an equality with the boys.

Modern education now became very popular. Provincial officials and the rich gentry pushed it in their various communities. In the capitals of the provinces normal schools both for men and women were started in order to train teachers for the much needed elementary schools which could not be opened because of the lack of teachers. These schools were boarding schools and the students were free from all expense. Chemistry, physics, algebra, geometry, English, were made a part of the curricula. The desire for a new code of laws modeled after the code of the West brought law schools. So great was the enthusiasm for modern education that here and there trade schools were started. In Hangchow, for example, a silk culture school was opened in a former house. A few girls (city girls, probably, for all country girls were well versed in the art) studied the culture of the silkworm. These students were very modern—wore their hair cut short—a great change.

The mission schools (elementary and middle) and colleges conducted by English and Americans became increasingly popular during this period. Many non-Christian families put aside their religious prejudices for the sake of the better training in English and modern sciences, which these institutions offered over the native schools.

Suddenly the young people of China seemed aflame with the cry of freedom from the old customs. Girls began demanding equal rights with men. They asked for the ballot in 1912, seven years before the Nineteenth Amendment gave women the franchise in the United States. Mere catchwords these—suffrage, even for men, was only a name. The one opportunity so far for voting had been in the choice of members for Parliament. It was well known that no real election had been held. In fact, in a country where only five per cent could read and write, exercise of the ballot was impossible. Other demands they were making. Men and girls were asking the right to choose whom they would marry and, the privilege of setting up a separate home—apart from the patriarchal home. They felt that they could not endure its minute rules and strict discipline.

Still the bedrock of China's old civilization held. The whole fabric of society was woven out of the human relationships of father and son, husband and wife, older brother and younger brother. This family life was tenaciously rooted in the people's thought. The patriarchal family and the village remained the governing units. It was they who furnished the discipline which kept peace and order in spite of a weakened central authority and the cry of the Radicals for change.

CHAPTER XXII

Students and War Lords

DURING these years of reform and revolution political upheaval was not the only matter to engage the thought of the thinking men of China. Hand in hand with the governmental reforms and the changes of the social life of the country went a Renaissance in intellectual life.

This movement had its beginnings many years before the days of the Republic. We remember that there had been a Renaissance of thought in the eighteenth century during the early virile days of the Manchu Dynasty but that the criticism then introduced was purely academic. The scholars at that time did not bring their criticism to bear on the content of the literature. They were simply interested in discovering which documents were real and which were spurious. And also there was no study of the humanities. Later on in the Manchu Dynasty there developed another Renaissance movement when Kang Yu-wei, Liang Chi-chao and others dared to criticize the content of the classics and to interpret Confucius as a reformer. These were the reformers who influenced the young Emperor, Kuang Hsü, to promulgate the edicts of the Hundred Days of reform. In the reaction which followed their books were banned. The idea of criticizing the sacred classics was intolerable to all but these few in the days of 1898.

Now, twenty years later, a third movement arose. The books that were banned in 1898 were reprinted and many scholars now considered them mild in their revolutionary doctrines. A new literature was appearing which brought criticism to bear on the very ideas of the classics, holding nothing too sacred to be investigated. China's modern scholars sought to turn their searchlight of criticism on the civilization of both East and West and to compare them, a thing which was foreign to every previous conception in China.

These modern scholars were not content to limit their investigations to the time-honored subjects of philosophy and theories of government but also studied social and economic conditions both in China and in the West. They invited men like Bertram Russell and John Dewey to come to China to lecture—the first time that scholars of China had invited scholars of the West to come and explain their philosophies. Translations were made of many Western books, even the most radical. This movement modern Chinese scholars call the Renaissance or New Thought Movement.

One of the most outstanding of this group of modern Chinese philosophers is Hu Shih, quotations from whose writings have already been given. It is he who has probed deep to find out what were the relative spiritual values of the Eastern and the Western civilizations. In a lecture on the subject, he said:

> "Is it necessary for me to remind my readers that neither the emancipation of women, nor democratic government, nor universal education has come from the so-called spiritual civilization of the East? Is it necessary for me to add that, after all, there is not much spirituality in a civilization which bound the feet of its women for almost a thousand years without a protest, nor in that other civilization which long tolerated the practice of suttee or cremation of widows and has maintained the horrible caste-system to this day?" [1]

The spirit of investigation and reform led the scholars to take up another problem, that of China's future literary language. Possibly the first gun in this battle was fired by the prominent writer, Huang Yuan-yung, in 1915 when he published an article in which he declared that Chinese thought should come into direct contact with world thought and furthermore that it should be brought to the average man as well as to the educated few. In order to spread these ideas among the masses of the population he suggested the adoption of a simplified written language to take the place of the old classical one. He pointed out that the Renaissance of Europe, when writers began to use the spoken language of the people, had overthrown Medievalism on that continent.

The proposal to bring world thought to the average man of China presented a knotty problem. Not only did the masses lack the ability to read; but also the written language of the classics, called *Wen Li,* differed widely from the spoken language. It was condensed to the last degree, each character or group of two or three characters standing for a whole thought or sentence. Only the students who were grounded in the classical studies could make anything out of the printed page, as it took years of study to master this cryptic style. The novelists had long ago refused to use it. They borrowed the characters from the *Wen Li* but followed the form of the spoken language. For generations the scholars had repudiated this use of the vernacular and felt it beneath their notice. But now a few fearless ones began to assert that the old classical language was dead or dying and to demand that the spoken language which the dramatists and novelists had used successfully should be substituted for it. They claimed that the language of the novels was capable of becoming the future literary language of the country; in fact, that the only obstacle was the failure of the scholar class to sanction its use. A more conservative group took the position that it would be a pity to discard the old classical literature. Furthermore they claimed that because of divergence of dialects *Wen Li* was the only language that all educated people could understand and that it was more beautiful than the spoken language, or *pai hua*.

By 1917 the reform movement gained a new impetus. Articles published in modern magazines in Shanghai asserted that the classical language had outlived its usefulness and praised the writers who were using the *pai hua* as a medium of expression. The National University at Peking assumed leadership of the movement and it spread quickly through the provinces.

The difficulty in the way of developing a uniform language for China was still great as the scholars were quite right in pointing out *Wen Li* was the only uniform language of the educated people. As China was a country of many dialects, printing in the colloquial did not produce a universal language. There would be as many printed languages as there were spoken dialects. So the question had to be faced: Which dialect should be adopted as the national language of China?

Because the capital had generally been situated in the north the dialects of this part of the empire had long been recognized as the official language and had come to be known as Mandarin. The middle and southwestern dialects, though differing some from the Mandarin, still could be understood. The southeastern dialects alone were incapable of being understood in other parts of the country. As the Mandarin dialects were understood by nearly ninety per cent [2] of the people of the eighteen provinces, the decision was made to accept Mandarin as the national language, the language of literature and school texts, and a language to be taught in the schools throughout the nation.

Following this decision, newspapers and periodicals printed in the vernacular appeared everywhere. By 1920 the movement had attained such momentum that the Ministry of Education ordered that the living national language should be taught in the first two grades of the primary schools. And in another eight years the national government declared that throughout the secondary school system all texts written in the classical language should be abolished and that only those in the *Kuo Yü,* national language, should be printed and used.

While many of the mature students were thus shifting their attention from politics to the New Thought Movement there were others who were inordinately interested in political questions. Since the triumph of an Eastern nation, Japan, over a European one, Russia, thousands of students had gone to Japan for study and hundreds to Europe and America, hoping in these foreign countries to gain the secret of power that Japan had shown. These young and immature students with quickly gained degrees returned to their native land, the land of the scholar's privilege. Scholars had always been the only ones eligible to office and on this account held a great prestige in the eyes of their countrymen. The old examination system had vanished, so it was natural that students with degrees from Japanese and Western colleges should consider that they had fallen heir to the privileges of the old students and demand appointment to offices as their right. It was natural, too, that the mass of the people should give to the new students the reverence which all students had always commanded in China. However, there was a group, those already holding office and the military leaders who did not value the new students so highly as they valued themselves, that balked them in their efforts to gain office. In retaliation the students turned to criticism of the government.

This spirit of criticism spread rapidly and soon reached down from the returned college students to the boys and girls in the secondary schools, and they too insisted that their opinion in public matters be seriously taken. To make themselves more effective, students of all ages organized into societies and unions, held mass meetings and parades, instituted strikes and boycotts. Whenever they thought things were going badly with the government they held demonstrations around the ministers' houses in Peking and around officials' *yamens* in other cities throughout the provincial capitals. The anniversary of the day on which the twenty-one demands were signed had come to be called "Humiliation Day" and on this date each year the students staged demonstrations in all cities to show their displeasure and chagrin. When their demonstrations became too violent and the police tried to quiet them there was often shooting and killing of one or more students. These students in the eyes of their fellows then became martyrs, martyrs who further incited the youth of the land.

The events of 1918 and 1919 roused the students to a national demonstration. At the Peace Table China's hopes were shattered and she failed to get an adjustment of the Shantung question. The Versailles Treaty had allowed Japan to retain Shantung. This was a bitter blow to China, and dissatisfaction was voiced in many ways and in many quarters. The most bitter cry of protest came from the students. In mass meetings and from the stump boys and girls proclaimed the perfidy of Japan and the injustice done to China by the Allies. In Peking they attacked two members of the government, burning their houses and denouncing them as traitors. They preached a boycott of Japan, haranguing the people neither to sell to Japan nor to buy from her. The students themselves did all they could to make this boycott effective by refusing to use Japanese articles, although they had become very much the vogue among the young moderns. For example, black cotton umbrellas on steel frames imported from Japan had been universally popular among the students but now were cheerfully discarded; the young people went back to the oiled-paper umbrella of old days, lately used only by the coolies. Straw hats, bits of finery, shared the same fate until Japan's trade was very much crippled.

Not only the students in China but those who were studying in Europe and America raised their voice of disapproval over the Versailles Treaty. Undoubtedly their bitter cry, in season and out, had great influence on members of the Disarmament Conference meeting in Washington in 1921-22. At any rate the Conference devoted considerable attention to Far Eastern questions. Agreements among the Treaty Powers were signed which gave back to China the leased territory of Kiaochow Bay and the chance to buy the Shantung railway. Foreign post-offices in Chinese territory were to be abolished and the way was opened for calling commissions to investigate the tariff and extraterritoriality questions. China, in the future, was to lease no more territory and the policy of the Open Door, equal commercial opportunities to all countries, was reiterated. Thus did China obtain what she failed to get at Versailles. The protests of the students regarding Shantung had been heard.

The great question of the future was: Would China, with this concession to her desire for freedom from foreign control, be able to strengthen her central authority, manage her railways, modernize her courts, protect life and property within the country?

Unfortunately the government of China was not becoming stable. Quite the reverse. Ever since Dictator Yuan Shih-kai's death, the central authority had been growing weaker and weaker. Not only Canton, but other sections, too, had declared their independence, refusing to pay any revenue to Peking. Yet the semblance of power remained at the capital for the foreign nations still brought their international problems before the government at Peking, thus giving it a certain amount of prestige. The President and Parliament had never been able to control the growing power of the war lords.

The war lords had become the actual rulers of China, veritable feudal lords. Backed by large armies they made and unmade government officials, collected established taxes, levied new ones, seized railroad revenues. They early found that opium revenues brought them more easy money than anything else. So they encouraged its growth! At times they even forced the farmer at the point of the gun to plant opium, sometimes confiscating the same crop from the hapless farmer later on. Often long lines of soldiers of this and that war lord escorted the carriers of the opium to the big shipping centers. And the opium habit, which had been largely stamped out during the Empress Dowager's days, was again fastened upon the people.

These ill-got moneys the war lords did not spend on railroad building or repair, on road building, reforesting, control of the Yellow River, or education. The funds, often great, which each war lord extracted from his region went to the upkeep of his army and the enriching of himself and his friends who would be worth while in furthering his ambitions. Each had his eye on Peking as his ultimate goal. Here each ambitious war lord dreamed he would sit in power and control the wealth of all China. In the north, the most conspicuous of the war lords were three— Wu Pei-fu, Chang Tso-lin, Feng Yu-hsiang. At times they were in alliance with one another, more often they were fighting one another.

Wu Pei-fu was a Chinese of good education. He had received a military training and possessed courage and ambition. Chang Tso-lin was a rougher type. As a boy there had been a price on his head because he had killed a whole family for revenge. During the Russo-Japanese War he served in the Japanese Army and afterward was taken into the Chinese Army in Manchuria. He proved to be a man of power and became virtual dictator in that province. Feng Yu-hsiang, quite generally known as the "Christian General," as he professed Christianity, was like Chang—a man without education. He maintained strict discipline of his troops, taught them bits of the Bible. As his army marched, they sang *Onward, Christian Soldiers*.

By 1924 Wu Pei-fu had high hopes of uniting all China under himself but was defeated by Chang Tso-lin near the Great Wall and betrayed by his subordinate, Feng Yu-hsiang, who marched into Peking and took it for himself. Wu Pei-fu fled to the Yangtse and made that his base.

Feng Yu-hsiang, though he gained military control of the capital, was unable to organize a government, so he allied himself with Chang Tso-lin. When these two war lords removed Tsao Kun (the last one to hold the office of president) and put Tuan Chi-jui in office as Provisional Chief Executive, even the outward show of a republic had vanished. Feng Yu-hsiang remained in Peking for two years at the head of his army called the People's National Army, and Chang Tso-lin, though he retired beyond the Wall into Manchuria, kept a close watch, as well he might, on Peking. Feng Yu-hsiang, no more loyal to Chang Tso-lin than he had been to Wu Pei-fu, leagued himself with one of Chang's subordinates for the purpose of invading Manchuria. This attempt was a failure and Chang now allied himself with Wu, and Feng was the one to flee—to the northwest on the Mongolian border, and in

March, 1926, on to Russia. Thus were the tables turned. But by this time matters in the south demanded Wu's return to Hankow on the Yangtse and Chang Tso-lin gained control of Peking where, with an improvised Cabinet, he ruled for two years until 1928, when Peking was taken by the Nationalists, which is another story.

During this period the Soviet Government began its negotiations with Peking. Deeming the recognition of its government by the nations of the Far East important, Russia, through its representative, Joffe, offered, in exchange for China's recognition, to give up the Boxer indemnity, concessions in treaty ports, extraterritoriality and tariff restrictions and to agree to a future adjustment of the Chinese-Eastern Railway, which extended across northern Manchuria connecting the Trans-Siberian with the Japanese railroads in southern Manchuria. Such an offer of wholesale surrender of treaty privileges on the part of Russia was very tempting to the Peking Government, and in 1924 they entered into a treaty with Russia in which Russia waived her old treaty privileges and China recognized the Soviet Republic.

The Soviet, now in possession of the old Russian property in the Legation Quarter, reopened the former Legation and raised it to an Embassy. From here, Ambassador Karakhan promoted pro-Soviet feeling among the intelligentsia of Peking. But on the whole the north was too conservative for the doctrines of the Soviets. Soviet Russia did not find the results commensurate with its efforts.

But though the north lent a rather deaf ear to Russia, the south proved to be much more eager to listen. It was during this time that Russia through Joffe made a tempting offer of funds and recognition to Sun Yat-sen, who was then president of the Southern Republic at Canton which had been set up by the Kuomintang or Nationalist Party.

CHAPTER XXIII

THE NATIONALISTS COME INTO POWER

DURING these years while the presidents were becoming mere puppets in Peking and the war lords were wielding military power untrammeled throughout the north, the southern leaders were trying to develop a republic which would maintain the ideals of the Revolution and one which would be strong enough to control the whole nation. When President Li had dismissed the national Parliament so summarily in 1917, the members of the Kuomintang had fled from Peking to Canton. Their attempts at setting up a government in Canton were many and varied. At times Sun Yat-sen was at the head of the government and at times some other leader gained the upper hand and Sun was exiled. Generally during such periods he took refuge in Shanghai and worked from there to advance the interests of the party.

Two notable additions strengthened the movement. The first was the adherence of the students who began to preach the doctrines of Sun Yat-sen. The other was Russian friendship and aid. In January, 1923, one of Russia's representatives, Joffe, met Doctor Sun in Shanghai and persuaded him that he could add the principles of the Soviets to the Kuomintang program without disloyalty to his ideal. At first they simply declared friendly relations but as time went on Sun received more and more aid from Russia. Doctor Sun had realized that if he was to launch a campaign for the control of all China he would be forced to borrow from foreign countries, but the Western powers had been unwilling to recognize his southern government or to lend him money. Feeling sorely this rebuff he more than welcomed aid from any quarter.

Following this declaration of friendly relations between Sun and Joffe, Sun returned to Canton, once more assuming the leadership of the southern government. In September, 1923, Comrade Borodin arrived in Canton and from then on financial and other help was received from Russia. The army was supplied with money, arms and advisers. Late in the year the Kuomintang Party was reorganized and in January, 1924, Communists, both Russian and Chinese, were admitted on condition that they adopt the principles of the Kuomintang. But Communist members added their own slogan of Communism, anti-capitalism, anti-imperialism, anti-Christianity. These new doctrines proved to be just the seed to sprout in the rich loam of a growing nationalism.

Sun Yat-sen's ever closer rapprochement with Russia, the accumulating power of the Communists and Sun's arbitrary actions in Canton were again making him unpopular in the south. What might have been the outcome is difficult to guess, but his death early in 1925 changed the situation somewhat. Organization of the Nationalist Party followed. A Central Executive Committee took the place of President Sun and Chiang Kai-shek became the military leader. Russian arms, money and advisers were freely supplied. The "three principles"[1] taken from the will of Sun Yat-sen became the spiritual program of the party. Concretely stated, these are: unification of the country, or nationalism; popular government of, by and for the people; and social and economic reforms. In his will, Sun impressed upon his followers the necessity for immediate abolition of "unequal treaties." Under the head of unequal treaties the

Executive Committee named extraterritoriality, foreign controlled customs, and all political rights which foreign nations had exercised in the country. In a land of ancestor worship Sun Yat-sen was quickly exalted. His picture was placed in every school and military camp and each morning his followers worshiped it and repeated the three principles.

To carry out the first principle of Sun Yat-sen the Nationalist Party determined to make China a unified republic free from foreign privilege. The movement developed along two lines: one an education of the oppressed masses to a realization of their wrongs, and the other, the military task of gaining possession of the National Government.

The work with the masses was carried on through propaganda by means of the slogans the Communists had introduced into the party—anti-capitalism and anti-foreignism.

Propaganda spread fast through the ranks of the students into the mass of industrial workers. The students themselves carried the flaming torch of resentment against the capitalists and especially against the foreigners to their brothers in industry. China's hand industry of centuries in the large cities, especially in Shanghai, was undergoing a revolution. Both foreigners and Chinese had built machine powered factories in which they employed Chinese labor. The kind of evils one might expect in factory life, uncontrolled by laws regulating the hours of labor, had grown up. Chinese owner and foreigner were alike culpable. Many efforts had been made in the foreign part of the city to improve conditions. But the argument of the owners was—as long as the Chinese owners in the native city are under no law for running their factories, we in the foreign city cannot compete with them if the foreign municipal council regulates the hours and other conditions in our factories. Factory life could only be improved by the con-

NATIONALISTS COME INTO POWER 311

certed effort of all concerned. A little headway had been made. But while legislation was taking its slow way, the factory worker (whose lot, it must in fairness be said, was not worse than in the hand industries throughout the nation) was roused by the new doctrine taught him by the students who in turn had been taught by their new friends, the Russians.

The various labor disputes that arose afforded an opportunity for agitators to turn antagonism against employers in general into hostility against foreigners in particular. In May, 1925, a labor dispute at a Japanese mill resulted in a riot and the death of a Chinese rioter at the hands of a Japanese guard. The students arranged the demonstration of May thirtieth as a protest, not against employers as such but against the foreigners as murderers. On that fatal day, although there was a law in the International Settlement against parades or political meetings, the students began lecturing on busy street corners and distributing anti-foreign literature. An unprepared police force, the head of police off at the golf links, proved to be the final letters to spell tragedy. Several agitators were arrested for violating the laws of the Settlement, their friends stormed the city jail where their comrades were held; the police, now thoroughly frightened at the growing chaos, fired into the crowd killing six and wounding several who later died. Before nightfall the dead students had become martyrs, victims of foreign aggression, and anti-foreignism was spreading like wild fire over the length and the breadth of China.

Less than a month later, when a parade was filing past Shameen, the foreign concession at Canton, Chinese students of the military academy, officered by Russians, aimed their rifles toward Shameen and fired, killing the French consul, whereupon British and French forces on Shameen answered with machine-gun fire. Forty-four Chinese were killed, among them twenty-two cadets and four students.

These and other incidents of a like nature had done their work. The Russian doctrines of anti-Christianity, anti-imperialism, anti-capitalism, anti-foreignism, were making their way fast throughout China. And they were slogans which aided in the military conquest of the country, for the masses were easily won over to join a cause which promised them the property taken from the rich and from the foreigners.

So the Nationalists set about their high mission of unifying the country. It was a tremendous task, for China in 1925-26 was a prey to war lords and bandits. There was no money; there was little communication of a modern type; there was little education; much poverty and official graft. Bandits and war lords swept over the country taking their toll of the people, confiscating the railroads and boats.

In August, 1926, Chiang Kai-shek, Commander-in-Chief of the Army, began the "march to Peking" traversing the selfsame route that had been taken by the red-turbaned Taipings. And strangely enough, the badge was again red—a red flag this time, with a blue corner, like in meaning to the red flag of Russia, for the radical left wing of the Nationalist Party was now in control. Through Kuangsi and Hunan, up to the three cities, Hanyang, Wuchang and Hankow, they marched with Galen, the Russian, as military adviser. The propaganda corps preceded them, promising lower prices and the blessings of prosperity if the foreigners were driven from the Flowery Kingdom and a Utopian land if the Nationalists were allowed to rule the country.

By the time the army arrived at any point the mass of the people had been won over. The privates in the opposing army and their officers went over to the Nationalists or fled. Wuchang alone underwent a siege before it came under the

NATIONALISTS COME INTO POWER

Nationalist banner. Everywhere there were demonstrations against the foreigners. In many cases boycotts made it impossible for foreigners to buy food or other necessities or get any one to work for them. In other places the demonstrations were of a more violent nature and there was looting and threat against life. In Hankow the mob forced the foreigners to flee from the British Concession and later Great Britain gave over the Concession to the Nationalist authorities. Wherever the armies of the Nationalists went that winter the cry was raised against the foreigners and often they had to flee. Mission schools and hospitals were confiscated; some closed, some taken on by the Chinese and some used by the military.

The radical wing now thoroughly in control of the party set up their civil headquarters at Hankow. Eugene Chen, a Chinese claiming British citizenship as he was born in Trinidad, and the Russian, Borodin, were the civil leaders. Commander Chiang Kai-shek moved on with the army.

Soon Hankow and all the districts back over the route the Nationalists had taken found themselves under the power of strange new doctrines. The millennium was not the millennium they had looked for. The shopkeepers were presented with rules and demands lessening the hours of labor of their employees. Some of these new rulings were just: Many were not, and shop after shop was obliged to close, the owner bankrupt, crushed between the heavy taxes and the demands of the employees. Under the preaching of the propaganda corps the farmers rose against their landlords, sometimes killing them, often refusing to raise rice except for themselves. The rich men of the cities grew more and more terrified as the doctrines against the capitalist took possession of the people. Soon the doctrine grew into action and here and there a rich man was beheaded or shot because he was a capitalist. Communism was running rife in the wake of the army. Now the power of the family father and the village elder, questioned by the young people since the Revolution, was broken.

Down the Yangtse the army marched. Other parts of the army took Fukien, Chekiang and Kiangsi. Chiang Kai-shek himself moved upon Shanghai. The International city of Shanghai, fearful of its fate, barricaded itself behind barbed wire. All the Powers hurried their navies to its protection. Naval boats of the various nations went up the Yangtse for the purpose of protecting their nationals if it were necessary. Everything in the army and in the towns the cry against foreigners became a slogan. Hatred grew into a kind of mania. Shanghai with its rich revenues fell. Only Nanking of all the great cities south of the Yangtse remained to be taken. The war lord who held Nanking had called upon the northern war lords to help him. Again the people of Nanking, as so many times in her history, watched the approaching armies.

An eyewitness says:

"One of the strangest events in history was happening right there before our eyes. The entire collapse of a huge army before propaganda. A hundred thousand strong, an army of good fighters, bandits many of them, who had been brought up on death and destruction and blood-shed, equipped with guns, field pieces, aeroplanes, giving up a fortified city without a shot fired, and the larger part of the opposing army still three days' journey away! Incredible. . . .

"It had been a gray day with no sunset. The city wall became a huge black cliff separating us from the crawling grey flood down on the marshes, but also shutting us into a like crawling grey flood of frantic humanity, thousands of them flowing in from all the streets, trying to get out two small funnels some twenty

NATIONALISTS COME INTO POWER 315

feet wide—the two North gates, five minutes' walk from our hill. . . .

"In the city down in the suburb, out on the marshes, rifle shots rang out, not the regular shooting of a battle, but shots fired at ragged uneven intervals. The firing of troops running amok. Looting? Raping? Killing their companions to get seats in the boats?"[2]

The unexpected had happened. The northern armies had retreated and early the next morning the Nationalists were in possession of Nanking.

A few hours afterward missionaries, business men and foreign officials were pleading for their lives. Six were killed; others were wounded; property was burned and destroyed and no Chinese official tried to stop the destruction. Another twenty-four hours and not a representative of the Powers remained in the ancient city of Nanking except those who had been killed and were hastily buried before their compatriots made their escape. The most accepted explanation of this event is that the Radical group in Hankow had ordered a massacre of all foreigners to discredit Chiang Kai-shek, the leader of the army, of whose popularity they were jealous.

This event, the Nanking Incident, halted for a year the progress of the Nationalist armies. The party itself became hopelessly divided. Chiang became leader of the Conservative group who repudiated the Russians and the Communists, and set up a government at Nanking. The Radicals remained at Hankow still faithful to the principles of Communism and to anti-foreignism. As the summer advanced, largely because of the finding of documents which proved that Moscow was planning the communism of China, the position of the Radicals became more and more desperate and that of the Conservatives correspondingly bright. By

July the group at Nanking had decided to expel the Communists from the party, to send Borodin and the other Russian advisers back to Russia, and to suppress radical doctrines. As a counter-move many Chinese Radicals made vehement attacks on the Conservatives and particularly on Chiang. Among these was Madame Sun who went to Moscow but before going issued a statement declaring that the Nationalists at Nanking, in giving up the social phase of the Revolution, had betrayed the Three Principles of her husband.

It soon became evident that the expulsion of the Russians and the Communists was not sufficient to unite the party. The strife for leadership went on but in the end Chiang Kai-shek secured the headship of both government and army. By the spring of 1928 he was ready again to embark on the conquest of the north.

The north in the meantime, though divided among several war lords, had been fairly peaceful. Chang Tso-lin remained in control of Peking as well as Manchuria. In the northwest, Feng Yu-hsiang, now returned from Russia, held Shensi Province. A Nationalist, at times he declared his loyalty to Chiang but no one seemed to be very certain of him or his movements. There was much rumor that he was backed by Russia. In Shansi, Yen Hsi-shan still kept his province neutral and independent. For years he had given his province peace and order and something of economic improvement. "The Model Governor" he was styled. Each of these three, strong in his own power, was weak against the oncoming Chiang Kai-shek and the Nationalists. But they could not unite against this common foe. In the end Yen and Feng decided to cast their lot with Chiang in his efforts to drive Chang Tso-lin from Peking. Except for some trouble with the Japanese in Shantung, there was little obstacle to the threefold march on Peking.

NATIONALISTS COME INTO POWER 317

Chang Tso-lin, possibly feeling the game was up with Yen and Feng and Chiang all in the field against him, or possibly as a result of a warning from the Japanese that he had best leave Peking, abandoned Peking on the night of June second. He left the capital over the Peking-Mukden railway line, his military trains filled: wife, concubines and children; treasure and soldiers. Just as he passed outside the Great Wall of China into his long held territory of Manchuria a bomb exploded under his train. The great northern war lord was dead.

After Chang Tso-lin's flight from Peking, Yen marched into the capital and raised the flag of the Nationalists. A month later Chiang himself arrived, followed a few days later by Feng and other government and military leaders.

On July 6, 1928, war lords, military leaders, government officials proceeded outside Peking to the temporary tomb of the Nationalist leader, Sun Yat-sen, and there announced to his spirit that his wishes had been fulfilled; the northern war lords had fallen before the Nationalists, Peking had been captured and the country was unified under a government dictated by his Three Principles. The Nationalists had acquired their first object, the conquest of China.

CHAPTER XXIV

THE NATIONALIST REGIME

THE Nationalists even with their triumphal entry into Peking and their quick conquest of the country were only at the beginning of their task. Many and serious problems confronted them. Could they keep the country under their military control? What type of government would they set up? What would be their attitude toward social welfare and toward the Communists? And how could they manage China's international affairs?

By gaining control of Peking the Nationalist Party became official heirs to the National Government of China. As the seat of the new government which they proposed to set up they chose Nanking. Though formerly known as the "southern capital" the city lies on the Yangtse midway between north and south. The "northern capital," Peking, beautiful city of the Mings, was abandoned and its name changed to Peiping, "Northern Peace." The foreign diplomats, however, continued to live at Peiping, the nations finding it onerous to move from their expensively equipped Embassies in the old capital, and perhaps wondering if the capital might again be established in the north. Here also, when Chiang Kai-shek departed for Nanking, remained Yen Hsi-shan, "The Model Governor."

In Manchuria Chang Hsueh-liang succeeded his father. While both Yen and Chang were in alliance with the Nationalist Government no one felt sure how much real loyalty they would give to the central government in Nanking. In the north also was Feng Yu-hsiang, "the Christian General," who came and went, an uncertain quantity. In the south conditions were equally insecure, for the southerners, always separatist in tendency, had since the break with the right wing of the Nationalists in 1927, after the Nanking affair, been particularly independent.

By the autumn of 1928 when the leaders at Nanking wished to put into effect some kind of civil government they found themselves in real control of but five provinces and these were all near Nanking in the central eastern area. In March, 1930, Finance Minister T. V. Soong stated that only four provinces, Kiangsu, Chekiang, Anhwei and Kiangsi, furnished reliable financial reports and that in only two of these provinces were the provincial authorities sending in any revenue to the capital.

As time went on it became increasingly difficult for the Nanking Government to keep even a semblance of national unity. The great war lords of the north at times seemed loyal to the Nanking Government and at other times were actually fighting it, either singly or in combinations of two or three. Matters came to the most serious crisis for Nanking and Chiang Kai-shek late in 1929 and continued critical through the first part of 1930. War Lords Feng Yu-hsiang and Yen Hsi-shan, pushed their armies south of Peking, assuming control of communications and revenues. In addition they recognized the southern leader, Wang Ching-wei, as legal head of the Nationalist Party in lieu of Chiang Kai-shek. Actual fighting between the two factions began by May, 1930, and continued for five months. For a time the advantage was on the side of the north and it almost seemed as if Chiang Kai-shek was doomed to failure, but in the end Nanking's greater prestige and larger supplies of funds, arms and munitions won out and the Nanking faction began to win back the places which had been captured by the northern war lords, Feng and Yen.

Chang Hsueh-liang had evidently been watching the game going on within the Wall from his stronghold in Manchuria. At length he decided to intervene in Chiang's favor, having obtained a promise of control of the northeastern seaports. To fulfill his part of the bargain he proceeded through the Great Wall, taking Tientsin and Peiping. This achievement made him ruler of the inner northeast provinces in addition to his own Manchuria, and both were held under an alliance with Chiang Kai-shek. The war lords who had planned the overthrow of the Nationalist Government then withdrew: Yen to Japan; Feng to his old stronghold, Shensi Province; and the southern insurgent, Wang, with whom the northerners had been plotting, to Europe.

Again Chiang Kai-shek was in control of the country and through his alliance with Chang Hsueh-liang he possessed a firmer hold on Manchuria than the Chinese Government had enjoyed for some time. If the alliance could be made to last it might mean a permanent and stronger union of the Nationalist Government with the north, both with the Chinese within the Wall and with Manchuria without. Chang Hsueh-liang was appointed a vice-commander-in-chief of the Nationalist Army, Navy and Air Forces, with instructions to reorganize China north of the Yellow River. What might have been the result of this close alliance between Nanking and Manchuria had no disruptive factors come into the situation it is hard to estimate. But in less than a year difficulties with Japan over Manchuria arose. But that is a later story.

According to the second of the Three Principles of Sun Yat-sen, the Nationalists were bound to set up a democratic form of government. A few months after the conquest of Peking, in October, 1928, "The Organic **Law**" was promulgated to serve as the law of the land until the permanent constitution could be drafted. This instrument placed the Nationalist Party in control of China during what is known as the second phase of the Revolution, called "the period of tutelage," during which time the people were to learn in their local governments how to exercise authority under a constitution. The Organic Law provided that the government should be divided into five departments, or Boards, called *Yuan,* namely Executive, Legislative, Judicial, Examination and Control. Each *Yuan* had its own president and Chiang Kai-shek was chosen as president or chairman of the National Government. The functions of the first three *Yuan* were adopted by the Chinese from the usage of the West and are similar to those of like name in other governments, but the last two are thoroughly Chinese. The duty of the Examination *Yuan* is to see that all public officials are to be appointed only after examination and after their fitness for the office has been determined by the *Yuan.* The Control *Yuan* is supervisory and controls criticism of officials, impeachment and auditing. The Examination *Yuan* has its precedent in Chinese government in the old examination system and the Control *Yuan* in the imperial censorate, which dates back to the third century B. C.

Even if, in this plan, there might be possibilities of a democratic form of government, in practice there has developed, since 1928, a system totally at variance with Doctor Sun's second principle of creating a government by and for the people. The government is a creation of the party, which numbers only one in every thousand of the population of China. Real power lies with a much smaller group than this—The Central Executive Committee of the Nationalist Party. The chairman of this committee, appointed by the party, is president of the National Government at Nanking and commander-in-chief of the army. These powers make him official ruler of China with the power of a dictator. To meet the criticisms against this autocratic tendency, plans were made at the Plenary Session of the Executive Committee held in November, 1930, for the opening of a National People's Convention which ultimately met during the next spring.

On May 12, 1931, the Convention adopted a provisional constitution[1] for use during the political tutelage period until the people should be ready to govern themselves. According to this constitution a national congress of the Kuomintang delegates shall exercise the governing powers on behalf of the National People's Congress and when Congress is not meeting the Executive Committee is to assume control. The people are to enjoy the rights of election and other political rights only in their local districts, called *hsien*, with no part in either national or provincial governments. Only when district autonomy has been carried out throughout a majority of the provinces is the National Government to summon a National People's Congress to decide upon the adoption of a permanent constitution. At the present rate of progress in the direction of self government, it would appear that many a day will pass before the people will be called upon to summon any such congress.

The third principle of Sun Yat-sen relates to social and economic reform. In that field, problems are quite as great as in those covered by the first two principles, namely unification of the country and development of a democratic government. And there was evidence of the same lack of harmony within the party toward this third principle as toward the other two. With the break-up of the Nationalist Party after the Nanking Incident in 1927 the more radical members of the party withdrew their support from the

Nanking Government and vehemently criticized Chiang Kai-shek for abandoning the principles of the founder, Sun Yat-sen. Madame Sun herself, in her denunciation of the right wing of the Nationalists who were in power when she left for Moscow, stated, "It is the third principle (of Doctor Sun), that of the livelihood of the people, that is at stake at the present time." Pointing out that her husband had worked many years for the betterment of the masses she added, "Yet today the lot of the Chinese peasant is even more wretched than in those days when Doctor Sun was driven by his great sense of human wrongs into a life of revolution. And today men, who profess to follow his banner, talk of classes and think in terms of a 'revolution' that would virtually disregard the sufferings of those millions of poverty-stricken peasants of China."[2]

This slow progress has created an unrest and dissatisfaction among the masses which have given the Communists an opportunity that they have been quick to seize. As we have seen, the Communists were officially expelled from the Nationalist Party in the summer of 1927. Since then, they have worked underground and have found the time ripe for their endeavors.

The directors of the Communist movement in China, realizing that the industrial workers were too small a group to use as a party around which to build up communistic activities, have taken the cause of the peasants as their rallying point. When we remember that eighty-five per cent of the population of the country is agricultural, the importance of such a decision is manifest. Let us look at the conditions of livelihood of these peasants. Authorities differ somewhat on the proportion who own their land. One says that of the whole country seventy-five per cent are tenants of absentee landlords. In sections such as the rich east-central districts it is claimed that as many as fifty per cent own their own land. On the average, the "farms" are pitifully small—not more than five acres per family, or less than one acre per person. These allotments would be meager indeed if they were unmolested in the enjoyment of them, but the peasants lose much of their produce through banditry and looting because of the disorderly condition of government. And beyond all this, able-bodied men are pressed into service in the armies.

In spite of a very small cash income—estimated at not more than two dollars and fifty cents per person—taxation is enormous. Taxation rates appear to be two or three times as heavy as in the times of the Manchus. Worse still, the tax in many places has been collected for from thirty to forty years in advance, leaving the people penniless and deprived of clothes, tools and almost every movable article. Everything of any value has been seized to satisfy the collection. Opium growing is made compulsory in many districts and a high tax is placed on it.

Under these conditions, it is easy to see that the peasants were easily impressed by the teaching of the Communists when they came into a community preaching, "down with the capitalists and large landowners; divide the land among everybody; lower taxation!" Impressive slogans these to take to an illiterate and oppressed peasantry.

Since the expulsion of the Russians in the summer of 1927, the party has been directed by Chinese Communists. The propaganda phase of the work is organized and executed by young Chinese intellectuals, many of whom have been trained in Sun Yat-sen University in Moscow and in similar institutions in China. These young men and women work among the masses and win them over by their enthusiasm and fair promises of land and lighter taxation. Then the Red Army appeared and worked with terrorist methods against the Nationalist Government, and also against any backsliders from among those who have once avowed themselves as Communists. Often the Red Army augmented its numbers by buying the army of some general who had no money to pay his soldiers.

The Communists seemed to have been successful in setting up a more or less permanent government in a few small sections called "Soviet Areas," but in the main they moved from place to place. In the Sovietized areas they indulged in burning of deeds and in parceling out of land among the peasants. The government expeditions sent against them were only moderately successful in combating Communism so there developed a sort of guerrilla warfare between the forces of the Nationalists and the Reds, between the "haves" and "have nots."

Just what were the dimensions of the movement in China at that time it would be hard to say. Those who are following it most closely fail to agree.[3] However, it seems clear that the central government had openly avowed its fear of the movement. President Chiang himself has said, "We dread the Communists more than we do sweeping floods and fierce beasts." The bankers and large merchants of the seaport cities agree with him, and many of the outside nations, especially Japan, have expressed themselves as equally fearful. It would seem to be not so much a danger of Communism in any strict sense of the term but rather of an anti-property movement which might threaten the power of the present Nationalist Government. Some think that the leaders of the movement use the Communist slogans to reach the masses and would throw them aside in the moment of victory quite as quickly as Chiang Kai-shek and his followers threw aside Russian advisers and principles when they became embarrassing. Others see in the movement the only hope of a true revolution, which would consider the welfare of the people of the nation. And these feel that the young intellectuals who are the leaders of the movement are some of the truest patriots that China has today.

Whether Communists or Nationalists are eventually entrusted with the solving of China's internal problems, either party will find itself confronted by menaces to social security.

Famine, China's age-old enemy, still stalks the land and problems which would tax the abilities of the most capable government. Every year many are dying of starvation and many others have scarcely enough to keep soul and body together. It is so much a part of Chinese life among the poor that they shrug their shoulders and remark that famines and wars are necessary if anyone is to have anything to eat. The causes of the ever-recurring famines have been summed up by the American Red Cross Commission, appointed by the Central Committee to examine into the causes and relief of famine in China. Their report (August, 1929) said, "The committee learns—that the destitution which prevails in the famine areas is the cumulative result of the chronic conditions of disorder, the crushing exactions of the war lords, the depradation of bandits, the enforced payment of confiscatory taxation, and the crippling and the consequent inability of railways to function beyond a fraction of their normal capacity."[4] The report points out that China's only hope of doing away with famines is through the establishment and maintenance of a strong central government.

Second comes the transportation difficulty. Means of transport are still most inadequate. Except in Manchukuo, there has been little railroad building since the early days of the republic. The Nationalists early laid out an ambitious campaign for motor road building. Under an American engineer they mapped out an elaborate system of roads for Nanking and vicinity and have completed some roads in the city and along the river front. Other cities also are building motor roads in the cities and immediate vicinity and roads are being built between towns. Sixty thousand miles of highway already built indicate that both the national and local governments are awake to the necessity of quicker and cheaper transportation than the time-honored methods. But to compare with the United States sixty thousand miles of road is only a little more than that maintained by the state of Virginia. For the whole United States with a population not one-third of that of China there were, in 1930, 155,343,529 miles of highway, which means that with an equal population the proportion is eight thousand to one.

Air mail and passenger service is also being advanced. Daily services connect Hankow with both Shanghai and Peiping while semi-weekly schedules serve other cities such as Changsha and Chengtu. These are being used by business men and government officials, both Chinese and foreign.

Education, another project of the Nationalists, is also developing slowly. Under the National Government there exists a Ministry of Education whose aims are to promote nationalism and democracy. It is roughly estimated that there are forty million children of school age who are not yet in school. To accommodate these there is need of a million and a half additional teachers and a million classrooms. Because of the lack of money little headway is being made on this program. Missionary education, which has often helped to fill in the gaps, has received a setback since the Nationalist military conquest of the country. For a while the anti-foreign and anti-Christian movement destroyed or closed many of these institutions. Disorders in various parts of the country have prevented the reopening of many of them and government restrictions are holding back others. All schools must be registered; in primary schools no religious instruction is allowed and in secondary schools religious courses may be offered but not made obligatory.

In addition to the children of school age without instruction, there are estimated to be two hundred million persons between the ages of sixteen and sixty who are unable to read. Realizing that for the present the teaching of these masses cannot be accomplished through the school system, several other schemes are being tried by individuals in various localities. A system of forty phonetic symbols was devised but this attempt did not meet with much popular favor probably because of the diversity in dialects. It is possible that with the growing knowledge of the *Kuo Yü* (national language) this method might develop further in the future. The next attempt and one meeting with considerable success is the "thousand character" method. By learning one thousand carefully chosen characters, a person is enabled to read the vernacular newspaper and ordinary business papers.

The chief obstacle in the way of promoting education, transportation and general well-being is the lack of money. A large part of the national income is eaten up by the maintenance of large armed forces. Besides the National Government troops and those of the war lords, there are the armed bandits and the Red Army. Plans have been drawn up to disband these forces, but little if anything was accomplished before foreign invasion threatened.

One of the greatest basic reasons for the poverty of the government is the lack of a self-denying patriotism among the people. The old and universal custom of official squeeze for the benefit of one's family is so ingrained in Chinese political and social life that it will be extremely difficult to eradicate. Some of the Chinese themselves recognize the seriousness of this practice. Chiang Kai-shek has issued mandates announcing the government's determination to eradicate corruption from the public service. Another leading Nationalist and high official of the Canton group, Hu Han-min, boldly declares that "squeeze is in the blood of

Chinese officials."[5] He suggests that the only remedy for it lies in educating the masses to resist its abuses but admits that it would take centuries of organized effort to accomplish such a result, that the blood that runs in the veins of the masses is of the same composition as that of the officials, that it is the squeezing instinct of old Asia. At the bottom of all Chinese economics is "the eternal question of the food supply and the idea of 'the enrichment of the family at the expense of other families.'" In the changes that are now taking place in the social structure, the family is one of the institutions that is being attacked most vigorously by the young reformers. Possibly social changes in this direction may pave the way for the coming of better political and economic attitudes.

In fact there is a notable trend in this direction. We are reminded of what happened during the Dark Ages when, notwithstanding constant war and destruction, the people developed their arts and crafts and literature to a noticeable degree. So now in spite of wars and banditry, in the face of famines and exorbitant taxation, reform is reaching down into the lives of the people as it has never done before. Ideals of universal education, a national language, hygiene and sanitation, higher standards of living are being spread among the masses by the newspapers and the enthusiasm of the younger generation. The installing of bus lines, air services and city improvements is giving in certain sections a new impetus to business, while the use of these new means of transportation is bringing the possibility of united action on the part of government officials. The Industrial Revolution, though a long way from touching the lives of China's four hundred million people, still is making its way slowly but surely.

Besides the internal difficulties with which the Nationalists have been beset, matters have been going badly in those semi-independent states, those ever troublesome areas on the northern frontiers. Russian influence has been gaining in Mongolia, but the most vexing problems have come in Manchuria, the old home of the Manchus. Let us go back a little to recall that the Manchus, when they conquered China in 1644, adopted a curious policy toward their native land. Large numbers of Manchus were drained from the state to fill the garrisons in cities of conquered China, leaving a mere handful in Manchuria. No attempt was made to fill up these vacant spots—indeed an entirely opposite policy was entered upon. Manchuria was closed to immigration even to the Chinese, so the land remained one of open wastes and small population—a possible future happy hunting ground for the Manchus. As time went on, immigration laws grew lax and their neighbors, Mongols, Russians, Koreans, Chinese, and lastly Japanese began to filter in and settle on the rich agricultural lands. By the end of the Manchu Dynasty the number of native sons was small compared to the immigrant population.

When the Chinese pushed the Manchus from the Dragon Throne in 1911, there was speculation in some quarters as to whether the Manchus might return to their old home. But this did not take place. The Imperial family took no lead in such a move but remained with the Boy Emperor in the Forbidden City in Peking and most of the Manchus scattered in those garrisons throughout the empire filtered in among the Chinese population. However, Manchuria did not go unpopulated. The opportunity that the Manchus failed to grasp was seized upon by Chinese peasants from North China who, turning their backs on the trying conditions in China, fled to Manchuria. This was partly the intensification of an old movement which began during the latter part of the Manchu Dynasty. Peasants and merchants from the northern inner provinces, especially Shantung, had long been accustomed to journey to Manchuria for the warm season, returning after the harvests were over to their ancestral homes in China. They worked for a season in a strange land only to gain funds to take back to China. In this immigration only the men went, journeying by sea across Pechili Gulf to the ports of Newchwang and Antung. But the immigration of the last few years is of a different character, for now whole families, the patriarch and all of the generations of the family migrate, abandoning the ancestral home and starting a new one in Manchuria. It is like the immigration into the Americas and the settling on the rich agricultural lands of the New World. Manchuria beckoned them, giving them land and peace and order under which they could develop economic safety. During the years 1926, 1927 and 1928, they came at the rate of a million and more a year.

The Governor of Manchuria for many years, the old war lord, Chang Tso-lin, followed a policy of friendliness with Japan. This arrangement gave Japan the opportunity to develop her sphere of influence and gave Manchuria a peace and order which China proper failed to achieve. Chang's successor, his son Chang Hsueh-liang, as we have seen, formed a closer alliance with the Chinese Government than his father and finally openly placed himself on the side of the Nationalist Government. He was established in Peking and assumed charge of the region north of the Yellow River. By so doing, his greatest interest lay south of the Wall and his reliance and cooperation with Japan became less than that of his father.

All of the old questions between China and Japan, dating back from the Sino-Japanese War and the days of the leased territories, now took on more sinister proportions. Difficulties over trade, protection of each other's nationals, disputes over treaty rights, clashes between Chinese and

Japanese soldiers—all these and many other questions disturbed the peace between the two countries. The troubles with Japan were not the only ones for those with Russia also were revived. In the summer of 1929 the Nationalist Government, claiming that the Russians had been using the Chinese Eastern railroad for Communistic propaganda, seized the railroad and imprisoned Russian officials of the road. The Russians protested and threatened war, and diplomatic relations were broken off between the two countries. At this juncture the United States stepped in, reminding both nations that as signatories of the Kellogg Pact they could hardly go to war. After months of negotiations and some fighting on the border, the two countries came to an agreement and restored matters according to the status of the 1924 Treaty. In 1935 the Chinese Eastern Railway was sold by Russia to Manchukuo.

The Sino-Japanese differences were not so easily arranged as the Russo-Chinese ones and finally came to a head in September, 1931. In the summer of that year a Japanese navy officer, Nakamura, had been killed and the Japanese had failed to gain the satisfaction they had demanded. Then occurred the now famous "September 18th Incident" in which the Japanese claimed that Chinese soldiers had blown up part of their South Manchurian Railway. The whole thing resulted in actual though not declared war between China and Japan in Manchuria and, before the end was reached, an outbreak in Shanghai when the Japanese failed to obtain the Chinese Government's official disapproval of the Chinese boycott against Japanese goods.

In Manchuria the Japanese were easily victorious but in Shanghai the Chinese Nineteenth Route Army, under General Tsai, surprised the world by putting up a stubborn resistance and might have won over the Japanese had they been able to get any help from General Chiang. For many a day, General Tsai blamed Chiang for refusing to send him help and denounced him as playing with the enemy against the interests of his own country. The whole affair was placed before the League of Nations. It was unable to stop the fighting but finally appointed a committee of investigation under Lord Lytton, which, after spending some months in the Far East, handed in a lengthy report. Neither country liked the report; the Chinese resented the admonition which was given them to maintain a more orderly country and the Japanese felt that the blame for the whole thing had been put upon their shoulders, especially as the world took the attitude that only the military power of Japan had made the independence of Manchuria possible. In the end, Japan sent in its resignation as a member of the League.

But before the League report was published, matters had advanced rapidly in Manchuria. She declared herself an independent state with a republican form of government. The last of the Manchus, the same who as a little boy had succeeded the Empress Dowager upon the Dragon Throne, came back to the land of his forefathers and was proclaimed head of the new state of Manchukuo. When the question of recognition of Manchukuo came up the powers took the stand that, as its creation had been contrary to treaty rights, it was not entitled to recognition. Japan, on the contrary, just before the Lytton report was made public, recognized the new nation. Since then the capital has been removed from Mukden, a little farther north to the former city of Changchun, now called Hsinking, or New Capital, and the last Manchu has been proclaimed Emperor Kang Teh in a ceremony following the old imperial rites.

But even this loss of large territory was not then a powerful enough sting to unite the different factions among the Chinese to repel the invader. For a while they are able to carry on a boycott in this section or that but lack the self-denying patriotism to unite in a sustained movement against a common enemy. A student of Manchurian and Chinese affairs, Owen Lattimore, has explained the apparent failure in the north in an interesting way.[6] He thinks that the Chinese do not fear the activities of the Russians deeply because that is a more or less accustomed menace. They have always had the barbarian on the north. The outsider on the north comes and goes, but after all he can be dealt with satisfactorily. Japan, however, is quite another matter. That country stands for a new threat from across the sea. It is a new kind of danger and the Chinese have not learned to deal with it as they have with that old menace beyond the Great Wall. Therefore, it is to be feared and it must be combatted.

At any rate, China would seem to be working out her salvation in much the same manner as she has always done. From the days of the Ancients we find her trying to break down separate state lines and build up a confederacy or an empire. Today she is striving for a united national government. From the time of the Ancients her second great problem has been to protect herself from the outside barbarian and often she succeeded by building a Great Wall or by conquest or assimilation. In this modern age she is trying to protect herself from this new menace from beyond the sea. It is a matter of repelling the Japanese invaders already upon her soil.

CHAPTER XXV

NATIONALISM PREPARES FOR A TEST

It has been frequently deplored, during the last quarter-century, that China seemed incapable of nationalism, that her people lacked true patriotism, their loyalties being directed to the family, to the village or *hsien,* at most to the province. Onlookers since the Revolution of 1911 have looked anxiously for the development of a national unity which would be adequate to protect the country in this modern world. And at length the change has come. In the last year or two the world has become aware that China has developed a nationalism. The people now are actuated by a sense of patriotism—loyalty to the country of China.

Hu Shih explains this new phase of national thought and feeling as follows:

> "Nationalism is a new word in the Chinese dictionary but national consciousness has never been absent in Chinese history. It has its firm foundation in the racial, cultural and historical unity of her vast population. It always asserted itself whenever China came into contact with a foreign race or culture, especially in those historic periods when she was conquered by a foreign invasion or dominated by an alien civilization. It was Chinese national consciousness that gradually revolted against Buddhism as an alien religion and finally killed it. It was Chinese nationalism which brought forth the numerous anti-Manchu secret soci-

eties and open revolts in the 18th and 19th centuries, and which finally overthrew the Manchu Monarchy twenty-six years ago.

"Frankly and truthfully speaking, what Japanese apologists loudly advertise to the world as 'anti-Japanese sentiments and acts in China' is simply Chinese nationalism resenting and resisting the real and undesirable aggressions of a foreign power, Japan. . . . The issue, therefore, is pure and simple: It is Chinese nationalism resisting Japanese invasion; it is the Chinese nation fighting for its very existence."[1]

Today, one often hears the statement, "Japan has caused Chinese unity." But besides the fact that foreign aggression stimulated the development of this new nationalism and unity, another factor that made its expression possible was the appearance of a recognized national leader, Chiang Kai-shek—China's George Washington. Perhaps we should say leaders, for Madame Chiang has been a real part of the leadership.

About the time he was coming into prominence as a Kuomintang leader in 1927, Chiang Kai-shek married Mei-ling Soong of the powerful Soong family, sister of Madame Sun Yat-sen and Madame H. H. Kung, and of T. V. Soong, the financier. The Soongs are a Christian family and Chiang Kai-shek has since his marriage joined a Methodist church in Shanghai. His wife has broadened his horizon materially, as she spent most of her early life in America and is a graduate of Wellesley College. She has brought him her knowledge of the West and serves as his interpreter of English and of foreign news.

Chiang himself spent some years abroad just after the Russo-Japanese war studying in Japan and later a year in Russia. The combined foreign experiences of Chiang and his wife have been invaluable in their efforts to modernize China, and the two have worked together in the furtherance of China's unity and advancement. Other counselors of Chiang are: W. H. Donald, an Australian, German military advisers, and Italian and American flying experts. In the civil government are a large corps of modernly educated Chinese. During the last ten years, Chiang Kai-shek has grown definitely as a leader. At times his methods have seemed harsh, but in the conditions which have confronted him, bold quick thrusts were necessary if the various factions scattered all over China were to be welded together for common action.

At the end of the Manchurian affair of 1931, China had many military leaders all waiting for a place in the sun. A military council was formed, over which Chiang was made chairman with full power to issue military orders. With him served several with whose names we are familiar—Chang Hsueh-liang, the erstwhile young marshal of Manchuria; Feng Yu-hsiang, the "Christian general"; Yen Hsi-shan, Shansi's "model governor," and the Kwangsi war lord, Li Tsung-yin.

Chang Hsueh-liang's position in Peiping was untenable after the loss of Manchuria. Certain leaders, T. V. Soong and Sun Fo, and some of his own troops, wanted him to try further resistance against Japan, but that was clearly impossible at the time. So Chang moved from Peiping west to Paoting-fu, but after the loss of Jehol in 1933 he realized that he and his troops were useless there, as a Manchurian campaign was more than ever out of the question. So Chang handed over his troops to become part of the national army under Chiang Kai-shek and he left for Europe. Yen Hsi-shan devoted himself to his own affairs as governor of Shansi. Feng Yu-hsiang was less tractable. He wanted Shantung but was sent to Chahar, where he followed a vacillating course. At one time he declared himself commander-in-chief of the People's Anti-Japanese Army and called on all China to resist Nanking. No one took him seriously, so he betook himself to a Buddhist monastery on the sacred mountain, Tai Shan, in Shantung, where one of his former underlings Han Fu-chu[2] was governor.

While all this unrest and shifting were going on among the military leaders of the North, the South was living up to its reputation of separatism. The southern provinces denounced Chiang for following a weak policy regarding Jehol and Japan but, taking the advice of one of their leaders, Pai Chung-hsi of Kwangsi, they decided not to embark on a military campaign against Nanking. In Fukien province, however, things took more alarming shape. There some of Chiang's old enemies held important positions and by the end of the year 1933 an independent government was set up. Eugene Chen was Minister of Foreign Affairs and Tsai Ting-kai, the former (1932) leader at Shanghai of the Nineteenth Route Army, was military chief. Otherwise the rebels failed to get the support they counted on. The Southwest Political Council and individuals on whom they had counted denied any sympathy with them.

In this situation, Chiang decided to act with vigor, first by an aerial attack on them and then by an advance of infantry. Both these movements proved the effectiveness of Chiang's military machine. In two weeks the fighting was over, and the whole rebellion was crushed within two months of its beginning. This affair served as an awakening to the Chinese war lords with individual aspirations and also showed the Japanese that unification might become a possibility in China. A man of the caliber necessary for national leadership had emerged from among the war lords.

Chiang's old enemies, the Communists, were next to be reckoned with. During the years since 1927 when the

NATIONALISM PREPARES FOR A TEST 339

Communists had been expelled from the Kuomintang, these two parties had been implacable foes and Chiang had sent many expeditions against the "Soviet areas."[3] The Reds carried on a sort of guerilla warfare in which their members were one moment soldiers and the next peasants, peacefully tilling the soil. The expeditions of the government accomplished nothing except cruel warfare and great loss of life on both sides. By 1933 when Chiang was free to launch another expedition, the Reds controlled a large area in Kiangsi and two smaller ones in Hunan and Anhwei. The government expedition was planned against the large Kiangsi Soviet. But new tactics were used. The Nationalists built motor roads leading to the area and erected a cordon of small forts around the district so as to keep out necessities, principally salt. Though a slow and expensive method it brought so much hardship that the Communists found their position untenable. However, they planned a well-ordered retreat and before the Nationalist Army were aware of it, the main Red Army, 90,000 strong, had been on the march for several days. A second army also escaped. Women and children followed the armies and Communist sympathizers joined them on the way.

The "long march" of about seven thousand miles will go down in history as one of the spectacular treks of all time. Led by Chu Teh, commander-in-chief of the Red Armies, they traveled west and south through Kuangtung, Kwangsi, Hunan, Kweichow and Yunnan provinces and then north into Szechuan, across the Yangtse and Tatu rivers, finally reaching Shensi slightly over a year after starting. Forty-five thousand of their original first army of 90,000 still survived. Their hardships at times seemed insurmountable; high mountain ranges, wide rivers, unfriendly tribes, lack of food, and the ever harassing government troops. They seized goods from merchants and landlords but paid for whatever they obtained from the farmers and did considerable teaching of democracy and social equality.

When the Kiangsi Red Army arrived in Shensi, they found a well-established Communist community. The Nationalists maintained a governor in the province and two armies. One of these was made up of the Manchurian troops driven out by Japan and now again under their old commander, Chang Hsueh-liang, who had returned from Europe. The other soldiers were Shensi native troops under Wang Hu-cheng, who served under the young Marshal Chang. Very soon it became noticeable that there was much passing to and fro between these two armies and the Communists. Another interesting fact was evident. The Communists were discarding their anti-landlord and anti-capitalist slogan for an anti-Japanese one. Until the invader was driven from the country, social welfare could not progress, they said. Also, they knew that the Nationalist government had met them on that issue in its new economic reconstruction program.

To return to Nanking, the Central Executive Committee had been busy consolidating the government machinery. Late in 1934 various economic matters had been put under control of the central authorities. Local mints were abolished and issuance of bank notes was put under regulations from Nanking. National taxes were to be collected by Nanking officials and provincial budgets approved by the central government. The opium revenue was made a state monopoly. As various local taxes, principally land taxes, were still allowed, there appeared to be no difficulty. The Generalissimo and his wife visited various parts of China as another phase of the unifying program. And early in 1936 one more step was taken in centralization. Provincial and local committees of the Kuomintang were replaced by

NATIONALISM PREPARES FOR A TEST 341

commissioners appointed by Nanking. At Nanking the party system continued and some of the members suggested that Chiang be made president of the Kuomintang, a position no one had held since Sun Yat-sen. This move seemed ill advised and was dropped. Patriotism still centers around the figure of Sun Yat-sen whose picture, draped by national and party flags, is seen in all official buildings and school rooms and auditoriums. The picture of Chiang is almost as often seen, but not given the same prominence.

These various unifying measures, both political and military, naturally called down criticism and complaints against Nanking and particularly Chiang. Those of separatist tendencies feared too strong a leader. So by early summer of 1936, taking advantage of Japan's inroads in North China, the southern military leaders from Kwangtung and Kwangsi were again in revolt, demanding that Chiang start measures immediately for military campaign against Japan. Possibly the overthrow of Chiang, not Japan, was their goal. When Chiang refused their plea, the Southerners began the movement of their troops northward toward Hunan, expecting its governor would allow them to pass through. But Chiang acted quickly and got the co-operation of the governor, who withstood the revolutionists with his own troops. Some claim that Chiang bought up the Hunan governor, but whatever he did, it preserved the nation intact. A civil war between north and south would have left the country wide open for Japan to enter. As a matter of fact, few if any supported the southern leaders and they discovered how unpopular dissension was becoming. They retired to their own borders. Chiang placed his own officials in Kwangtung. Kwangsi retained its own leaders, Li and Pai, apparently on an understanding of good behavior.

With the collapse of the Southern Rebellion the country

settled down to a renewed confidence in Chiang Kai-shek, which they showed in great festivities on his fiftieth birthday in October, 1936. The most spectacular part of the celebration was the gift of fifty-five war planes which performed exemplary manoeuvers above Nanking.

And then in scarcely six weeks, December, 1936, occurred the kidnapping of Chiang which all the world remembers. The capture took place at Sian-fu in Shensi, where we have seen Communists and Shensi and Manchurian troops, all of them strongly anti-Japanese. The reason for this strange event lay, probably, in the fact that Generalissimo Chiang, long-time enemy of the Communists, had ordered Chang to go against the Red settlements in Shensi. But his soldiers refused because they felt that Japan, not the Communists, was their enemy. The news of the German-Japan alliance against Communism had further excited them. Upon news of their refusal, Chiang went up to try to coerce them to do his own bidding, but failed. And then early one morning firing drove him from bed. There was no escape except over a wall and to a cave where he was later in the morning captured. Apparently the Reds had nothing to do with Chiang's capture, though they had a voice in the ensuing negotiations. That was the work of Chang or, rather more, his subordinates, Yang Hu-cheng and his Shensi troops.

Chiang and Chang could not find a basis for agreement, for Chiang insisted it was mutiny and they must either surrender to him or kill him. The story goes that the captors had read Chiang's diary and become convinced of his sincerity and so were loathe to kill him. Then Mr. Donald, who had been adviser to Chang for several years before accepting that position to Chiang, flew up from Nanking. Both trusted him; both were relieved to see him; and conversations began. In the meantime matters were crucial in Nanking. The government wished to send up

NATIONALISM PREPARES FOR A TEST 343

an expedition against the rebels, but the Chiang family feared that such a course would mean the death of the Generalissimo and advised against it. Donald persuaded Chiang to send word to Nanking to send no expedition. Chiang though in captivity was head of the Military Council.

Then Madame Chiang and her brother, T. V. Soong, flew up to Sian. While they were conferring, feeling over China rallied around Chiang. Feng Yu-hsiang now in Nanking as vice-chairman of the Military Affairs Committee acted in the Generalissimo's place and urged Chiang's release, promising to throw his support toward urging upon Chiang anti-Japanese action. Yen Hsi-shan, the Kwangsi leaders so lately in revolt, Sung Cheh-yuan of the Chahar-Hopei Autonomous Council, governors of provinces, and intellectuals, all rallied to the Generalissimo's support.

Finally, Chang Hsueh-liang broke the seeming deadlock by offering to go to Nanking with the Chiangs. That action would show he wanted no ransom, and by taking the blame upon himself he would free Yang Hu-cheng and his Shensi troops from any fear of punishment.

The party arrived in Nanking on December 25, 1936, and the city and the whole country went wild with jubilation. Guns, firecrackers, sirens made the wildest Chinese New Year mild in comparison. Chiang had, it seemed, suffered no loss of face. Then only did the country really know how much they had come to lean on their strong man. He, of course, in Chinese fashion took the blame and recited his own shortcomings—laxity over his men and personal faults—and resigned all his offices the conventional three times. He was reinstated each time. Chang was given a sentence of ten years and the next day was pardoned. In the spring of 1937 he was in retirement in Chekiang Province.

The upshot of the Sian Affair has been a *rapprochement* between Communist and Kuomintang parties, which had been separated and fighting each other since 1927. The so-called Soviet Republic of China is now (1938) called "The Bordering Districts of Shensi, Kansu, Ningsia." The Red armies now constitute the "Eighth Route Army of the National Army of China." The Red flag, insignia and cap are gone and in their places are the Nationalist flag and symbol, Kuomintang regulation uniforms and caps. And the erstwhile Red Army is fighting on the "popular front" against the common enemy.

It is interesting to read some of the statements made by Red leaders. Mao Tse-tung, their chairman, in August, 1936, said, "that the property of rich farmers would not be confiscated by the Communists if these wealthy men supported the movement to resist Japan. Property and factories of merchants and of larger and smaller capitalists will not be confiscated. On the contrary we will protect such enterprises and even help them to develop their business."[4]

Nym Wales reports that in the new elections which have brought about this change there is universal suffrage above the age of sixteen. Landlords and capitalists are allowed to vote, although it is admitted there is some difficulty in granting them this right. Different individuals have thus expressed their views. "In this crisis we must support the unification of China. . . . We cannot have two separate class governments at such a time, so we must give up all forms of Soviet power." And again another leader says: "The people all liked the Soviet better. It was simple and easy for them. The landlords will perhaps like the new democracy better, but there are few landlords left here to enjoy it."[5] The "new democracy" is a form of representative democracy, the village electing its representatives, those representatives in turn electing district representatives, and

NATIONALISM PREPARES FOR A TEST

these in their turn electing members of a governing body for the whole area.

The Soviets have prepared a ten-point program for cooperation with Nanking. The first seven points refer to national defense and mobilization of armies against Japan. The last three call for improvement and reconstruction of the life of the people, including removal of the many unjust surtaxes, decrease of taxes, and decrease of rents, development of the anti-Japanese national defense education, and organization of a united front of the whole country, with the unification of the two parties (Kuomintang and Communist) as the basis of the struggle against Japan.

In commenting on the receipt of this program, Chiang Kai-shek in September, 1937, said that the Nationalist government would gladly accept the services of any political organization which sincerely desired to stem foreign aggression and work for the cause of the Nationalist Revolution under the leadership of the Kuomintang. The aim of the Revolution was to seek for China freedom and equality. With this in view, Sun Yat-sen had years before enunciated the Three People's Principles. And again Chiang said:

> "The manifesto recently issued by the Chinese Communist Party is an outstanding instance of the triumph of national sentiment over every consideration. The decisions embodied in the Manifesto, such as the abandonment of violence, cessation of Communist propaganda, abolition of the Chinese Soviets, and the disbandment of the Red army are all essential measures towards the mobilization of national strength for the purpose of repelling attacks on our national existence.
>
> "These decisions embody the spirit of the Manifesto and resolutions adopted by the last plenary session of the Kuomintang. The allegiance now openly avowed by the Communists to the cause of the Three People's

Principles has happily closed the last gap in our national armour. The entire nation shall henceforth strive in one common direction."[6]

The "one common direction" had already been charted by the enemy who by this time were carrying on undeclared war in North China and at Shanghai.

While the military and political elements involved in the making of a new China have necessarily occupied so much attention, social and economic needs have by no means been neglected. These have been dealt with under two heads—the New Life Movement and the National Economic Reconstruction Movement.

The New Life Movement was officially launched by Chiang Kai-shek in February, 1934, at Nanchang, capital of Kiangsi. From that beginning it has spread all over the country. It has an almost puritanic flavor, enjoining abstinence from excesses of all kinds, gambling, drinking, smoking, and elaborate entertaining. Often one hears a guest in fun chide his host or hostess, "This is no 'New Life' dinner." The symbols for right conduct, one aim of the movement, are four Chinese characters *Li, I, Lien, and Chih*—"*Li*, which means courtesy; *I*, meaning service towards our fellow men and ourselves; *Lien*, representing honesty and respect for the rights of others; and *Chih*, or high-mindedness or honor—virtues which made the Chinese nation great in remote times."[7]

Sun Yat-sen's principle of the Livelihood of the People forms an important phase of the movement. Attention is given to more sanitary and hygienic conditions in the cities and villages. To provide more adequately for these needs, people are exhorted to give up old expensive habits in celebration of births, weddings, and burials. New Life posters are hung up in schools, especially those in backward rural districts. The pictures—showing children exercising, taking baths, brushing teeth, sleeping—are held up as patterns by the teachers and visiting nurses. Undoubtedly, it has been a useful device for raising the standard of living; certainly the aspect of the people on the streets shows marked improvement over conditions ten years ago.

Education, both private and public, has progressed tremendously. In an interview granted the author, the Minister of Education was most enthusiastic over the results of co-education, saying it was proving successful "beyond all expectations." In the cities, the character of school buildings varies greatly, some being old Chinese structures and others of modern types. Playgrounds and gymnasium apparatus are plentiful, which is especially necessary where buildings are heated but poorly, if at all. School readers are attractively got up in the simplified national language. The greatest need is for more trained teachers to supply the ever-broadening demands.

In the Economic Reconstruction Movement, there is a wealth of undertakings: conservation work, reforestation, highway and railway building, financial reforms, and rural rehabilitation. Of these, perhaps the rural rehabilitation is the most interesting and vital. The movement began, so one of the Nanking officials promoting the movement told me, several years ago in voluntary meetings of university men called to discuss social questions. Interest increased and, after several conferences, the decision was reached that any plan to help China must be based on agriculture, as such a large part of the population is rural. Finally the government embraced the movement and incorporated it in a department at Nanking. The program, as it had developed by the spring of 1937, included six objectives: crop improvement, land utilization, rural education, co-operatives, credit, self-defense. The movement, besides being very much needed, has proved to be exceptionally astute as it furnishes the people much the same benefits as they had hoped for under Communism.

Unity and reconstruction made 1937 (until the armed conflict) a banner year in prosperity. Julian Arnold, American commercial attaché, reports that:

> "China's financial stability was maintained, unification of the currency system advanced; China's credit strengthened by the augmentation of gold reserves abroad, and until the commencement of hostilities with Japan next year's fiscal year was promising. . . . Rice crop products, cotton, and tung oil were excellent; up to the middle of July the general outlook for trade throughout the country was more encouraging than at any time for some years past . . . the total imports over the first six months increased by thirty per cent and exports by forty-five per cent compared with the same period last year."[8]

In July the outbreak of hostilities began to test the unity and patriotism of the "popular front" of China.

CHAPTER XXVI

THE "POPULAR FRONT" FACES JAPAN

THE YEARS from the Manchurian Incident until the starting of military operations between Japan and China in the summer of 1937 were, as we have seen, crowded ones for China. She had not only to battle with the problems of perfecting the government machinery and promoting social welfare, but also to provide national defense against a powerful Japan, grown more aggressive since the creation of her puppet state of Manchuria.

The severance of Manchuria from China did not satisfy the Japanese authorities, and they continued to take occasion to further their interests at the expense of China whenever they found it possible. Japan claimed that for defense purposes she needed the section lying to the southwest of Manchuria, known as Jehol. Formerly, this territory constituted the eastern part of Inner Mongolia. Japan seized Jehol in 1933 and added it to Manchukuo, thereby giving herself a convenient base from which she has frequently started military operations south of the Great Wall. This seizure was promptly followed by the Tangku Truce which provided for a demilitarized zone between Manchukuo and North China. A line was drawn through northern Hopei, just north of Peiping, beyond which line Chinese troops were to withdraw to the south and southwest. The Chinese were allowed police but no soldiers, while the Japanese were given the right to oversee the withdrawal of Chinese troops.

On the other hand, Japanese soldiers were not to go south of the Great Wall.

For two years relations were fairly smooth. Intellectual leaders such as Hu Shih called upon the Chinese to bend their energies to internal reconstruction, and the Chinese government issued a "good-will mandate" forbidding provocative acts against foreign peoples in China and urging good will toward the country's neighbors. Japan also made declarations of good will and economic co-operation. Mr. Hirota, then Minister of Foreign Affairs, was the leader in these protestations of friendship, but his Three Principles regarding China which he issued in 1935 must have seemed anything but reassuring to the Chinese. They read:

1. China shall not again utilize the influence of Europe and America to embarrass Japan.
2. Relations between China, Japan, and Manchukuo shall be adjusted. China shall recognize Manchukuo and promote economic co-operation with Manchukuo and Japan.
3. China and Japan shall co-operate in defense against Communism, especially along the northern border of China.

The peace was short-lived, and in 1935 there occurred several events which destroyed these good-will efforts. Suddenly a slogan, "North China for Northern Chinese," was heard. This movement culminated in the creation of several autonomous régimes. The first, the East Hopei Autonomous Council, was set up in the demilitarized zone, north and east of Peiping, with Yin Ju-ken as the chairman. Tungchow, fifteen miles east of Peiping, became the headquarters. Peiping, which had been the capital of China until its removal to Nanking in 1928, harboring by 1935, almost under its walls, a separatist régime! Another such set-up farther

THE "POPULAR FRONT" FACES JAPAN 351

to the north was the Hopei-Chahar Political Council, with General Sung Cheh-yuan at the head.

The policy of Japan in establishing these autonomous governments was to work directly with local officials in an attempt to divorce them from the central government at Nanking. The Tangku Truce had the legal if unwilling backing of the Nanking government, for it was signed by the central authorities. But later ones were not. For example, the so-called Ho-Umetsu Agreement, a letter from General Ho to the Japanese general, Umetsu, was never published and never ratified by the Chinese government. At first, the plan of autonomous states met some success, as Japan was able to influence certain Chinese to support her course, but by 1936 there was a stiffening in the attitude of Nanking, which declared that only those agreements and arrangements which were ratified by the Nationalist government could be recognized.

General Sung Cheh-yuan, the head of the Hopei-Chahar Political Council, affords an interesting study. He was not only chairman of the Council but also head of the Hopei Provincial Government and commander of his own provincial army, the Twenty-ninth Army. No Nanking troops were allowed in Hopei, so he was supreme military leader of the province. He was in a most baffling position. Japanese, of course, were counting on his being their handy man and co-operating with them. A man of little education, he showed real ability in handling the situation, and for two years stood as a sort of buffer between Japan and the Nanking government. In his army were patriotic officers and soldiers, and the loyal intellectuals and other groups in Peiping were naturally at times pressing him hard for resistance against Japan. Nanking was not able to send him military support, so he followed a middle course; on the one hand keeping the most vociferous patriots from open demonstrations, and on the other avoiding issues with the Japanese. Both sides counted on him, strangely enough, but when war came he was found to be a patriotic Chinese. Not all were as able or loyal as he. Yin Ju-ken, head of the East Hopei Autonomous Régime, put himself on record as opposed to its dissolution.

The two greatest problems in the autonomous sections were smuggling and narcotics. Japanese and their subjects, the Koreans, had the advantage of extra-territorial status and thus, under the protection of Japanese courts, did about as they pleased. Japanese goods were landed at Tientsin and other nearby small Chinese ports without paying duty. This distressed many foreign nations as well as the Chinese, for interest on loans is paid from the customs receipts. Also, it vitiated the Open Door policy for trade in China. The Chinese government, of course, protested its loss of revenue, which they estimated at about eight million dollars (U. S. currency) a year. The Chinese were able to combat the evil somewhat by invoking the death penalty for those handling the smuggled goods beyond the demilitarized zones. Trains and busses leaving the autonomous and demilitarized regions were searched.

The narcotic menace has grown apace in these regions where Japanese nationals are protected by their officials. To quote an American onlooker at Tientsin in 1936:

"In the Japanese Concession at Tientsin last year [1936] I counted over forty tables on one street where opium-smoking and drug-taking paraphernalia were openly sold. I secured the names of 134 shops in the Japanese concession, under euphemistic names, where narcotics and injections were sold. The price was very cheap, often free, for the first injections, until the habit was formed. There were 800,000 drug addicts in the Tientsin area. Doped cigarettes were sold through the villages under Japanese influence. The Chinese made protests in vain."[1]

Japan's major objectives became clearer as time went on. She wished to establish a single economic bloc of Japan, Manchukuo and North China. "North China," as interpreted by the Japanese, means the five northeastern provinces: Chahar and Suiyuan, Inner Mongolian provinces, and Shansi, Hopei, and Shantung, the northeastern three of the eighteen provinces of China proper. To make "cooperation" effective in this region, she felt that she must have control of its railways and natural resources. The natural resources which she is desirous of controlling are coal in Shansi, iron in Chahar, and cotton, which may be grown in Hopei and Shantung. Under this scheme North China would become another Manchukuo and just as much cut off from China as is that state and would form a buffer between Russia and China as Manchukuo does between Russia and Japan proper.

By the summer and autumn of 1936, things did not seem to be going so smoothly for Japan as they had from 1931 to 1935. Heretofore, when Japanese had been killed in China, the Japanese government had been able to make protests and gain advantages for its own policy in China. As I read in the newspapers in Tokyo in the latter part of 1936 the meager accounts of various incidents as they occurred in China, I sensed a surprisingly mild attitude on the part of Japan. In Szechuen in West China, two Japanese journalists were killed, in Pakhoi in southwest China a Japanese druggist was murdered; a Japanese policeman in Hankow and a Japanese sailor in Shanghai met similar fates. But China, instead of the former acceptance of Japanese demands, was now insisting that her side of the story be heard and that thorough investigation by both parties be made. In the end, China paid indemnities for the killings in Szechuan and at Pakhoi but refused any responsibility for the last two which had occurred in foreign concessions, where she had no jurisdiction. Beyond this

China would not go. This stubborn resistence was novel in the recent relations of the two countries.

On the military front also Japan received a check in the Inner Mongolian provinces. Over Chahar, she had been able, in 1935, to gain military supremacy and had drawn it into the Hopei-Chahar Political Council. In 1936 she decided on the same course in Suiyuan, just west of Chahar. Japanese officers had been active for years in stirring up the Mongols against the Chinese under the guise of the slogan "Inner Mongolia for the Inner Mongolians." In May, 1936, Prince Teh,[2] with Japanese advisers, organized a military government of Mongolia at the same time that he was professing loyalty to the Chinese government. In the autumn he led an expedition into Suiyuan from Chahar. It is known that the Japanese Kwantung Army of Manchuria backed this attack against the Chinese government in Suiyuan. But the Chinese military commander was able to resist them and drive them back into Chahar. The whole affair aroused patriotism throughout China, where women's clubs and other organizations raised money for the soldiers in Suiyuan.

Events in China: Chiang Kai-shek's capture and release in the northwestern province of Shensi in December, 1936, the subsequent rallying of all classes and sections in China round him as a common leader, and the *rapprochement* of the Nationalist and so-called Red armies so long fighting against each other, had a varying effect on different Japanese leaders. Some saw in it an opportunity for peaceful constructive relations between the two countries. Others were alarmed and feared that their whole aggressive plan for North China might be jeopardized. Through the first half of 1937 the former group seemed to be in the ascendancy. Japan's ambassador to China, Kawagoe, kept reiterating that in China there was a new type of man at the

THE "POPULAR FRONT" FACES JAPAN

helm, patriotic, well-informed, and efficient, and that Japan would do well to recognize that fact in her dealings with the country. Naotake Sato, with a long experience in diplomacy, was called from France to be foreign minister in General Hayashi's cabinet. He was a liberal and openly declared himself in favor of treating China on a basis of equality instead of presenting demands at the point of the sword. His efforts were directed along the line of developing collaboration between the two countries on economic matters. Unfortunately the wise and intelligent views of these gentlemen were heeded only for the moment, for with the fall of the short-lived Hayashi cabinet in May of 1937, Sato was out of office and the views of Kawagoe unheeded.

The Japanese government, unable to take the advice of its own peacefully minded statesmen, clung to the policy of acquiring control over North China. On the other hand, the Chinese, with the great progress they had made in unity and patriotism and in developing political and economic strength, naturally resisted Japan's policy and refused to recognize any other control than Nanking's. They knew that if they relinquished the North China provinces, in time they would be called upon to do the same farther south. Thus it is not surprising that Japan was finding that the morale of local leaders, such as Yen Hsi-shan, Sung Cheh-yuan and Han Fu-chu, was stiffening and they were referring questions to Nanking instead of following the former practice of making local arrangements on their own responsibility.

With relations between the two countries thus strained another incident arose. At Lukuochiao, Marco Polo Bridge, near Peiping on July 7, 1937, Japanese soldiers were engaged in night maneuvers which resulted in a skirmish with a band of Chinese soldiers. This occurrence unimportant in itself became a major issue when Japan demanded that the Chinese government consider it a matter for local settlement.

The clearest understanding of the situation is gained by reading the statements of government officials of the two countries.

Chiang Kai-shek on July 19, less than two weeks after the Lukuochiao affair, announced the Nanking government's conditions for settlement:

> "First, any kind of settlement must not infringe upon the territorial integrity or sovereign right of China.
> "Second, the status of the Hopei-Chahar Council was fixed by the Central Government and we will not allow any illegal alteration. [Chiang agreed to sanction the local agreement on July 7 in an effort to make peace.]
> "Third, we will not agree to the removal by outside pressure of those local officials appointed by the Central Government, such as the chairman of the Hopei-Chahar Council. [Sung Cheh-yuan held this position.]
> "Fourth, we will not allow any restriction to be placed on the positions of the 29th Army [Sung's army]."[3]

The Japanese answered that China must assume responsibility for the Lukuochiao incident and punish the guilty, withdraw troops from the Peiping-Tientsin area, eradicate all acts of anti-Japanism and enforce, in co-operation with Japan, measures against Communism. These terms, of course, China could not accept as they infringed upon her own sovereignty.

Ten days later, Generalissimo Chiang issued the statement that "Japan's army has completely ignored China's wishes and therefore China is determined to fight to the last man. I call upon the people to mobilize their total resources and struggle hand-in-hand to save the country."

In reply to Secretary Hull's plea for peace to both nations, Premier Konoye replied on August 28: "Japan entertains no intention of resorting to diplomatic means of settlement. We favor a comprehensive punitive campaign against China," and on October 8, General Matsui proclaimed, "The Japanese army is now prepared to use every means to subdue its opponents."[4]

Foreign Minister Hirota in his statement before the Japanese Diet on September 5 makes clear the Japanese attitude:

> "Ever since the beginning of the present China affair, the Japanese Government in pursuance of its policy of *local* settlement and non-aggravation, exerted every effort to effect a speedy solution. The Nanking Government whose prompt reconsideration was invited failed to manifest a grain of sincerity but concentrated its armies in North China to challenge Japan, while in the Yangtse Valley and elsewhere in South and Central China, they embarked in an anti-Japanese campaign of the most vicious kind, which not only prevented our nationals in that region from engaging in peaceful pursuits but also jeopardized their very existence."[5]

A Nine-Power Treaty Conference was called at Brussels in November. Though a signatory of the Nine-Power Treaty which promised to protect China's sovereignty, Japan refused to appear. A condemnation of Japan as the aggressor was all that was accomplished. The League could do no more.

CHAPTER XXVII

CHINA AT WAR

WITH THE inability to settle the Lukuochiao affair, China and Japan found themselves in an all out though undeclared war. The Japanese undoubtedly expected a quick victory as in the previous Sino-Japanese war of 1895. By vehemence of attack they hoped to terrify the Chinese people into quick and complete submission. However, their estimates went awry and they were surprised to find that the Chinese refused to "bend the knee" before their military invasion.

Peiping and Tientsin fell without delay as the Nationalist armies were not able to reach the northern cities in time to prevent occupation. The greatest loss of property occurred at Tientsin and the most deplorable of all losses was Nankai University, which was destroyed by bombing. Nankai had been established years before by one of China's most forward-looking educationalists, Chang Bo-lin. The university's scholarship had become widely known as its publications were interchanged with universities in Europe and America. Moreover, it had come to be a force in China through its graduates, many of whom held offices in the various departments in the central government at Nanking. The Japanese feared its influence and that of all educational institutions. At Peiping, Tsing Hua College, the American Indemnity School, was partly destroyed and not allowed to open.

Within a month after the beginning of hostilities, the war was carried to a second front, Shanghai. The Chinese armies put up a splendid fight. Three months passed before

Shanghai fell, and then the victory was robbed of any decisive character because the defeated armies, instead of being annihilated or captured, slipped through the enemies' lines and escaped to the interior. It is a military maxim that a war against an enemy who possesses a large territory and vast resources cannot be won unless its army can be conquered. China is one of those countries which is blessed with a vast hinterland to which her armies can escape and live to fight another day.

Following the fall of Shanghai, the neighboring large cities, Hangchow, Soochow and Nanking fell before the invader within a few weeks. But again the armies and the official government slipped away to the inexhaustible west and a new capital was set up at Hankow, farther up on the Yangtse. The brutal treatment by the Japanese armies of the civilian population, especially at Nanking, strengthened the resistance of the Chinese all over the nation and aroused sympathy throughout the world. As these cities fell, the Chinese freely used the scorched-earth policy, destroying anything which might aid the invader, factories, water-works, bridges, as well as flooding large areas before the approach of the enemy.

After a lull Japan undertook to connect her conquests in the north with those in the Yangtse region. To this end she set out at both ends of the Tientsin-Pukow railway, aiming at the junction with the Lunghai railroad. This move was hotly contested by the Chinese over a period of five months, during which they won a decisive victory at Taierchwang. Though this victory merely delayed the Japanese, it was of great psychological significance to both sides. To the Chinese it gave a great lift in morale to know that they could win a battle in spite of the superior equipment of the enemy. To the Japanese it brought humiliation to suffer the first defeat in their modern history. When the junction, Süchow, fell during the next month "not a single Chinese division was destroyed nor a valuable gun acquired." As at Shanghai and Nanking, the Chinese army was not annihilated but only pushed back into the interior.

After the fall of Süchow, the Chinese opened the dikes in the Yellow River, thus preventing the Japanese from marching overland to Hankow, the new capital and their next objective. This move forced the Japanese to take the slower route up the Yangtse and one which might bring them into difficulties with foreign powers who had long had the right to patrol the river with their gunboats in order to insure free navigation. Thus another five months was consumed in reaching Hankow, and when the Japanese marched in (October 26, 1938) they found that the government and the Chinese army were well away to the west in Szechuen province. There a new capital, Chungking, was established, above the Yangtse rapids, which the Japanese have never reached except by bombing.

Four days before the fall of Hankow the Japanese army surprised the world by marching into Canton. All but a meager ten thousand of its inhabitants had fled to the west. The Japanese, who now had control of both ends of the Canton-Hankow railroad, failed to gain the entire line.

During the summer of 1939 naval operations played a more active role. Although a blockade of the whole China coast had been declared when hostilities opened in the sumber of 1937, it had not been systematically enforced. However, in February, 1939, three months after the fall of Canton, naval vessels seized the Chinese island of Hainan, which lies between Hongkong and Singapore. Two months later Japanese appeared in the Spratly Islands, claimed by France, which lie off the coast of Indo-China. This action was followed shortly by the successive closing of the Chinese ports of Swatow, Amoy, Fuchow, Wenchow and Ningpo to foreign trade, though it is well known that many goods have been smuggled through these ports. Not until November was Japan able to enter the extreme southern port of Pakhoi, and this victory was offset by the army's defeat at Changsha, where the Chinese pushed them back to Hankow.

From then on the war settled down to a more or less routine procedure, with very little in the way of territorial changes. Japanese have made attacks, and Chinese, both regular army and guerillas, have counterattacked. Chungking has been repeatedly bombed and as repeatedly rebuilt. The Japanese have attempted to build up defenses against the guerilla bands and to protect the railways which they hold. They have tried to cut all roads over which supplies could come from other countries and to destroy all airdromes which might be used in attacks against Japan.

China, since the war, has been divided into two parts, occupied and free China. In territories occupied by her armies, Japan has set up local puppet-governments with Chinese officials nominally at the head but with numerous Japanese advisers the power behind the throne. The success of these has been meager as has been indicated by the fact that many of the Chinese puppet-officials have been assassinated. Japan almost immediately tried to find someone to assume the position of federal puppet-chief. Her first efforts were to procure a man of reputation and ability, one in whom the Chinese would have confidence. But this was not so easy. For months she endeavored to enlist the services of Wu Pei-fu, a war lord of the twenties, educated, prominent and respected by the Chinese. He refused time and time again and finally died in Peiping.

Wang Ching-wei was the next to be approached. Wang had been a fiery Revolutionist in the early days of the Republic, a follower of Sun Yat-sen and later a member of the leftist group at Hankow. During the thirties he made peace with Chiang Kai-shek, even holding office under the Nationalists. Early in 1939 he flew from Chungking to Indo-China, where he denounced Chiang and outlined possible peace terms between China and Japan. Of course, he was thereupon expelled from the Nationalist party. Wang and the Japanese carried on negotiations for a long period before he was finally installed in Nanking (March 30, 1940) as head of the Chinese government under the control of Japan. The Kuomintang (Nationalists) straightway branded Wang as a traitor to his country. Through their foreign minister they notified the various embassies and legations in China of their position, saying, "The Chinese government desires to take this opportunity to repeat most emphatically the declaration already made on several occasions that any act done by such an unlawful organization as has just been set up in Nanking or any other puppet body that may exist elsewhere in China is *ipso facto* null and void and shall never be recognized by the Chinese government or people."

Since then many cities of free China have erected statues of Wang Ching-wei and his wife kneeling, the Chinese way of symbolizing utter scorn. This is said to be the second time in China's history that a traitor has been the subject of a "kneeling statue." The first one, about one thousand years ago, recorded the treachery of Chinhui, who betrayed the Sungs to northern invaders.

The lot of the Chinese in occupied territories is a difficult one. Japanese have swarmed into the cities, one hundred thousand in Peiping alone, to govern, to run the businesses of the community, to spread the use of narcotics. Higher institutions of learning are closed, and in the lower schools a process of Japanization is carried on through the teaching of the Japanese language, history and religion. Shinto teaches the cult of the Sun Goddess and the mission of the superior race, the Japanese, to bring the world to great peace and the duty of the world to follow Nippon.

One of the most important results of the war is the migration of from forty to sixty million people from the eastern occupied areas to the west into free China. The students were the first to go. When Nankai and other colleges were bombed, all students knew there was virtually a price upon their heads and certainly no freedom of thought. Accordingly they left by whatever route possible to go to free China, carrying with them books and laboratory equipment. Some went to Yenan, the Communist capital, where they maintain the Northwest University, which sponsors the mass education movement and agricultural reforms.

Many of the American-established Christian colleges fled to Chengtu, Szechuen, where they operate as the Christian colleges of China. The war has made the colleges more practical and realistic in their approach to education. During vacations the students spend much time and effort in the rural districts spreading information on economic and social problems. The Peiping and Tientsin Chinese colleges escaped to Kunming and amalgamated under the name of the Southwestern University. Before Japan began war with America and Britain, seventy-seven of one hundred and one colleges had fled to the west. Since then the remainder have been forced to move out of occupied territory. The number of students in the colleges is greater than that before the war started.

Following the students to the west journeyed large numbers of the industrial population from the eastern cities. All equipment which could be transported was taken with them, what could not be moved was destroyed in the scorched-earth policy. Machines and mining equipment were knocked down and carried by raft, by cart, and on human backs to the far west, where they were reassembled and put to work. It is said that nearly five hundred manufacturing and mining units were thus sent to the west.

And behind the students and artisans and industrial workers traveled many of the lowly of the cities and the peasants whose homes and few possessions had been destroyed by bombs and fires.

The migration of so large a number of people brought many problems; the first, maybe, the problem of assimilation. The people from the east were accustomed to styles and ways of the modern ports where foreigners had brought many innovations, which had not yet reached the people of the west. It was like setting a large number of New Yorkers in a state like Wyoming or Nevada. They had to learn to understand one another's ways and ideas. For the west it has meant a hastening of the industrial and social revolution which had been coming very slowly to them; for the easterners it probably has meant the sloughing off of some non-essentials. The people of the two sections have been of help to one another and have broken down sectional barriers, thus increasing the unity so much needed.

The question of livelihood was of immediate concern. Fortunately the southwestern provinces have an abundance of food crops and several minerals of value—coal, iron, tungsten and antimony. The industrial machinery that was brought from the east was scattered and set up in fifteen different centers. The results have been good. Annual coal production rose to over two million tons. Textile and chemical industries were started. Arsenals have made China independent in small-arms production—rifles, machine guns, grenades and ammunition.

Of great aid in helping the refugees to obtain a livelihood have been the Chinese Industrial Co-operatives. They are small scale, decentralized, co-operatively owned societies of at least seven members, each manufacturing some one product. The central government has given money for their establishment and much has been raised in America. The movement has proved very successful and a most effective device for making the refugees who have poured into the west productive and self-supporting. The range of industry is great; spinning and weaving, making of army blankets, soap, toothpaste, all sorts of electrical appliances, metal fixtures and utensils, lathes, machine-shop tools, medical kits, printing presses and fountain pens. In less than two years, twenty-five co-operatives have been established. Thirty thousand is the goal. They are scattered throughout sixteen provinces. The decentralization has been of great value in avoiding wholesale destruction during the bombing season. It has also spread industrial development throughout the western provinces.

Since the days of the Mings, China's communication with the outside world has been through her eastern ports. But since the war began, by losing her seaports and the use of the Yangtse, she virtually lost her normal means of transport. In spite of these losses, much material has come through by smuggling, even under the eyes of the Japanese military, who connived at it for the financial gain accruing to the officers. But these importations were not sufficient for China's wartime needs and so she has had to build up new lines of communication through her western land frontier to connect on the north with the Soviet Republics or on the south with Indo-China, Burma and India and thence to the southern Pacific and Indian Oceans. It reminds us of the days of the Hans and the T'angs and the Mongols, when China was connected with Europe by the "Silken Way" across central Asia.

In the early days of the war one of the best routes extended from northwestern China through Sinkiang to Russia. Materials were carried part of this way by motor transport, but much of it by camel caravans and donkey and mule trains.

A due-north route to connect with the Trans-Siberian is under construction. The northern route was probably the most valuable at first, but since the Russian-German war the flow of materials has greatly decreased. With the completion of the Alaskan highway, the northern route will regain its importance.

Another route was by railroad through French Indo-China, then by motor road to Kunming, capital of Yunnan. After the Japanese began to get privileges in northern Indo-China and finally got control of the whole territory, this route was lost to China. But fortunately the Burma Road had been built. This road, built by hand labor, was a hazardous enterprise, winding in hairpin curves around the mountains and over gorges. It ran from Chungking through Yunnan to Lashio and then connected with the railroad running through Burma to the port of Rangoon. Finished in 1938, the Burma Road was most important (except for six months when the British closed the Burma part of it) until 1942, when the Japanese got control of Burma. Since then the Chinese have been building roads into India. Not waiting for the completion of these, huge United States transport planes are carrying war material from India to China. It is said that the volume is equal to that formerly carried over the Burma Road.

Air service for passenger travel and mail has been maintained between different parts of Free China and with foreign countries.

China has been at war over five years. Although she has lost territory to the invader and control of much of her seacoast as well as river and railroad transportation facilities, she has gained much by the development of the west which had hitherto constituted a backward part of the country. Now this large section is alive and progressive. It is a huge frontier region with all the marks of any frontier—vigor, independence, progressiveness, freedom and toleration, a land where achievement is what counts. In this atmosphere a new China has been born, self-reliant and resourceful. In the postwar reconstruction all this new-found energy and resourcefulness will be needed for the projects which must be attempted: education, for seventy per cent of the populace is still illiterate, and modernization of agriculture, for farming is carried on by human labor and hand tools and the peasants feel the weight of high rents and oppressive taxation. Reforestation and river and harbor improvements are crying needs. The meagerness of transportation facilities demands the building of railroads and motor roads, which in turn demand trucks and automobiles and rolling stock. All this development will require industrialization of the country, which continues to be eighty-per-cent agricultural, with what little industry there is largely of a hand-tool and domestic type. The Chinese will have to use all the endurance and sacrifice which they have acquired during the war period to make a China to fit their dreams.

Free China's government is under the Kuomintang, and the Party chief, Chiang Kai-shek, who has grown in stature in the eyes of his people. They look up to him and have gained confidence in his policies. The various departments of the government and the National Economic Council are staffed by a rising group of young men, able and patriotic. Men, now in their forties, they were boys when the Revolution first came to China and have been brought up and educated under the new democratic ideal. Women, too, girls of the Revolution, are working in all kinds of enterprises and are treated as equals by the men. The time that has elapsed since the Revolution has now given to China a well-trained group with progressive ideas—a fact which should not be overlooked in considering the strength of China today. It is interesting to recall that in 1936 the Japanese ambassador to China, Kawagoe, warned his people that there was a new type of man at the helm in China. Needless to say, they did not heed his warning.

Besides the Kuomintang there exist several minor groups or parties, the strongest among them the Communists. Nationalists and Communists have continued in the common policy, upon which they agreed after the Sian kidnaping affair, of opposing Japan. The government's development of mass education, the industrial co-operatives, agricultural reforms and local democracy have created more trust in the Nationalists and maintained a certain amount of unity between the two groups. The Eighth Route Army (Communist) has carried on a most effective guerilla warfare in the northern occupied regions. They sometimes complain that the central government does not give them a fair share of supplies, but on the whole the two parties get on without too much difficulty which, it is hoped, augurs well for the future. The test will come when the end of the war relieves the country of the Japanese menace.

The criticism that the constitution has not yet been drafted and that the Kuomintang holds the monopoly in the government has to a large extent been met by the formation in 1938 of the People's Political Council (P.P.C.). The Council is composed of two hundred and forty members and represents various groups. About one-third of the members come from the provinces and special municipalities, a few from Mongolia and Tibet, and six represent the overseas Chinese. The majority of the members represent cultural, professional and economic bodies who have been active in political leadership though not officials of the Kuomintang or of the government. There are some Communist members, and thirty are women. They are not chosen by a popular election but appointed by some council or commission of the group they represent, with some oversight by the Kuomintang. A

CHINA AT WAR

group of five members furnishes the presiding officer for the meetings, which occur twice yearly. One of these five is a woman.

The P.P.C. has three powers: the right to deliberate on all important measures, domestic or foreign, before they are enacted into law, the right to submit proposals to the government, and the right to demand and hear reports from the ministries and to interrogate the officers of state. Chiang, himself, either attends the meetings or reads the reports. Though not a legislative body, it is considered a most promising approach to the realization of the completion of democracy in the federal government. Possibly the P.P.C. may be a more Chinese or Oriental form of democracy than the popular assemblies the Western world has adopted. So far, the Orient, neither China nor Japan, has been successful in the use of a Western-type parliament. It may be that some such form as the P.P.C. is better adapted to Chinese needs and may indicate the lines along which Eastern democracy may run.

China's foreign policy rests upon the necessity to resist Japan and to ally herself with all nations who are willing to oppose Japanese aggression and to safeguard peace in the Far East. She has received aid from Russia, Great Britain and the United States.

Chinese-American relations have improved steadily during the war period. Since the Manchurian affair we have always declared that we would recognize no territory acquired by force. Such puppet states have no legal status in the eyes of international law. Therefore, in our eyes, Manchukuo and other sections which the invader has occupied are considered parts of China.

What remain of old treaty rights seem to have automatically disappeared under the exigencies of war, but still they exist legally. For some time it has been advocated by many Americans that China's role in the war has earned her relief from the irksome bonds of the past and that therefore the United States should take the lead in a move to waive formally extra-territoriality and any other rights which might infringe upon China's sovereignty. When Wendell Willkie was in Chungking it was reported that he and Chiang Kai-shek discussed the matter at length. A few days after this report came the news that the United States and Great Britain had informed the Chinese government that they were ready to negotiate new treaties which would relieve China of the burden of extra-territoriality. The move is based on the assumption that in any settlement of Asian affairs the people of Asia have the right to shape the future of Asia rather than to be dictated to or controlled. China with her complete independence will be able to contribute her full share in the development of East Asia as she never could if she were only half-master in her own house. Now she can co-operate fully in a world arrangement of free nations.

The American government has given aid to China at crucial moments. At the time of Japan's entry into Hankow it extended a small loan of twenty-five million dollars, and again, when Japan recognized the puppet state of Wang Ching-wei, made a loan of one hundred million dollars to the government at Chungking.

When the American Congress passed the Lend-Lease bill in March, 1941, Great Britain, China and Greece were especially named as those to whom aid should go. Estimates indicate that about six-hundred-million-dollars' worth of supplies were allocated to China during the last months of 1941. And then Japan attacked the United States and our aid to China became accelerated. A five-hundred-million-dollar loan was made to bolster her currency; technical advisers and a military mission went to Chungking. More than a hundred P-40-fighter planes with American pilots under Colonel

Chennault, known as the American Volunteer Group (A.V.G.), flew to southwest China for active service. Later our planes and pilots were operated directly under the American army with General Stillwell in command.

On July 2, 1942, Secretary Hull and the Chinese Foreign Minister, T. V. Soong, signed an agreement for economic collaboration during and after the war. It obligates the United States to continue Lend-Lease aid to China and brings China into discussions of postwar economic conditions throughout the world. Similar to an agreement presented to Russia, it brings the United States, Great Britain, China and Russia into an economic front. It will mean the working together of over a billion people on the problems confronting the world.

To the onlooker it would seem that China may be entering on another period of leadership, which position she lost after the T'ang Dynasty. During the war she has been a member of the A B C D (American, British, Chinese, Dutch) group conferring in Washington on Far Eastern developments. Her relations with Indian leaders have been cordial. Nehru, the leader of the Congress party in India, visited Chiang Kaishek in Chungking and, when the Japanese were drawing near in Malaya and Burma, Chiang flew to New Delhi to confer with Gandhi and Nehru. For China to become a leader in Asian affairs it can only be as a liberal democratic state and as a leader of free peoples. Japan has tried to erect a new order in Asia under a cruel and oppressive dictatorship. The opportunity for liberal leadership in Asia in co-operation in a world federation of free nations lies before China. Her progressive development during the war would give her the backing of the United States in such a role.

CITATIONS

CITATIONS

Chapter III

LEGENDARY HEROES

[1] The accounts of the legendary heroes and rulers were written at various times between the fourth century B. C. and the third century A. D. The order in which they are given in this chapter places them as they would come in an orderly account of the development of civilization. See *Autobiography of a Chinese Historian,* Ku Shih Pien. Translated and annotated by Arthur W. Hummel.

[2] SACRED BOOKS OF THE EAST, edited by Max Müller. Vol. XXVIII, Book XXI, Section 8. Oxford Clarendon Press, 1879-1910. Vols. XXVII, XXVIII, *Li Ki,* translated by James Legge.

[3] SACRED BOOKS OF THE EAST, Vol. III, Part I, Book I, *Shu Ching.*

[4] Edith Simcox, *Primitive Civilizations,* Vol. II, p. 46. Macmillan Co., 1894.

[5] SACRED BOOKS OF THE EAST, Vol. III, Part II, Book I, pp. 42-43.

[6] H. A. Giles, *A History of Chinese Literature,* p. 8. William Heinemann, London, MCMI.

[7] *Ibid.,* p. 8.

[8] A. W. Hummel, *Autobiography of a Chinese Historian,* pp. 113-114. E. J. Brill, Ltd., Leyden, Holland, 1931.

[9] A. W. Hummel, "What the Chinese Are Doing in Their Own History," *The American Historical Review,* July, 1929, pp. 715-24.

Chapter IV

ARCHAEOLOGY FINDS THE SHANGS

[1] George Cressey, *China's Geographic Foundations,* p. 184. McGraw-Hill Book Company, New York, 1934.

[2] J. G. Andersson, "A Prehistoric Village in Honan," *China Journal of Science and Arts,* September, 1923.

[3] C. W. Bishop, "The Neolithic Age in Northern China," reprinted from *Antiquity* for December, 1933.

[4] F. H. Chalfant, *Early Chinese Writing,* Carnegie Museum Vol. IV, No. 1, pp. 32 and 34.

[5] J. H. Ingram, "Civilization and Religion of the Shang Dynasty," *China Journal of Science and Arts,* September, 1925.

[6] *Ibid.*

[7] W. Percival Yetts, "The George Eumorfopoulos Collection," *The Catalogue of the Chinese and Corean Bronzes, Sculpture, Jewelry and Miscellaneous Articles,* Vol. I, p. 19.

[8] *Ibid.,* Vol. I, p. 21.

[9] Hu Shih, "Religion and Philosophy in Chinese History," *Symposium on Chinese Culture,* edited by Sophia H. Chen Zen, p. 33. China Institute of Pacific Relations, Shanghai, China, 1931.

[10] C. W. Bishop, *Preparatory Notes on the Worship of Earth Excavation of a West Han Dynasty Site,* pp. 2-5. Kelley & Walsh, Ltd., Shanghai, China, 1931.

Chapter V

THE CHOU DYNASTY. THE FIXING OF CUSTOM

[1] C. W. Bishop, "The Chronology of Ancient China," *The Journal of the American Oriental Society,* Vol. 52, No. 3, September, 1932.

[2] H. A. Giles, *A History of Chinese Literature,* p. 25.

[3] Edith Simcox, *Primitive Civilizations,* Vol. II, p. 50.

[4] C. W. Bishop, "The Beginnings of North and South in China," *Pacific Affairs,* September, 1934, p. 312.

[5] Marcel Granet, *Chinese Civilization,* p. 176. A. A. Knopf, New York, 1930.

[6] Edith Simcox, *Primitive Civilizations,* Vol. II, p. 67.

[7] H. A. Giles, *A History of Chinese Literature,* p. 18.

[8] E. Simcox, *Primitive Civilizations,* Vol. II, p. 73. Sacred Books, *Li Ki,* Vol. XXVII, Book X, Sec. 1; Book III, Sec. V.

[9] S. Wells Williams, *The Middle Kingdom,* Vol. I, p. 511. John Wiley, New York, 1861.

[10] V. K. Ting, "How China Acquired Her Civilization." *Symposium on Chinese Culture,* p. 11.

CITATIONS

Chapter VI

THE EASTERN CHOU DYNASTY. AN AGE OF CREATIVE THOUGHT AND LITERATURE

1 Hu Shih, "The Development on the Logical Method in Ancient China," p. 5. *Book of Poetry,* Part I, Book IX, I, Oriental Book Co., Shanghai, 1922.

2 Hu Shih, *ibid.,* p. 7. *Book of Poetry,* Part III, Book III, X.

3 H. A. Giles, *A History of Chinese Literature,* p. 17.

4 Hu Shih, "Religion and Philosophy in China," *Symposium on Chinese Culture,* p. 36.

5 H. A. Giles, *A History of Chinese Literature,* p. 61. W. H. Stuart, *The Use of Material from China's Spiritual Inheritance in the Christian Education of the Chinese Youth,* p. 127.

6 *Analects,* Legge, translated by James, Book VIII, Chapter II, THE CHINESE CLASSICS, Trübner & Co., London, 1861-72.

7 *Great Learning,* Legge, Chapter IX, p. 3.

8 *Analects,* Legge, Book XII, Chapter VII.

9 *Ibid.,* Book VII, Chapters XIX and I.

10 *Ibid.,* Book II, Chapter XXII.

11 Stuart, p. 165. *Analects,* Book XV, Chapter XXIII.

12 H. A. Giles, *A History of Chinese Literature,* p. 40.

13 Hu Shih, *Symposium,* p. 39.

14 *Ibid.,* p. 36.

15 C. W. Bishop, "Bronzes of Hsin-cheng Hsien," *Smithsonian Report of 1926,* pp. 457-68.

16 P. C. Hsu, *Ethical Realism in Neo-Confucian Thought,* p. 2.

Chapter VII

THE CH'IN DYNASTY. A UNIFIED EMPIRE

1 H. A. Giles, *A History of Chinese Literature,* pp. 107-08.

Chapter VIII

THE HANS

[1] H. A. Giles, *A History of Chinese Literature*, translated from Ssu-ma Ch'ien, p. 105.

[2] *Ibid.*, p. 104.

[3] M. Aurel Stein, *Ruins of Desert Cathay*, Vol. II, p. 153. Macmillan Co., New York, 1912.

[4] T. F. Carter, *The Invention of Printing in China and Its Spread Westward*, p. 89. Columbia University Press, 1925.

[5] Hu Shih, *Symposium*, p. 46.

[6] *Ibid.*, p. 47.

[7] T. F. Carter, *The Invention of Printing*, p. 3.

[8] *Ibid.*, p. 3.

[9] Raphaël Petrucci, *Chinese Painters*, p. 50. Coward-McCann, Inc., New York, 1920.

[10] E. F. Fenolossa, *Epochs of Chinese and Japanese Art*, Vol. I, p. 26. Frederick A. Stokes & Co., New York, 1912.

[11] H. A. Giles, *A History of Chinese Literature*, p. 105.

Chapter IX

THE DARK AGES IN CHINA

[1] Hu Shih, "Religion and Philosophy in Chinese History," *Symposium*, p. 47.

[2] Fa Hsien, *The Travels of Fa Hsien, 399-414 A. D.*, re-translated by H. A. Giles, p. 2. Cambridge University Press, London, 1923.

[3] *Ibid.*, p. 2.

[4] *Ibid.*, pp. 14-15.

[5] *Ibid.*, p. 15.

[6] *Ibid.*, p. 17.

[7] Raphaël Petrucci, *Chinese Painters*, p. 57.

CITATIONS

Chapter X

THE GOLDEN AGE OF THE T'ANG DYNASTY

[1] Florence Ayscough, *Tu Fu, The Autobiography of a Chinese Poet*, p. 355. Houghton Mifflin Co., Boston.

[2] M. Huc, TRAVELS THROUGH ASIA. *A Journey through the Chinese Empire*, Vol. I, p. 155. Harper & Bros., New York, 1855.

[3] *Ibid.*, Vol. I, p. 153.

[4] Hu Shih, *Symposium*, p. 52. Also see Giles, pp. 198-203.

[5] Hu Shih, *ibid.*, pp. 53-54.

[6] *Ibid.*, p. 55.

[7] M. Aurel Stein, *The Thousand Buddhas*, p. 11. Published under orders H. M. Secretary of State for India and with co-operation Trustees of British Museum, London, 1921.

[8] Raphaël Petrucci, *Chinese Painters*, p. 58.

[9] L. A. Cranmer-Byng, *Lute of Jade*, Introduction. J. Murray, London, 1911.

Chapter XI

THE FIVE LITTLE AGES AND THE SUNG DYNASTY

[1] T. F. Carter, *The Invention of Printing in China and Its Spread Westward*, p. 50.

[2] *Ibid.*, p. 41.

[3] *Ibid.*, p. 51.

[4] *Ibid.*, p. 5.

[5] Hu Shih, *Symposium*, p. 56.

Chapter XII

THE MONGOL RULE

[1] D. C. Boulger, *History of China*, Vol. I, pp. 303, 310, 318. William Thatcher & Co., London, 1898.

[2] *The Travels of Marco Polo the Venetian*, Everyman's Library, pp. 167-68. E. P. Dutton, New York, 1925.

³ *Ibid.*, pp. 189-90.

⁴ *Ibid.*, pp. 209-10.

⁵ *Ibid.*, pp. 283-84.

⁶ Pearl Buck, Translation, *All Men Are Brothers*, Vol. I, p. VII. John Day Co., New York.

Chapter XIII

THE MING OR BRIGHT DYNASTY

¹ Mabel Ping-hua Lee, *The Economic History of China*, p. 105. Columbia University Press, New York, 1921.

² *Ibid.*, condensed from Report, p. 358.

Chapter XIV

THE CHINESE AGAIN A CONQUERED PEOPLE

¹ G. M. Steiger, *A History of the Orient*, p. 39. Ginn & Co., New York, 1928.

² *The Sacred Edict*, with a translation of the colloquial rendering by F. W. Baller, p. 1. American Presbyterian Mission Press, Shanghai, China, 1907.

³ *Ibid.*, p. 2.

⁴ *Ibid.*, p. 3.

⁵ *Ibid.*, p. 15.

⁶ C. E. Chapman, *A History of California: the Spanish Period*, Chapters III, IV. Macmillan Company, New York, 1921.

⁷ C. A. Beard, Editor, *Whither Mankind*, p. 32. Longmans Green & Co., New York, 1928. Hu Shih, "The Civilizations of East and West."

⁸ G. C. Sellery and A. C. Krey, *The Founding of Western Civilization*. Harper & Brothers, New York, 1929.

⁹ E. T. Backhouse and J. O. P. Bland, *Annals and Memoirs of the Court of Peking*, pp. 322-25. William Heinemann, London, 1914.

CITATIONS

Chapter XV

FOREIGN TRADE ADVANCES

[1] S. and M. L. Greenbie, *Gold of Ophir*, p. 162. John Day, New York, 1925.

[2] *Ibid.*, p. 168.

[3] H. F. MacNair, *Modern Chinese History, Selected Readings*, pp. 50-51. Commercial Press, Ltd., Shanghai, 1923.

[4] *Ibid.*, pp. 26, 27.

[5] Li Ung Bing, *Outlines of Chinese History*, p. 492. Commercial Press, Ltd., Shanghai, 1914.

[6] MacNair, *Selected Readings*, pp. 86-88.

Chapter XVI

THE TAI PING REBELLION

[1] W. J. Hail, *Tsêng Kuo-fan and the Taiping Rebellion*, p. 256. Yale University Press, New Haven, 1927.

Chapter XVII

THE EMPRESS DOWAGER

[1] J. O. P. Bland and E. T. Backhouse, *China under the Empress Dowager*, p. 90. J. B. Lippincott Co., Philadelphia, MCMX.

[2] *Ibid.*, p. 95.

Chapter XIX

REFORM AND REACTION

[1] Chang Chih-tung, *China's Only Hope*, pp. 125-26. Fleming H. Revell Co., New York, 1900. Translated by S. I. Woodbridge.

[2] *Ibid.*, pp. 125-26.

[3] Bertram Lenox Simpson, *Indiscreet Letters from Peking*, p. 100. Dodd, Mead & Co., New York, 1907.

⁴ *Ibid.*, 278-81.

⁵ *Ibid.*, 298-301.

⁶ Refer to Chapter XIV.

Chapter XX

THE EMPRESS DOWAGER AGAIN AND THE LAST MANCHU EMPEROR

¹ Morse, H. B., *The Trade and Administration of China*, pp. 291-307. Kelley & Walsh, Ltd., Shanghai, 1913.

Chapter XXI

REFORM CHANGES INTO REVOLUTION

¹ C. A. Beard, Editor, *Whither Mankind*, p. 29. Longmans, Green & Co., New York, 1928. Hu Shih.

² Paul Linebarger, *Sun Yat-sen.*

³ W. E. Soothill, *A History of China*, p. 71. Ernest Benn, Ltd., London, 1927.

Chapter XXII

STUDENTS AND WAR LORDS

¹ C. A. Beard, Editor, *Whither Mankind*, p. 40. Longmans, Green & Co., New York, 1928. Hu Shih.

² Hu Shih, "The Literary Renaissance," *Symposium on Chinese Culture*, p. 134.

Chapter XXIII

THE NATIONALISTS COME INTO POWER

¹ H. F. MacNair, *China in Revolution*, Chapter VI. University of Chicago Press, Chicago, 1931. J. O. P. Bland, *China: The Pity of It*, Chapter IV. Doubleday, Doran & Co., Garden City, N. Y., 1932. W. H. Stuart, *The Use of Material in China's Spiritual Inheritance in the Christian Education of the Chinese Youth*, pp. 82-93.

² Alice Tisdale Hobart, *Within the Walls of Nanking*, pp. 189-92. Jonathan Cape, London; Macmillan Co., New York, 1928.

CITATIONS 383

Chapter XXIV

THE NATIONALIST REGIME

[1] H. F. MacNair, *China in Revolution,* Appendix, p. 228.

[2] *Ibid.,* pp. 122-23. Reprinted by permission of University of Chicago Press.

[3] *Ibid.,* Chapter XII. J. O. P. Bland, *China: The Pity of It,* Chapter XIV. U. A. Yakhontoff, *The Chinese Soviets.*

[4] Bland, p. 317.

[5] *Ibid.,* pp. 312-13.

[6] Owen Lattimore, *Manchuria, Cradle of Conflict, pp.* 296-97. Macmillan Company, New York, 1932.

[7] V. K. Ting, "How China Acquired Her Civilization," *Symposium,* p. 26, China Institute of Pacific Relations, Shanghai, China, 1931.

[8] *Ibid.,* p. 26.

Chapter XXV

NATIONALISM PREPARES FOR A TEST

[1] "Documents Concerning the Sino-Japanese Conflict," *Trans-Pacific News Service,* January, 1938, p. 57.

[2] Tried by Court Martial in Hankow, January, 1938, and shot for not leading his troops against the enemy in Shantung.

[3] See pp. 325-26. Conditions up to 1933.

[4] "Facts about Communism in China," *Peoples' Tribune* (China), November, 1937.

[5] *Asia,* February, 1938, special section, p. 141.

[6] *People's Tribune* (China), November, 1937.

[7] "The New Life Movement," *Information Bulletin* (published by Council of International Affairs, Nanking, China), December 21, 1936.

[8] M. H. Lin, *The Sino-Japanese Conflict,* Chinese Cultural Society, New York, 1937, p. 16.

Chapter XXVI

The "Popular Front" Faces Japan

[1] Frank W. Price, "Japan's Continental Policy," *China Faces Japan*, Chinese Students' Christian Association in North America, 1937, p. 14.

[2] Reported killed, New York *Times*, March 8, 1938.

[3] *Trans-Pacific News Service*, January 28, 1938, p. 4; and New York *Times*, July 20, 1937.

[4] Information Service, Federal Council of the Churches of Christ in America, October 16, 1937.

[5] "Documents concerning The Sino-Japanese Conflict," *Trans-Pacific News Service*, January, 1938, p. 14.

[6] M. H. Lin, *The Sino-Japanese Conflict*, Chinese Cultural Society, 1937, p. 21.

ADDITIONAL BIBLIOGRAPHY

ADDITIONAL BIBLIOGRAPHY

Ashton, Leigh, *An Introduction to the Study of Chinese Sculpture*, Charles Scribner's Sons, New York, 1924.

Ayscough, Florence, and Lowell, Amy, *Fir-Flower Tablets*, Houghton Mifflin Company, Boston, 1921.

Baker, John E., *Explaining China*, D. Van Nostrand Company, Inc., New York, 1927.

Binyon, Laurence, *Painting in the Far East*, Longmans, Green & Company, New York, 1924.

Biot, E., *Le Tcheou-li ou Rites des Tcheou*, Paris Omprimerie Nationale, 1851.

Burgess, J. S., *The Guilds of Peking*, Columbia University Press, New York, 1928.

Carus, Paul (translator), *Lao-tzu's Tao-teh-king*, 1909.

Cormack, Mrs. J. G., *Chinese Birthday, Funeral and Other Customs*, China Booksellers, Ltd., Peking, 1922.

Dennett, Tyler, *Americans in Eastern Asia*, The Macmillan Company, New York, 1922.

Giles, H. A., *Confucianism and Its Rivals*, Charles Scribner's Sons, New York, 1915.

Gems of Chinese Literature, Kelly & Walsh, Ltd., Shanghai, 1884.

(translator) *Strange Stories from a Chinese Studio*, Kelly & Walsh, Ltd., Shanghai, 1908.

Hirth, Friedrich, *The Ancient History of China to the End of the Chou Dynasty*, Columbia University Press, New York, 1908.

China and the Roman Orient, Kelly & Walsh, Ltd., Shanghai, 1885.

KARLGRAN, BERNHARD, *Philology of Ancient China,* Harvard University Press, Cambridge, Mass., 1927.

KING, F. H., *Farmers of Forty Centuries,* Harcourt, Brace & Co., New York, 1927.

KING-HALL, STEPHEN, *Western Civilization and the Far East,* Charles Scribner's Sons, New York, 1924.

KULP, D. H., *Country Life in South China,* Teachers' College, New York, 1925.

LAMB, HAROLD, *Genghis Khan, The Emperor of All Men,* Robert McBride Company, New York, 1927.

LATOURETTE, K. S., *A History of Christian Missions in China,* The Macmillan Company, New York, 1929.
> *The Chinese: Their History and Culture* (2 vols.), The Macmillan Company, New York, 1934.

LAUFER, BERTHOLD, *Archaic Chinese Jades,* Field Museum, Chicago, 1912.
> *Chinese Clay Figures,* Field Museum, Chicago, 1914.
> *Chinese Grave Sculptures of the Han Period,* F. C. Stechert & Company, New York, 1911.

MASPERO, HENRI, "The Origins of the Chinese Civilization," translated by C. W. Bishop, *Smithsonian Report, 1927.*

MENZIES, J. M., "The Culture of the Shang Dynasty," *Smithsonian Report, 1931.*

MORSE, H. B., *The Gilds of China,* Longmans, Green & Company, New York, 1909.
> *Trade and Administration of China,* Longmans, Green & Company, New York, 1908.

NORTON, HENRY KITTREDGE, *China and the Powers,* John Day Company, Inc., New York, 1927.

REICHWEIN, ADOLF, *China and Europe; Intellectual and Artistic Contacts in the Eighteenth Century*, Alfred A. Knopf, New York, 1925.

SIREN, OSVALD, *A History of Early Chinese Art*, E. Benn, Ltd., London, 1929.

SMEDLEY, AGNES, *Chinese Destinies*, The Vanguard Press, New York, 1933.

SMITH, ARTHUR H., *Chinese Characteristics*, Fleming H. Revell Company, New York, 1894.

> *Village Life in China*, Fleming H. Revell Co., New York, 1899.

SOOTHILL, W. E., *The Analects of Confucius*, Fukuin Printing Company, Yokohoma, 1910.

> *The Three Religions of China*, Hodder & Stoughton, New York, 1933.

STEIGER, G. N., *China and the Occident*, Yale University Press, New Haven, Conn., 1927.

STEIN, M. AUREL, *Ancient Khotan*, T. F. Unwin, London, 1903.

> *Sand-Buried Ruins of Khotan*, T. F. Unwin, London, 1903.
>
> *Innermost Asia*, Oxford Clarendon Press, 1928.
> *Serindia* (5 vols.), Oxford Clarendon Press, 1921.

WALEY, ARTHUR, *An Introduction to the Study of Chinese Painting*, Charles Scribner's Sons, New York, 1923.

WANG, CHI-CHEN (translator), *Dream of the Red Chamber*, Doubleday, Doran & Company, New York, 1929.

WEALE, PUTNAM, *Why China Sees Red*, Dodd Mead & Co., New York, 1925.

WERNER, E. T. C., *Myths and Legends of China*, Farrar & Rinehart, Inc., New York, 1933.

WILLIAMS, E. T., *China, Yesterday and Today,* Thomas Y. Crowell Co., New York, 1923.
> *A Short History of China,* Harper Brothers, New York, 1928.

WILHELM, RICHARD, *A Short History of Chinese Civilization,* G. G. Harrap & Co., London, 1929.
> *Confucius and Confucianism,* Harcourt, Brace and Company, New York, 1931.

YAKHONTOFF, VICTOR A., *The Chinese Soviets,* Coward-McCann, Inc., New York, 1934.

ZUCKER, A. E., *The Chinese Theater,* Little, Brown & Company, Boston, 1925.

NEW BOOKS OF INTEREST

AYSCOUGH, FLORENCE, *Chinese Women Yesterday and Today,* Houghton Mifflin Company, Boston, 1937.

BERKOV, ROBERT, *Strong Man of China,* Houghton Mifflin Company, Boston, 1938.

CHIANG KAI-SHEK, MADAME, *General Chiang Kai-shek; the Account of the Fortnight in Sian, etc.,* Doubleday, Doran & Co., New York City, 1937.

CHAMBERLIN, W. H., *Japan Over Asia,* Little, Brown & Company, Boston, 1937.

HUDSON, G. F., AND MARTHE RAJSHMAN, *An Atlas of Far Eastern Politics,* John Day Company, New York, 1942.

LINEBARGER, PAUL M. A., *The China of Chiang Kai-shek,* World Peace Foundation, Boston, 1941.

MACNAIR, H. F., *The Real Conflict between China and Japan,* The University of Chicago Press, Chicago, 1938.

MORSE, H. B., AND MACNAIR, H. F., *Far Eastern Inter-*

national Relations, Houghton Mifflin Company, Boston, 1931.

SCHERER, JAMES A. B., *Japan Defies the World,* The Bobbs-Merrill Company, Indianapolis, 1938.

SNOW, EDGAR, *Red Star Over China,* Random House, Inc., New York, 1938.

STEIN, GUENTHER, *Far East in Ferment,* Methuen & Co., Ltd., London, 1936.

WALES, NYM, *China Builds for Democracy,* Modern Age Books, New York, 1942.

INDEX

INDEX

Adventurers, Merchant, 177
Agriculture
  Manchu Dynasty, encouraged, 187, 196
  Ming revival of interest in, 162
  Neolithic Age, 38
  products, 19
Air mail, 327
Air passenger service, 327
Altar of Heaven, 168-169
A-lu-te, 232, 233
American Red Cross Report, 326
Amoy, 21, 212
Amur River and Valley, 191, 244
An Lu Shan, 128
An Yang
  excavations at, 39, 41
  site of Oracle Bones, 41
Analects, the sayings of Confucius, 65
Ancestor worship, 45, 57, 72, 107, 196
Ancients, 64, 75, 76, 334
  five, 24-25
Andersson, J. G., discoveries of, 38
Andrade, Fernando Peres de, 175, 176
Andrade, Simon, 176
Anhwei, 319
Anking, 220, 224
Annam, 144, 194
  lost to France, 240
Anti-capitalism, 310-311
Anti-dynastic movement, 216. *See also* Tai Ping rebellion
Anti-foreignism, 310, 311, 313, 315, 327
Antimony, 19
Antiques
  of China, 36
  of Egypt, 36
Antung, 331
Arabs, 90, 91
Aral Sea, 111
Archaeological discoveries
  Han period, 96-99
  Neolithic Age, 37-38
  preservation of, 37

Archaeological discoveries— *continued*
  Shang Dynasty, 36-44
  Sung Dynasty, 36
  T'ang Dynasty, 122-125
Archaeology Finds the Shangs, chapter on, 36-44
Archaeology, study of, Manchu Dynasty, 195
Architecture
  Ming Dynasty
    buildings, 170
    tombs, 169
  stimulated by Buddhism, 107
Army, edict for modernization of, 269
Arnold, Julian, 348
Art
  Buddhistic, 107, 122, 123
  Chou Dynasty, 69-70, 71
  Manchu dynasty, 194
  Sung dynasty, 140
Asia, Central, 88
Astronomical instruments, 190
Astronomy, Jesuit work on, 190-191
Attila, 102, 141
Autumn Annals, 45, 46

Bactria, 87
Baffin, explorer, 177
Baikal, Lake, 141
Bamboo, 85
  staves of, 87
Bamboo Annals, 42, 45
Bandits, 102-103, 131, 156, 312
Bas-reliefs, 98, 170
Battering-ram, 114
Beans, 18
Beard, C. A., *Whither Mankind,* quoted, 195-196, 281, 299
Beginnings (Mythical), chapter on, 23-26
Bhaisajyaguru, Paradise of, 123
Bishop, C. W.
  discoveries of, 38, 70
  History of Chinese Literature, A, quoted, 46

Bishop, C. W.—*continued*
  Preparatory Notes on the Worship of Earth Excavations of a West Han Dynasty Site, quoted, 43, 51
  quoted, 43
Bland, J. O. P., *China under the Empress Dowager,* quoted, 231-232
Board of Admiralty, 240, 253
Bodhar, 119
Bokhara, 87
Bo-lin, Chang, 358
Book of Change (sacred book), 56
Book of History, 70, 94
Book of Poetry or *Odes,* 49, 52, 53, 58, 70, 71, 94
Book of Rites (Li Ki), 52, 53, 58
Books
  block printing of, 132, 133
  first official book, 133
  oldest printed book, 133, 134
  wooden, 96
Borodin, Comrade, 309, 316
Boston, 197
Boulger, D. C., *History of China,* quoted, 142
Boundaries, 17
Boxer uprising, 258-265
  attack on Peking, 260-265
    description of by Putnam Weale, 262-263, 264
  beginning of, 258
  death sentence for leaders of, 265
  massacres during, 259
Boxers, 258
Boycott
  Chou Dynasty, 55
  of Japanese goods, 303-304
Breaking Up of the Chinese Empire, The, 245
Bridge, scaling, 114
British Museum, 97, 123
Bronze
  casting of, 42
    perfected, 171
  inscriptions of, 43
  shapes of, 98
Bronze Age, 39, 42
  art of, 70
  date of, 44
Buddha, 62, 68, 104-105, 105-106, 107
  relics of, 106

Buddha—*continued*
  sacrifice to, 104-105
  veneration for, 105-106
Buddha Guatama Sakyamuni, statues of, 107
Buddhidharma, 104
Buddhism, 93
  and development of art, 107, 122
  Ch'an or Zen school, 121, 122
  changes in, 121
  fills wants, 93-94, 104
  flourishes, 120
  legends of, 91
  persecution of, 121
  preparations for, 93
  protests against, 121
  toleration of, 99
  Zen, revolt against, 137
Buddhist canons, *see* Sutras
Buddhist paintings, 123
Buddhist temples, *see* temples
Burlingame, Anson, 235
Burmah, 194
  lost to Great Britain, 240

Cabot, Sebastian, 177
Calendar, 28
  corrected, 190
  lunar, abolished, 295
  solar, adopted, 295
Calendar tree, legend of, 32
Calligraphy of Han Dynasty, 97
Cambron Ware, 173
Cambuluc, 142, 145, 161
  palace at, 146, 147, 156
  renamed Peking, 165
Canal, Grand, The, 108, 150
  rebuilding of, 150
Canals, 21, 108-109, 150, 178, 236
  Sui Dynasty, 108
Cannon, 182
Canton, 21, 90, 189, 192, 197, 200, 202, 203, 210, 211, 212, 213, 215, 221, 222
  government at, 295, 307, 308, 309
Canton River, 175
Capshuymun, 209
Caravan trade, Manchu Dynasty, 192
Caravans, 88, 89-90, 99
Cards, 115
Carter, T. F., *The Invention of Printing in China and Its Spread Westward,* quoted, 89, 96, 133, 134
Carvings, 98

INDEX

Caspian Sea, 141
Cave of a Thousand Buddhas, 133, 134
Central Board of Control of Railways, 275
Ceramics
  clay for, 171
  factory famous for, 171
  See also Pottery, Porcelain, Urns, Sacrificial Vessels
Certificates, negotiable, 113
Ceylon, 91, 105
Chairs, 114
Chalfant, F. H., 39, 40
  discoveries of, 40
  Early Chinese Writing, quoted, 41
Ch'an, double road, 121, 122
Chancellor, Richard, 177
Ch'ang An, 46, 48, 59, 85, 105, 110, 112, 115, 165
Chang Ch'ien, General, 87, 91
  interest in foreign lands, 88
Chang Chih-tung
  advocate of reform, 251
  aids organization of school system, 269
  China's Only Hope, quoted, 252, 253
  death of, 275
  doctrines of, 252, 253
Chang Hsueh-liang, 318
  gives up command, 337
  involved in kidnapping of Chiang, 342-343
  member military council, 337
  returns, 340
  supports Chiang Kai-shek, 320
Chang Tso-lin, 305, 316
  abandons Peking, 317
  activities of, 303
  death of, 317
Changsha, 218
Chapel, 212
Chapman, C. E., *History of California, A,* 190
Charcoal, 85
Chavannes, translator, 86
Cheefoo, 21
Chekiang, 171, 184, 271, 314, 319
Chen, Eugene, 313, 338
Ch'eng I, 138
Chengtu, conquest of, 84
Ch'i, 65, 84
Chiang Kai-shek, 312, 313, 314, 315, 316, 319, 328, 336

Chiang Kai-shek—*continued*
  averts civil war, 341
  crushes rebellion, 338
  heads military council, 337
  kidnapping of, 342-343
  President of National Government, 321
  quoted, 325
  quoted on national unity, 345, 346
  resigns offices, reinstated, 343
  ultimatum to Japan, 356
  unifying program, 340
Chiang, Madame, 336, 337, 340, 343
Ch'ien Lung, 194, 195, 196, 198, 200, 201, 202, 205
Chih, see Writing material
Chihli, Gulf of, 78
Ch'in Dynasty
  emperors, 75-79, 82, 84
  Literati of, 76, 77
  provincial division of, 76
  religious changes, 80
Ch'in Dynasty, A Unified Empire, chapter on, 75-82
Ch'in, state of, 75, 76
China, origin of word, 77
"China Ware," 173
Chinese-Japanese difficulties, 331, 332
Chinese Nineteenth Route Army, 332
Ching Teh Chen, ceramic factory, 171-172
Ching Tsai, mother Confucius, 64
Chinkiang, 212, 220
Chins, *see* Kins
Chou, Duke of, 56
Chou Dynasty
  art of, 69-70, 71
  chapter on, 45-58
  classes of people, 50-51
  culture of, *see* Shang-Chou culture
  customs of people, 48-49
  date of, 45
  division of, 48-49
  gods of, 57
  government of people, 50
  land division of, 47, 49, 50
  names kings, 47
  relations of people, 52-54
  religion of, 56-58
  ruling methods, 46-53
  symbol of, 47

Chou Dynasty—*continued*
  social classes of, 59
  trades, 54-55
Chou Dynasty, Eastern
  An Age of Creative Thought and Literature, chapter on, 59-72
Chou Dynasty, Eastern division
  ancestor worship among masses, 72
  education, 59-60
  excavations, 70
  language developed, 72
  literature, growth of, 61-62, 72
  mural decorations, 71
  philosophy, spread of, 63-72
  writing developed, 60-61, 72
Chou Kung, 71
Chou Li, 49, 55, 58, 70
Chou state, 46
Christ, 68
Christian doctrine, perversion of, 217, 218
Christianity, 213, 214, 217, 218, 222, 277
  Nestorian, 89
  tolerance of, 222
Ch'u, 83
Chu Hsi, 138
Chu Kui-tao, 216, 217
Chu Teh, 339, 359, 360
Chu-Yuan-chang, 156
Chuang-tzŭ, 63-64
Ch'un, Prince, 274, 275
Civil service examinations, *see* Examinations
Civilization
  advance in, 113-114
  Western, recognition of value of, 251
Classics, 68, 69, 91, 95, 100, 112, 132, 133, 137, 195, 235
  block printing of, 133
  destroying of, 76
  examinations in, *see* Examinations
  orthodox editions, 133
  preserved in stone, 132
  rubbing of, 132
  Standard Text or Confucian Canon, 95
Climate, 19
Coal, 19
Cochin China, 77, 90, 91
Co-hong merchants, 203, 210
  homes of, 204

Co-hong system, 193, 194, 197, 198, 200, 203
Coins, copper, 113
Colors to denote rank, 114
Commentaries, Han, repudiated, 138
Commerce
  facilities for, 21
  foreign, 17
  modern, 21
  seaports, 21. *See also* Trade
Communists
  admitted to Kuomintang, 309
  Chinese direct Communistic work, 324
  expelled by Nationalists, 316
  government fears, 325
  join forces with Kuomintang, 344
  "long march," 339-340
  promote own doctrines, 309
  success of, 325
  ten-point program of, 345
  work underground, 323
Confucianism, 277
  canon approved by Hans, 95
  changes in, 92
  destruction of literature, *see* Classics
  Five Classics, 162
  Four Books, 162
  loyalty to, 252
  official language, 101
  protests against, 92
  state religion, 92
  texts reinterpreted, 138
Confucius, 34, 56, 62, 63, 69, 71, 72, 92, 93, 103, 104, 130, 138, 163, 188, 218, 234, 298
  Analects, 65
  life-sketch, 64-68
  teachings and writings, 66-68
Coolies, 282
Copper, 19, 88, 113. *See also* Coins
  mines, 113
Corvino, John de Monte, 145
Cotton, 88
Couch, Turkish, 114
Cranmer-Byng, *Lute of Jade,* quoted, 126
Creation, story of, 23
Cressey, George, *China's Geographic Foundations,* quoted, 37
Crimea, 145
Cumsha, 209

INDEX

Cups, 113, 115, 173. *See also* Porcelains, Ceramics
Cushing, Caleb, 213

Dancing-girls, 115, 152
Dare-to-Dies, 284-285
Dark Ages
  chaos of, 101-102
  fortifications, 102-103
  literature of, 103-104
Dark Ages in China, chapter on, 100-109
Dark Lord, 24
Darkness, Period of Utter, 102-103
Defeat, causes of, 252
Degrees
  Chin Shih, 112
  Hsiu Ts'ai, 112
  Ming Ching, 112
Devastation of towns, 217, 226
Dewey, John, 299
Dialects, 21, 22, 100, 301
Dice, 115
Dictionary compiled, 189
Disarmament Conference, 304
Disunion, 134
Division of China
  into two parts, 139
  into thirty-six provinces, 76
Divination, 40, 56, 72
Dollars, pay for opium, 211
Dominicans, 191
Donald, W. H., 337, 342-343
Dragon
  emblem on flag, 26
  myths regarding, 23, 25, 26
Dragon God, 77
Dragon Throne, 26, 59, 84, 100, 101, 111, 119, 134, 181, 274, 276, 330
Drama
  Khan Dynasty
    development of, 151-154
    Orphan of Chow, The, 153
    Sorrows of Han, The, 153
    Story of the Western Pavilion, The, 153
  Ming Dynasty, 164
Dream of the Red Chamber, The, 189
Dress
  Ming Dynasty, 162
  Tang Dynasty, 114
Dutch attempt settlement, 176
Duties, 193, 220

Dynasty, *see* Ch'in, Chou, Han, Ming, Mongol, Shang, Sui, Sung, T'ang, Tsin, Yin

Earth Mother, 92
East Hopei Autonomous Council, 350, 352
East India Company, English, 177, 206, 210
Edicts
  Hundred Days', 255
  Imperial, 208
  modernization, 269-271
  slaughter, 259
Education
  Eastern division, Chou Dynasty, 59-60
  ideals of universal, 329
  modern, becomes popular, 296
  obstacles to promotion of, 327-328
  reforms of Wang An-shih, 136
Edward VI, 177
"Eight Legs" essay form, 162-163, 253
Elgin, Lord, 223
Elixir of Life, 80
Emperors
  divine, 27-29
  legendary, classes of, 27
  naming of in Ch'in Dynasty, 76
Empress Dowager, The, chapters on, 227-238, 267-276
  See also Tsu Hsi
Empress of China, The, 197
Encyclopedia
  of agriculture, 164
  written, 189
Encyclopedia, The Great, 164
Engineers, 145
England, 206
  attempts to reach China, 176-177
  leases Wei-hai-wei, 245
English
  and French war with Chinese, 222, 223
  merchants, 204-205
  war with Chinese, 212
Envoys
  Flemish, 145
  French, 145
  Indian, 91
  Italian, 117, 145
  Javanese, 91
  Persian, 117

Envoys—*continued*
  Roman, 90
  Russian, 192
  Turkish, 117
Equality of nations, 210, 213
Erh Huang Ti, 81-82
Erh Shih, 82
Eulogy on Mudken, The, 195
Eunuchs, 179
  bribery of, 174
  perfidy of, 275
  power of, 173-174, 230
Euphrates valley, 145
Examinations, civil service, 69, 100, 101, 111, 112, 136, 162-163, 185, 215, 235, 253, 321
  system abolished, 269
Examination halls
  Peking, described, 163
  razed, 269
Excavations, 37, 70
Execution, 202
Expansion, 111, 141, 142, 143, 144, 194
Exports, 193, 272
Extraterritoriality, 192, 213, 278, 304, 307, 310

Fa Hsien, 105-106
  quoted, 105
Family in social system, 51-54
Family life, 297
Famine, 101, 131, 326
  causes of, 326
  Ming Dynasty, 178-180
  specie, 211
Fan Yeh, 96
Fang Shih, see Magicians
Fashiba, Japanese *daimyo,* 175
Feng Shui, superstition, 107-108, 237, 258
Feng Tao, 133
Feng Yu-hsiang, 319
  and Chiang kidnapping, 343
  enters Buddhist retreat, 338
  joins Chiang Kai-shek, 316, 317
  member military council, 337
  recognizes Wang Ching-wei as Nationalist leader, 318
  withdraws to Shensi, 320
Fenolossa, E. F., *Epochs of Chinese and Japanese Art,* quoted, 98
Fertility, 18, 19
  of Yangtse Valley, 85
Finances, Manchu Dynasty, 214

Five Classics, Confucius, 162-163
Five Little Ages and the Sung Dynasty, chapter on, 130-140
  bright spot in, 132
  economies of, 131
Flail, 114
Flax, taxable commodity, 130
Flood, 131, 200
  legend of, 33
Folk-songs, 103
Foochow, 176, 212
Foot-binding, 184, 296
  abolished, 270
  beginning of, 115
Forbidden City, 166-167, 201, 224, 261, 289, 330
Foreign affairs, Manchu Dynasty, 196-200
Foreign policy
  Manchu Dynasty, 191-192
  Ming Dynasty, 174-178
Forests, 85
Formosa, 115, 185
Fortifications, 102-103, 223, 240
Four Books, Confucius, 162-163
France leases coaling station, 245
Franciscans, 191
Freer Gallery of Art, 42
French and English war with China, 222, 223
Frobisher, 177
Fu Hsi, 27, 28
Fu Sheng, 94
Fukien, 171, 185, 314, 338
Funeral rites, religion in, 93
Fur
  exported, 272
  imported, 197
Furnishings, change in, 113-114
Fusan, Korea, 175

Genii, 80, 92
Genoa, 146
George III, King of England, 198
George IV, portrait of, 205
Germany
  coöperation with China, 244
  leases Kiaochow Bay, 244
Giles, H. A.
  Gems of Chinese Literature, quoted, 126
  History of Chinese Literature, A, quoted, 33, 53, 62, 63, 80-81, 84, 85, 99, 105, 106
Ginseng, imported, 197
Glazing, 171-173

INDEX 401

Gobi, Desert of, 105
Gods
  of Chou Dynasty, 57
  of five elements, 80
  of Han Dynasty, 92
Gold, 19, 88
Gold of Ophir, 203
Golden Age, 33, 64, 103
Golden Age of the T'ang Dynasty, chapter on, 110-129
Golden enclosure, 138
Gordon, Chinese, 226
Government
  Canton, 295, 307, 308, 309
  criticism of, 302-304
  edict for reform of, 269
  Manchu, 185-186
  Nanking, 315, 318, 319, 323
  National, 318-323
    provisional constitution, 322
    democratic form, 320-321
  Peking, 290, 305, 307, 316
  provincial, 295
  reason for poverty of, 328-329
  reform in, 290-297
  strife for united, 334
  unstable, 304-305
Governor Findlay, 207
Governors, military, *see* War lords
Grain Loans, 136
Granet, Marcel, *Chinese Civilization*, quoted, 51
Great Wall, 22, 77, 78, 79, 84, 86, 87, 93, 96, 108, 117, 169, 182, 334
Green Sprout Law, 136
Gros, Baron, 223
Guilds, origin of, 54

Hail, W. J., *Tseng Kuo-fan and the Taiping Rebellion*, quoted, 226
Hamada, Mr., Japanese scholar, 42
Hami, 87
Han Dynasty, 88, 89
  calligraphy, 97
  campaigns against Huns, 86
  date of, 83, 100
  expansion of, 84-85
  founded, 82
  literature of, 94-95, 96
  origin of rulers of, 83
  painting, 97

Han Dynasty—*continued*
  pottery, 98-99
  sculpture, 98
  size, 110
Han rule, 145
Han, state, 83
Han Fu-chu, 338
Han Yü, 120
Handicrafts, 283
Hangchow, 108, 142, 150, 195, 217
  bombarded, 286
  surrenders, 286
  taken by Japanese, 359
Hankow, 307, 312, 313
  burning of, 286
  captured by Revolutionists, 285
Hanlin Academy, 128, 136
  fired by Boxers, 261
Hanyang, 312
  captured by Revolutionists, 285
Hart, Sir Robert, quoted, 19, 220, 243
Hay, John, 247
Hayashi, General, 355
Heaven, *see Ti'en*
Heavenly Lamp, 218
Heavens, thirty-three of P'an Ku, 24
  Taoist adoption, 120
Hedin, Sven, discoveries of, 96, 97
Hells, eighteen, Taoist adoption of, 120
Heroes, Legendary, chapter on, 27-35
Heroes of Liang Shan, The, 154-155
Hind, 177
Hirota, Japanese Minister of Foreign Affairs, 350, 357
Ho-Umetsu Agreement, 351
Hobart, Alice Tisdale, *Within the Walls of Nanking*, quoted, 314-315
Honan, 34, 37, 38, 48, 62, 98, 100, 139, 179
Hong merchants, *see Co-hong*
Hongkong, 224
Hongkong, island of, ceded to Britain, 212
Hopei-Chahar Political Council, 343, 351
Horace, 89
Horseback riding, 85
Horse-racing, 115
Horses, 149, 150
Houqua, merchant, 203, 204

Houses, materials for, 20
Hsien Feng, 225, 227
Hsien Yang, 79
Hsiung-nu, see Huns
Hsu, P. C., 137
Hsuan Tsung, 127, 128, 129
Hsuan T'ung, see Pu Yi
Hu Han-min, quoted, 328-329
Hu Shih
   Civilizations of East and West, The, quoted, 195-196, 281, 299
   quoted, 43, 61, 63, 69, 335
   Symposium, quoted, 92, 103, 121, 137, 284
   urges national reconstruction, 350
Huang Ti, 28
Huang Yuan-yung, 300
Huc, Abbe, *A Journey through the Chinese Empire,* quoted, 118
Hudson, explorer, 117
Hull, Secretary, 357
Hummel, A. W., *Autobiography of a Chinese Historian,* quoted, 34
Hunan, 216, 217, 218, 275
Hunan Braves, 219
Hung Hsiu-ch'uan, 215, 216, 219, 226
Hung Wu, 160, 161, 162, 165, 169, 170, 173
Huns, 77, 86, 87, 93, 102
   campaigns against, 86-87
   evils of invasion, 86
Hupeh, 275
Hwai River, 108

I Ching, see Book of Change
Idols, destroyed, 216
Immigration to Manchuria, 331
Imperial Chinese Railway Administration, 238
Imperial City, 168
Imports, 173, 197, 198, 205, 206
Indemnity, 222
   Boxer Uprising, 265-266
   to England, 212
   to Japan, 243
Indemnity College, *see* Tsing Hua College
India, 87, 91, 105, 111, 206
Industrial revolution, fight against, 237-238
Industries, fostering of, 187, 188

Industry, hand, undergoes revolution, 310
Infanticide, female, 53
Ingram, Dr. J. H., translations of, 41
Institute of History and Philology, 41
Intercourse, foreign, 145, 192
   passing of, 157. *See also* Trade
Intermarriage, 186
International affairs
   interest of Kuang Hsü in, 239-240
   new conception of, 278
Iron, 19, 56, 85
Iron Age, 56
Ismaloff, M., Russian embassy head, 192
Ito, Count, 241

Jade, 88
Japan, 116, 143
   acquirements from Russia, 268
   alarm over Russian activities, 242
   annexes Korea, 268
   attacked by Mongols, 143-144
   boycott of, 303-304
   copies China, 116-117
   difficulties with, 175, 331, 332
   gains Asiatic foothold, 175
   lands troops on Formosa, 241
   military operations in China, chapter on, 349-361
   refuses to appear at Nine-Power Conference, 357
   resigns from League of Nations, 333
   seizes Chinese territory, 292
   Twenty-one Demands of, 292
Japan-China compact regarding Korea, 241
Java, 105
Javanese, 91
Jehol, 198, 224, 225, 227, 228, 338, 349
Jenghis Khan, 141, 142
Jesuits, 182, 191
   enter China, 177-178
   interest in astronomy, 190-191
Joffe, Russian representative, 307, 308, 309
Jung Lu, 256, 259
Junk, Malay, reaches China, 175
Junks, 20, 149, 150, 178, 202, 207, 209, 220, 234

INDEX

Kai-feng fu, 157
K'ang Hsi, 186, 187, 188, 189, 190, 191, 192, 193, 194, 195, 196, 202
  astrology, interest in, 190
  bans missionaries, 191
  compared with Louis XIV, 188-187
  death of, 194
Kang Teh, 333
Kang Yu-wei, 254, 298
  conspiracy of, 256
  flight of, 257
  leader of Revolution, 283-284
Kansu, 37
Kaoliang, 18, 39, 50
Karakhan, Ambassador, 307
Kashgar, 88
Kataba, General, 119
Kawagoe, Ambassador, 354, 355
Kellogg Pact, 332
Kerosene oil, 296
  imported, 272
Khan Dynasty
  adopt Llamanism, 144
  conquer Annam, 144
  defeat Burmese, 144
  gifts to China
    Grand Canal, 150
    patronage of drama and novel, 151-155
  Mongols control China, 143
  repelled by Japanese, 144
  sea campaign, 144
Khan of Persia, 146
Khans, 145, 150
Kharezm, 141
Khitans, struggles with, 135, 138
Khotan-Lobnor, southern route, 87
Kiangsi, 171, 314, 319
Kiangsu, 225, 319
Kiaochow Bay, 244
  seized by Japan, 292
Kimono, 117
Kins, 138, 139, 140, 141
Kiu kiang, 149
Kiusiu, 144
Konoye, Premier, 357
Koran, 120
Korea, 37, 84, 109, 141, 143, 144, 182, 194
  difficulty over, 241, 242
Kow-tow, ceremony of, 192, 197, 198
Koxinga, pirate, 176, 184, 185
Ku K'ai-chih, 97, 107

Kuang Hsü, 233, 298
  burial of, 273-274
  conspiracy of, 256
  death of, 273
  interest of, in international affairs, 239-240
  joins reformers, 255-256
  made a prisoner, 256-257
  reform proclamation of, 255-256
  reign of begins, 239
Kublai Khan, 142, 143, 144, 145, 146, 155, 162
  power of, 147, 148
Kuan Kin, Goddess of Mercy, 123, 124, 172
Kung, Madame, 336
Kung, Prince, 224, 228, 229, 230
Kung An-kuo, 94
Kung Ti, 142
Kuomintang (People's Party), 289, 295, 307, 308
  admits Communists, 309
  Communists unite with, 344
  plans republic, 289
  reorganized, 309
  under the leadership of Chiang, 336 ff.
Kwan, Admiral, 212
Kwang-tzŭ, philosopher, 72
Kwolvon Point, 224
Kyoto, 116

Labor
  disputes, 311
  forced
    lessened, 113
    Ming Dynasty, 178
    on canals, 108
    on Great Wall, 77
    reforms in, 137
    revived, 130
Lamanism, 144
Lamps, 296
Land division, 47, 49, 50
Language, 21, 22, 60-61, 72
  common, 100
  literary, 300-301
  national, 302, 329
  spoken, 300-301
  written, 300-301
Lao-tzŭ, 62, 63, 64, 68, 69, 72, 92, 104, 110
  See also Yellow Ancient
Lao-tzŭ school of philosophy, 84
Lacquer-work, perfected, 171

Lattimore, Owen, 334
League of Nations
  condemns Japan, 357
  Japan resigns from, 333
  report of on Chinese-Japanese difficulties, 333
Learning
  privilege of a few, 195
  revival of, Manchu Dynasty, 196
Lee, Mabel Ping-hua, *The Economic History of China*, quoted, 179
Legge, James, 33
Li, C., 41
Li Hung-chang, 225, 226, 240, 241, 251
  interest in railway, 236
Li Ki, see *Book of Rites*
Li Lien-ying, 231
Li Po, 126, 127
Li Shih-chen, *Materia Medica*, 164
Li Ssu, 76
Li Tsung-yin, 337
Li-Tzu-ch'eng, 180, 181, 184
Li Ung Bing, 31, 58
  Outlines of Chinese History, quoted, 206, 207
Li Wang, 45, 48
Li Yuan, 110
  emperor T'ang Dynasty, 110, 111
Li-Yuan-hung, 294, 308
Liang Chi-chao, 254, 283-284, 298
  flight of, 257
Liang Kiang, 225
Liaotung Peninsula, 242, 243, 244, 268
Lin Tse-hsi, 211, 212
Ling, 114
Literati, 76, 77, 94-95, 189, 201, 232, 234
Literature
  Chou Dynasty, 61-62, 72
  concordance of, 189
  Eastern Chou Dynasty, An Age of Creative Thought and Literature, chapter on, 59-72
  Manchu Dynasty
    development of, 194, 195, 196
    flourished, 189
  Ming Dynasty
    conventionality of, 163-164
  of Dark Ages, 103-104
  reconstruction of past, 95

Literature—*continued*
  remains, Han, 95
Little Emperor, 289, 294
Liu Chiu Islands, 240-241
Liu Pang, 82, 83
Living conditions, 279-283
Lo Yang, 48, 59, 71, 100, 133, 165
Loans by government, 136
Long-Haired Rebellion, 216
Looting by international troops, 265
Lorcha Arrow, 221
Louis XIV, 186-187
Lu, 45, 65
Lukuochiao, 355
Lü Hsin-yen, 118
Lumber supply, 19-20

Ma Tsu, 121
Macao, 176, 189, 193, 202
Macartney, Lord, 198
  quoted, 266
Mac Nair, H. F.
  China in Revolution, quoted, 323
  Modern Chinese History, quoted, 204, 205-206, 226
Magicians (*Fang Shih*), 79, 80
  influence of, 91, 92
Malarial fever, 115
Malay Peninsula, 90, 91
Manchu Dynasty
  abdication, 289
  agriculture, sponsoring of, 187
  art, development of, 194
  badge of servitude to, 183-184
  chaos of, 202-203
  chapter on, 182-200
  conquests of, 182
  corruptness of, 227, 243
  decline of, 201-202
  dress of, 184
  efforts to cope with Revolutionists, 288-289
  expansion, 194
  finances, 214
  foreign affairs, 196-200
  foreign policy, 191, 192
  governmental policy of, 185
  industries, sponsored, 187, 188
  ineffectiveness of, 227
  literature of, 189, 194, 195
  military organization, 186-187
  weakness of, 243
Manchukuo, 19, 22, 37, 138, 326, 333, 349

INDEX

Manchuria, 77, 84, 111, 161, 194, 242, 244, 245, 316, 317, 320, 330, 331, 332
  Chinese-Japanese trouble in, 332
  declares independence, 333
  problem of, 330
Manchus, 179, 180
  defeat Mings, 179-181
  displease Chinese, 274-275
  early rebellions against, 183-185
  hold all offices, 274
  last of, 333
Mandate, The Imperial, to King George, 198-200
Manuscripts, 86, 122, 133, 164
Mao Tse-tung, 344
Marcus Antonius, 89
Marcus Aurelius, 90
Maritime Customs Service, Chinese, 220, 221, 246, 266
  function of, 273
Massacres, 120
Media of exchange, 56, 113
Mencius, philosopher, 68, 72, 138, 163
Menzies, James Mellon, 41
Merchants, English, homes of, 204-205
Military
  organization, Manchu, 186
  People's National Army, 306
  service compulsory, 113
  system of Tai Pings, 217
Millet, *see* Kaoliang
Mineral resources, 19
Mines in Shantung Province, 244
Ming Dynasty, 157, 162-173, 176, 177, 194, 201
  agriculture, interest in revived, 162
  ancient customs, revival of, 162
  architecture, 170
  arts, lesser, 171-173
  causes of downfall, 178
  chapter on, 161-181
  date of, 157
  defeated by Manchus, 179-181
  economic conditions, 177-178
  eunuchs, 173-174
  examinations, revival of, 162
  famine, 178-180
  foreign policy, 174-178
  government, 161-162
  land restoration, 164
  literature of, 163-164
  painting of, 170-171

Ming Dynasty—*continued*
  relief measures of, 178-179
  silk culture, revival of interest in, 162
  simplification of dress, 162
  strife of, 164-165
  tax exemption, 164
  tombs of, 169-170
  victories of, 161
Ming Huang, *see* Hsuang Tsung
Ming Ti, 91
Mission Societies, 215
Missionaries, 117, 118, 145, 218
  banned by K'ang Hsi, 191
  first Protestant, 214
Missions
  educational features, 215
  evangelical activities, 215
  expansion, 215-216
  medical activities, 215
Mo School of thought, 69
Model Emperor Lore, 34
Mohammed, 68
Mohammedanism, 89, 119
Mohammedans, 117, 119
  Chinese, attitude toward other religions, 120
Monasteries, destruction of, 121
Money, 56, 113
Mongol Dynasty, 140, 154
  conquests of, 141-144
  cultural life, 144-145
  foreign intercourse, 145
  unsatisfactory to people, 155, 156
Mongol rule
  adoption of Chinese culture, 144-145
  chapter on, 141-157
  nature of, 144
Mongolia, 22, 37, 77, 111, 142, 161, 182, 194, 244, 330
  Russia gains influence in, 330
Mongolian language, 145
Mongols, 140, 141, 161
  conquer China, 143
  repelled by Japanese, 144
  stirred up by Japanese against China, 354
Monks made diplomats, 145
Morrison, Robert, 214, 215
Mosque, 119, 120
Most favored nation clause, 212, 247
Mother of Metals, 24

Mo-ti, 62, 68, 69, 72
Mural decorations, 71
Myths
  regarding dragon, 23, 25, 26
  regarding origin of people, 23-26

Nankai University, 358
Nanking, 102, 156, 161, 163, 165, 184, 185, 219, 220, 224, 225, 246
  beseiged by Nationalists, 314, 315
  capital, republic, 289
  evacuation of, 286-287
  government, 315, 318, 319, 323
  taken by Japanese, 359
Nanking Incident, 315, 319
Nantucket, 197
Napier, Lord, 210
Nara, 116
National Academy, 133
National Economic Reconstruction Movement, 246 ff.
National University, Peking, 301
Nationalists, The
  attempt unification, 312
  chapter on, 308-317
  cities taken by, 313, 314
  control few provinces, 319
  demonstrations of, 312, 313
  doctrines against capitalists, 313-314
  organize, 309
  propaganda, 310
  regain control, 320
  split in party, 315-316, 322-326
  take Peking, 316-317
Navigation, 150
  of rivers, 21
Navy
  edict for modernization, 270
  funds for diverted, 240
  modern, advocated, 253
Neo-Confucianism, 137, 138, 170
Neolithic Age, 37, 38, 42, 171
Nerchinsk Treaty, 191, 213
Nestorian Christianity, 89, 119
Nestorian priests, 117
Nestorians, 119
  driven out, 121
New Life Movement, 346
New Thought Movement, 299-301
New York, 197
Newchwang, 331
Nine Dots, *see* Chou Dynasty land division

Ning Yüan, 182
Ningpo, 175, 176, 212
Nirvana, 107
"North China," Japanese interpretation of, 353
Northern China, 18-19
  excavations in, 37
Northwest Passage, 177
Novel, 104, 151, 153-155
  of Manchu Dynasty, 189
  of Ming Dynasty, 164
  origin of, 153
Nurhachu, Prince, 182

Ocean routes, 90-91
Old Buddha, *see* Tsu Hsi
Omega, 207
Onon River, 141
Open Door Policy, 247
Opium, 115
  admitted without duty, 224
  crop confiscated, 305
  destruction of, 211, 212
  growing compulsory, 324
  importation of, forbidden, 206
  revenue from, 305, 340
  silver paid for, 210-211
  smuggling of, 206, 207, 212, 352 ff.
  suppression of trade, 210-211
Oracle Bones
  archaeological site, 39-42
  for divination, 40-41
Organic Law, The
  provisions for government, 321
Orphan of Chow, The, 153
Oxus River, 87

Pagodas, 107, 108, 116
Pai Chung-hsi, 338
Painting, 97, 107, 122-125
  Buddhistic, 123
  Ming Dynasty, 170-171
  monochrome, 124, 125
  Sung Dynasty, 140
  T'ang Dynasty, 122, 124
Palaces
  A Fang Kung, 79
  Cambuluc, 146, 147, 156
  Intense Brilliance, 116
  Jehol, 198, 224, 225, 227, 228
  Prosperous Felicity, 116
  Summer, 224, 239, 240
  Yuan Ming Yuan, 223

INDEX 407

Pan family, historians, 95, 99
P'an Ku, 23, 24, 27
Panay affair, 359
Panoramic Glimpse of China, A, chapter on, 17-22
Panoramic view northern China, 18-19
Panoramic view southern China, 17-18
Paper, invention of, 96
Parkes, Harry, 221, 223
Parthia, 89
Pearl River, 194, 202, 221, 237
  center trade activities, 204
Peasants
  cause of, taken up by Communists, 323
  Chou Dynasty, 51
  conditions of, 323-324
  mode of living, 281, 282
  poverty of, 131
Pechili Gulf, 331
Peiho, 178
Peiping, see Peking
Peking, 70, 146, 150, 163, 178, 193, 219, 222, 234, 239, 246
  beauty of, 165-166
  becomes Peiping, 318
  building of a financial drain, 178
  government at, 290, 305, 307, 316
  looting of, 265
  plan of, 166-167
  taken by Manchus, 184
Peking Legations attacked by Boxers, 260-265
People
  coolies, 282
  crafts of, 55
  execution of, 202
  immigration of, 331
  peasants, 131, 281, 282, 323-324
  relations of, 52-54
  scholars, 279-280, 299
  speech of, 21, 22
  students, 298-307
  types of, 21, 22
  upper class, 279-280
    Chou Dynasty, 51
    T'ang Dynasty, 115
People's National Army, 306
Pepper, import, 175
Perestrello, Rafael, 175
Perpetual Astronomy of K'ang Hsi, The, 191
Persia, 146

Persian Gulf, 89, 91
Peter the Great, 192
Petrucci, Raphaël, *Chinese Painters,* quoted, 97, 107
Philadelphia, 197
Philippines, 176
Philosophers, 62
Philosophy
  Chou Dynasty, 63-72
Pilgrimages, Buddha priests, 105
Pirates, 156, 202
Pit dwellings, 38
Pliny the Elder, 89
Po, 34
Po Hsi, see Fu Hsi
Poetry, 103
  Manchu Dynasty, 195
  Ming Dynasty, 164
  reached heights, 125
  volume of, 125
Poets, 61-62, 103, 116, 125
Polo, Marco, 145-150, 217
  quoted, 146-150
Polo (father and uncle of Marco), 145, 146
Pope Nicholes IV, 145
Poppy, 115
  cultivation of forbidden, 206
Population, 21, 22, 190
  increase, 188
  Manchu Dynasty, 196, 201
Porcelain
  Han Dynasty, 98-99
  Ming Dynasty, 172-173
  Sung Dynasty, 140
  T'ang Dynasty, 113, 116
Port Arthur, 240, 244, 245
  Japan acquires, 268
Portuguese, 175, 176, 182
Position, comparison with United States, 17
Pottery, 42, 98-99, 113, 115, 116, 140, 171-173
  clay for, 171
  Han Dynasty, 98-99
  Ming Dynasty, 171-172
  Neolithic Age, 39
Priest-king (Son of Heaven), 57
Priests, travels of, 118
Printing, 132-134
  beginnings, 132, 133
  block printing, 132, 133, 134
Produce, 18
Property, private ownership of, 113
Prosperity, Manchu regime, 187

Provinces, 22
Provincial system, 161
Psalms translated into Mongolian, 145
Ptolemy, 89, 90
Pu Yi, 274
Pyramids, 36, 78

Queue
  abolished, 288
  badge of servitude, 183

Railroads, 21
  building of, 326
  China's first, 237-238
  Chinese Eastern, 244, 267, 307, 332
  control of, lost by China, 245-246
  dissension over schemes for, 275-276
  financing of, 245-246
  gains from, 246
  necessity for, 253
  Peking-Hankow, 246
  riots, 275-276
  Shanghai-Hangchow, 275
  Shantung lines, 244, 246
  Southern Manchurian, 332
  Tientsin-Pukow, 246
  Trans-Siberian, 244
Rebellions
  Manchu Dynasty, 185
  Ming Dynasty, 179-180
  sporadic, 214
  Tai Ping, chapter on, 214-226
Red Lord, 24
Reform
  edicts
    issued, 255-256
    rescinded, 258
  first movement, 237-238
  first talk of, 234
  Movement, program sponsored, 269
Reform and Reaction, chapter on, 251-266
Religion, *see also* Confucianism, Buddhism, Taoism
  Chin Dynasty, 80
  Chou Dynasty, 56-58
  denominational quarrels, 191
  fusing of, 93
  tolerance in, 118, 119
Renaissance
  intellectual life, 298
  literary, 195

Republic
  first parliament, 290-291
  rapid change in presidents, 294
  recognized, 290
  second president, 294
Republican government, 183
Residence, foreign, in Peking, 222
Revolt, 275-276
  causes for, of 1911, 277, 283
Revolution, chapter on, 277-297
  industrial, 329
  leaders of, 283-284
  of 1911, 183
  of 1913, 291
Revolutionists
  declare republic, 289
Ricci, Matteo, 177
Rice
  food of China, 18, 19, 85, 149, 150, 196, 217
  imported, 272
Riots over railway troubles, 275-276
Rivers
  floods of, 20
  navigability of, 20, 21
  waterpower of, 21
Roads
  automobile, 21, 326-327
  cart, 21
Roman Empire, 89
Roman writings, containing Chinese references, 89, 90
Romance of Three Kingdoms, The (San Kuo), 104, 154
Romans, 90
Rome, 88, 89
Royal Asiatic Society, 39
Rubbing, ink, 132
Russell, Bertram, 299
Russia, 191, 192, 242
  advances Manchurian interests, 267-268
  aids China, 308
  difficulties with, 332
  fleets lost by, 268
  leases Liaotung Peninsula, 244
  leases Port Arthur, 244
  wars with Japan, 267-268
Russians, expelled by Nationalists, 316

Sacred Edict, The, 188
Sacrifice, human, 104-105
Sacrificial vessels, 42, 58, 98

INDEX

Saghalien Island, 268
Salem, 197
Salt, taxable commodity, 130, 237
San Yan Fu, 149
Sandalwood, 197-198
Saracens, 157
Sato, Naotake, 355
Schaal, Joannes Adam, 190
Scholars, modern, 299
  mode of living, 279-280
School system
  advocated, 252
  established, 269-270
Schools
  establishment of, 277
  for study silk culture, 296-297
  increase in, 296-297
Science of Catastrophe, 92
Sciences, high development of, 195
Sculpture
  development of, 122
  Han Dynasty, 98
  Ming Dynasty, 169
  state of Wei, 107
  T'ang Dynasty, 122
Sea communication, 90
Seaports, principal, 21
Secret societies, 156, 258
  anti-dynastic, 202
  Dare-to-Dies, 284
Sellery, G. C., and Krey, A. C., *The Founding of Western Civilization*, quoted, 196
September 18th (1931) Incident, 332
Shang, 34
Shang-Chou culture, 72
Shang Dynasty, 35, 42, 72
  archaeological discoveries of, 36-44
  bronze, 42, 43
  pottery, 42, 171
  social diversions, 43
Shang Law, 75
Shang, Lord, 75
Shang Ti (Supreme Deity), 32, 44, 72, 80, 91
Shang Ti Hwei, 215
Shanhai-Kuan, 181, 183
Shanghai, 21, 40, 175, 212, 220, 223, 225, 308
  arsenal captured, 286
  Chinese-Japanese trouble in, 332

Shanghai—*continued*
  falls before Nationalists, 314
  falls before Japanese, 359
Shansi, 37, 316, 337
Shantung, 98, 105, 240, 245, 294, 303
  German concessions seized by Japan, 292
Shê, *see* Yü
Shen Nung, 28
Shensi, 37, 46, 115, 179, 180, 184, 316, 340, 360
Shih Chi, 95
Shih Huang Ti, 75, 76, 77-79, 81-82, 83, 91, 94
  builds Great Wall, 77, 78, 79
  burial of, 80-82
  burns classics, 76, 79
  destroys feudalism, 76, 79
Shih Min, 110, 111
Shih Nai-an, 154
Shu Dynasty, 180
Shu, State of China, 101, 133
Shu Ching, 34
Shun, 30, 31, 32, 33, 34, 64, 71, 103, 130, 164
Sian, 115, 116, 126, 133, 180, 265, 267, 342
Siberia, 37, 141
Sickle, 114
Silk, 19, 28, 205
  beginning of industry in Europe, 118
  culture, 162
  factories, 127
  medium of exchange, 56, 113
  paintings on, *see* Paintings
  pieces, 113, 117, 123, 205
  routes, 88, 89, 99
Silken Way, 117, 157
Silkworm, 18
  culture of, 297
  legends of, 29, 30, 118
Silver, 19
Simcox, Edith, *Primitive Civilizations,* quoted, 51, 53
Simpson, Bertram Lenox, *Indiscreet Letters from Peking,* quoted, 260-261, 262-263, 264
Sitting-mat, 114
Size, 190
  comparison with United States, 17
  Han Dynasty, 100
  lost territory, 239-248

Smuggling in autonomous sections, 352 ff.
Socrates, 62
Soeul, 175
Soil, 18-19
 conservation, 131
 depletion, 131
 loess, 37, 38, 46, 51, 85, 116
Soochow, 175, 359
Soong, T. V., 319, 336, 337, 343
Soothill, W. E., *History of China, A,* quoted, 291
Sorrows of Han, The, 153
Southern China, 17-18
Soviet Republic
 doctrines of, promoted, 307
 negotiations of, 307
 recognized by China, 307
Speech, 21, 22
Spheres of Influence, 245, 247
Spices, 193
Spring Annals, 45, 46
Squeeze, 193, 214, 225, 273, 274, 328-329
Ssu-ma Ch'ien, 80-81, 84, 86, 95, 99, 100, 137, 201
 Shih Chi, 95
Ssu-ma Kuang, *The Mirror of History (T'ung Chien),* 137
States, warring, 59, 75
Steiger, G. M., *History of the Orient, A,* quoted, 186-187
Stein, Sir Aurel
 discoveries of, 89, 96, 122, 123
 excavations of, 86, 90, 114
 Ruins of Desert Cathay, quoted, 86
Stone Age, 42
Story of the Western Pavilion, The, 153
Story-tellers, professional, 153
Straits of Malacca, 91
Students
 boycott Japan, 303-304
 chapter on, 298-307
 criticize government, 302-304
 demand offices, 302
 disapprove Versailles Treaty, 303, 304
 influence Disarmament Conference, 304
Su Ling, 28-29
Su Shun, 229
 arrest of, 228-229
 conspiracy of, 228
Sui, Duke of, 108

Sui Dynasty, 108
Sui emperor, 108-109
Sui Jen, 27, 28
Sumatra, 91, 105
Sun Fo, 337
Sun Hao, 114
Sun Yat-sen, 283-284, 291, 307, 308, 323
 aided by Russia, 308, 309
 death of, 309
 elected president 1921, 295
 honored after death, 341
 provincial president, 289
 sketch of early life, 284-285
 "three principals" of will of, 309-310, 316, 317, 320, 322, 345, 346
Sun, Madame, 336
 denounces right wing of Nationalists, 316, 323
 quoted, 323
Sun Yat-sen University, 324
Sung Dynasty, 36, 135-140, 142, 143
 archaeological discoveries of, 36
 art, 140
 chaos of, 135
Sung Cheh-yuan, 343, 351
Sungs, 135, 139, 140, 142
Superstitions, 91, 107-108, 180
Sutras (Buddhist canons), 106-107, 120
Swatow, 21
Szechuen, 77, 87, 88, 275

Ta Ch'ing dynasty, *see* Manchu
Table, high, 114
Tai Ping Rebellion
 leaders, 215, 216, 217
 temporal power, 216
 militaristic movement, 216, 217-218, 219, 224
 Nanking captured, 219
 ravages of, 217, 218, 226
 religious movement, 216
Tai Ping Tien Huoh, 216
Tai Shan, 68
Tai Tsu, 157. *See also* Hung Wu
T'ai Tsung, 111, 118, 128
Tai Yuan-fu, 265
Taku, Fort, 222, 223, 224
T'ang, 30, 34, 35
T'ang Dynasty
 architectural remains, 115-116
 court renamed, 115-116
 date of, 110

INDEX

T'ang Dynasty—*continued*
  dress, 114
  expansion, 111
  extravagance, 115
  furniture, 114
  Nestorian Christianity enters, 118
  opium introduced, 115
  painting, 124
  poetry, 125
  social life, 112
  tools, 114
  utensils, 113, 115
T'ang Dynasty, Golden Age of, chapter on, 110-129
Tangku Truce, 349, 351
T'angs, 130, 133, 145, 157, 194, 201
Tanguts, 135, 138
Tao, 63
Taoism, 64, 93
  corruption of ideas of Lao-tzŭ, 69
Taoists
  imitate Buddhists, 120
Tarim River Valley, 87
Tartar City, 166
Tartars, 85, 102, 123
Tax, 130, 200, 214, 324
  exemptions, 164, 187
  lessens forced labor, 113
  levied, by *Co-hong*, 193
  Ming Dynasty, 178
  on shelves, 130
  reform, 135, 136, 137
  relief from, 131
Taxable commodities
  flax, 130
  graduated tax, 137
  salt, 130
  tea, 114, 130
Tea, 85, 89, 126
  as beverage, 114-115
  export of, 271
  taxable commodity, 114, 130
Tea, 195
Teh, Prince, 354
Temples, 91, 216
  Buddhist, 107
  Taoist, art in, 120
  Temple of Earth, 169
  White Horse, 91
Ten Stone Drums, 70
Territory lost, 239-248
Testament, New, translated into Mongolian, 145
Three Kingdoms, period of, 101

Three Principles of Sun Yat-sen, 309-310, 316, 317, 320, 322
Tibet, 22, 111, 144, 194
Tibetans, 115, 123
Ti'en (Heaven), 44, 57, 69
Tien Shan (Tien mountains), 87
Tientsen, 21, 150, 222, 223, 265, 352, 357
Tigris River, 89
Tobacco, 115
Tolerance in religion, 118-119
Tombs
  Han Dynasty, 98
  Ming Dynasty, 169-170
Tools, 114
Trade, foreign, 88, 174, 192, 193, 196-200, 223, 224, 234
  Advances, chapter on, 201-213
  treaties, mark of, 212, 213
  caravan, 192
  change in character of exports and imports, 271-273
  increase in volume, 271
  Lorcha Arrow affair, 221
  regulation restrictions, 221
  relatives, 220
  restrictions of, 202, 203
  routes, 88, 89, 90, 117, 118, 190, 194
Trading posts, 192, 193
Transportation
  Han Dynasty, 100
  means of, 55, 85, 100, 236-237, 326-327
Travel, 85
  during Han Dynasty, 100
  of priests, 118
Treaty
  American, 222
  first with European power, 191
  French, 213, 222
  fulfillment demanded, 221, 222
  Nanking, 212
  Nerchinsk, 191, 213
  Peking, 223, 224
  Portsmouth, N. H., 268
  Russian, 222
  second English, 212
  Shimonoseki, 242-243
  Tientsin, 222
  Versailles, 303, 304
Treaty ports, 212
  increased, 222, 224
Tribute
  from Annam, 194
  from Burmah, 194

Tribute—*continued*
  from Chinese people, 216
  from provinces, 267
  to Khitans, 135
  to Mongols, 144
  to Tanguts, 135
True Prince, *see* White Jade Ruler
Tsai Ting-kai, 332, 333, 338
Ts'ao Ts'an, 83
Tseng Kuo-fan, 218, 219, 220, 225, 226, 240, 251, 288
  constructive reformer, 235
  death of, 235
  memorial of, 236
  victories over Tai Pings, 220, 225, 226
Tsin, 102
Tsing Hua College, 266
Tsingtao, 21
Tso Chuan, 33
Tso Tsung-tang, 225, 253
  death of, 238
  memorial of, 238
Tsu Hsi
  death of, 273
  degeneracy of court, 233-234
  diverts funds for navy, 240
  dominates son, 232, 233
  edicts for modernization, 269-271
  flight after Boxer movement, 264-265
  frenzy of, during Boxer movement, 258-259
  gains control, 257
  gains control second time, 227, 228, 229
  gains control third time, 233
  influence of eunuchs over, 230, 231-232, 259
  joint regent, 229
  problems of regency, 234
  reactionary program of, 257-258
  relinquishes second regency, 239
  rescinds reform edicts, 257
  return after flight, 267
  sponsors Reform Movement program, 269
  tribute collected by, 233
Tsung li Yamen
  formation of, 224
  reorganized, 265
Tsushima Island, 144
Tu Fu, 126, 127

Tuan, Prince, 259, 262, 265
Tuchuns, see War lords
Tun Huang, 122
Tung Chih, 227, 232-233, 257
Tungchow, 223, 350
Turfan, 88
Turkestan, Chinese, 22, 85, 111, 117, 194
Turkey, 117
Turkie, 110, 111
Twenty-one demands of Japan, 292
  published, 293, 303
Tzu Kung, 67

Unicorn, 177
United States, 17, 85, 197, 198, 206, 222, 265, 266, 272, 294, 327, 332
  and *Panay* sinking, 359
  fears restriction of trade, 246-247
  plea for peace, 357
  race for trade, 197, 198
Upper class
  Chou Dynasty, 51
  mode of living, 279, 280
  T'ang Dynasty, 115
Urns, 99
Utensils, 42
  change in, 113-114
  first, 28

Vegetation, 18
Venice, 145, 146
Verbeist, Dutch astrologer, 190-191
Virgil, 89
Vladivostok, 242, 244
Von Kettler, Baron, 260-261

Wade, Sir Thomas, 241
Wales, Nym, 344
Wall, Mongol, remains of, 165
Wang An-shih
  education reforms, 136
  plans for social reforms, 136
  taxation reforms, 135, 136
Wang Chich, 134
Wang Ching-wei, 319, 320
Wang Ch'ung, 92
Wang Hu-cheng, 340
Wang Wei, 124
War
  Russo-Japanese, 267-268
    effect on China, 268-269
  Chinese-Japanese, 242

INDEX 413

War—*continued*
  English-Chinese, 212
  French and English against China, 222
War lords
  ambitions of, 305
  chapter on, 298-307
  divert revenue funds, 305
  fight with Nationalists, 319-320
  gain control, 294, 295
  growing power of, 305
  leaders, 305
Ward, General, 225-226
Wastelands, reclamation of, 196
Water power, 21
Weakness of China, Han Dynasty, 100
Weale, Putnam, *see* Simpson, Bertram Lenox
Weapons, 114, 182
  battering ram, 114
  of Ch'ins, 79
  of Chous, 47, 56
  of Huns, 77
  of Manchus, 287
  of T'angs, 114
Wei, 101
  sculpture of, influenced by religion, 107
Wei-hai-wei, 240
  naval battle of, 242
  leased to England, 245
West River, 20
Wheat, 18
White Jade Ruler, 24
White Lily Society, 156
White Sea, 177
Williams, S. Wells, *The Middle Kingdom,* quoted, 54
Willoughby, Sir Hugh, 177
Wine
  rice, 115
  Snow Bubble, 127
Wood Prince, 24
Women's rights, 296, 297
Writing, 72
  archaic, 40
  materials for, 60, 72
  picture, 28
Wu, 101
Wu Fu, Empress, 111
Wu Pei-fu, 305
  activities of, 306
Wu San-kuei, 181
Wu Tao-tzu, 124

Wu Ti, 84, 85, 87, 91
  interest in foreign lands, 88
Wu Wang, 46
Wuchang, 102, 220
  besieged by Nationalists, 312-313
  captured by Revolutionists, 285

Xavier, Saint Francis, 177

Yang, 23
Yang Hu-cheng, 342, 343
Yang Kuei-fei, 127, 128, 129
Yang Shao Ts'un, 38
Yangchow, 139, 146, 195
Yangtse River and Basin, 18, 20, 77, 85, 90, 102, 108, 139, 142, 146, 149-150, 185, 212, 216, 217, 219, 220, 225, 234, 237, 245, 306
Yao, 30, 31, 32, 33, 34, 64, 71, 103, 130, 164
Yarkand, 88
Yehonala, *see* Tsu Hsi
Yellow Ancient, 24, 25
Yellow River, 19, 20, 22, 30, 32, 37, 46, 85, 90, 108, 109, 131, 200
Yellow Sea, 77, 78, 80
Yen Hsi-shan, 318
  and Chiang kidnapping, 343
  joins Chiang Kai-shek, 316, 317
  member military council, 337
  recognizes Wang Ching-wei as Nationalist leader, 319
  withdraws to Japan, 320
Yetts, W. Percival, quoted, 43
Yin, 23
Yin Dynasty, 35
Yin Ju-ken, 350, 351
Yü, 30, 33, 34
Yuän-hsing period, 96
Yuan Shih-kai
  betrays Kuang Hsü, 256
  death of, 294
  mistake of, 294
  opposed by Parliament, 291
  power increased, 291
  provisional president, 289-290
  recalled by Dynasty, 289
  retirement of, 275
Yüeh Chih, 87
Yu-hsiang, 305
  activities of, 306
Yunnan, 245
  revolts, 293

Zoroastrians, 119
  driven out, 121